Happiness and Economics

Happiness and Economics

HOW THE ECONOMY AND INSTITUTIONS AFFECT WELL-BEING

Bruno S. Frey and Alois Stutzer

PRINCETON UNIVERSITY PRESS

PRINCETON AND OXFORD

Library of Congress Control Number 2001095821

ISBN 0-691-06997-2 (cloth : alk. paper)
ISBN 0-691-06998-0 (paper : alk. paper)

British Library Cataloging-in-Publication Data is available

This book has been composed in Palatino
Printed on acid-free paper.∞
www.pup.princeton.edu

Printed in the United States of America

1 3 5 7 9 10 8 6 4 2

1 3 5 7 9 10 8 6 4 2
(Pbk.)

CONTENTS

CONTENTS

PREFACE

EVERYBODY wants to be happy. There is probably no other goal in life that commands such a high degree of consensus. "The pursuit of happiness" is even called upon in the American Declaration of Independence, and the Kingdom of Bhutan endeavors to maximize "Gross National Happiness."

Yet, curiously enough, economists have shied away from dealing with happiness. They have long considered it to be an "unscientific" concept. Instead they have based their microeconomic theory on utility that has no material content but that allows the successful analysis of human behavior. In the past few years the situation has changed: A number of economists see an advantage in measuring subjective well-being as expressed by individuals themselves.

This book reports the state of happiness research from the point of view of economics. To our knowledge, this is the first book establishing the link between happiness and economics. We discuss how the concepts of utility and happiness are related and show how micro- and macroeconomic conditions in the form of income, unemployment, and inflation affect happiness.

But our text certainly is not restricted to economics. Rather, one of the main elements is to integrate insights and empirical results from the other fields involved—in particular, psychology, sociology, and political science. Happiness research can be considered to be one of the few examples of successful interdisciplinary research.

Happiness is often seen as a purely personal issue. We argue that this is not the case. Individual happiness is strongly determined by the society one lives in. An original contribution of this book is to empirically show that the more democratic and the more decentralized a country is, the happier people tend to be.

This book builds on the invisible college of scholars of various disciplines who have paved the way. We particularly want to mention Richard Easterlin, Robert Frank, and Andrew Oswald in economics, Daniel Kahneman, Ed Diener, and Tom Tyler in psychology, Ruut Veenhoven in sociology, and Robert Lane in political science.

The many other scholars on whose shoulders we stand are discussed in the text.

We are grateful to Stephan Meier, Hanspeter Schmid, and especially Rosemary Brown for helping us in the preparation of the manuscript and to Matthias Benz and Reto Jegen for their helpful comments.

ACKNOWLEDGMENT

Chapter 8 of this book draws on material contained in our article "Happiness, Economy and Institutions" published in *The Economic Journal* 110(466): 918–38. We are grateful to the Royal Economic Society for permission to use this material.

Happiness and Economics

PART I

Setting the Stage

Chapter 1

HAPPINESS

1.1 The Ultimate Goal?

"WHAT IS HAPPINESS?" This question is probably as old as mankind itself. The greatest human minds have struggled with this issue. A large part of philosophy has been concerned with defining what a good and happy life is. Similar efforts have been made by psychologists, who have dealt with what particular ingredients and circumstances make people happy or unhappy.

But there has certainly not been any consensus as to what happiness is. It means different things to different people. It is open for everyone to define for themselves what happiness is. Some people are prepared to argue that it is the ultimate goal in life. All other influences on life (and even afterlife) are taken to be reflected in the notion of happiness. Therefore all that we do is pursue happiness. One author even proclaims, "How to gain, how to keep, how to recover happiness is in fact for most men at all times the secret motive for all they do" (James 1902, p. 76).

Some people disagree about happiness being the ultimate goal of human life; they see it as just one ingredient in the recipe for a good life. Thus, for example, three ultimate goals have been distinguished, none of which can be merged with, or be made subordinate to, another. They are subjective well-being (another term for happiness), human development (which is taken to include virtue), and justice (Lane 2000). Other authors mention companionship and freedom as ultimate goals on a par with happiness. Yet others consider an even larger set of factors to be important in addition to happiness. Examples of these factors are trust, self-esteem, absence of pain, satisfaction with one's work, and satisfaction with one's family life and marriage. In addition to these states or outcomes, procedural aspects may play a significant role. Most persons derive great pleasure from engaging, challenging activities. The emphasis on process rather than outcomes has been called the flow aspect of life.

Because happiness is such an elusive concept, it makes little sense to proceed by trying to define what happiness is. Fortunately, there is a useful way out. Instead of trying to determine what happiness is from outside, one can ask the individuals how happy they feel themselves to be. In general, it can be assumed that they are the best judges of when they are happy and when they are unhappy. While there are limits to how well people are able to evaluate their future state of well-being, it corresponds to a sensible tradition in economics to rely on the judgment of the persons directly involved, so that will be the procedure followed in this book.

1.2   CONCEPTS OF HAPPINESS

In this book, we follow a subjective notion of happiness. Even if we are restricted to such a notion of happiness, there are a number of concepts on how to capture it. It is useful to look at two polar concepts of happiness: subjective happiness and objective happiness. (See Figure 1.1.) At one extreme, we have the concept of *subjective happiness*, which can be captured by surveys, and is indicated on the right-hand side of Figure 1.1. With the help of a single question (single-item) or several questions (multi-item) of global self-reports, it is possible to get indications of individuals' evaluations of their life satisfaction or happiness. Behind the score indicated by a person is a cognitive process by which he or she evaluates happiness compared to other persons, past experience, and expectations of the future.

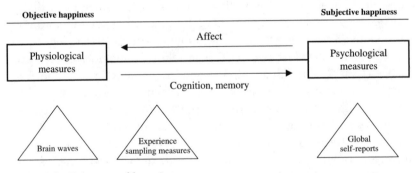

Figure 1.1. Concepts of happiness.

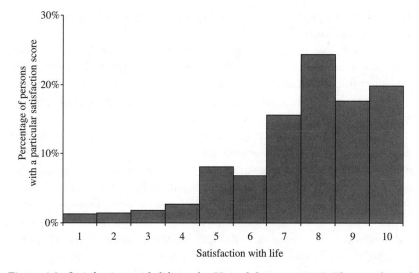

Figure 1.2. Satisfaction with life in the United States in 1995. The number of observations is 1534. Data from World Values Survey 1995–1997, ICPSR 2790.

Figure 1.2 presents an example of the measurement of subjective happiness via global self-reports. The example refers to the distribution of life satisfaction scores for 1,534 persons living in the United States in 1995. They were asked, "All things considered, how satisfied are you with your life as a whole these days?" Respondents had to indicate on a scale ranging from 1—corresponding to dissatisfied—to 10—corresponding to satisfied.

Most people in the United States indicate that they are reasonably happy; 20 percent of the respondents even consider themselves to be very happy (satisfaction score of 10); and no less than 62 percent report a satisfaction score above 7. In contrast, very few persons report themselves to be dissatisfied. Only about 5 percent of all respondents place themselves in the lowest three categories. On average, Americans have a life satisfaction score of 7.67.

At the other extreme, we have the concept of *objective happiness*, which is indicated on the left-hand side of Figure 1.1. It refers to physiological approaches, which endeavor to capture subjective well-being, especially by measuring brain waves. This approach comes close to the idea of a *hedonometer*, which directly measures cardinal utility. Objective happiness measures relate to a particular individual, but they are technical procedures that identify the extent of happiness.

They are objective in the sense that the judgment of happiness is made according to external rules.

Figure 1.1 also indicates another concept of happiness in between the polar extremes of subjective and objective happiness: experience sampling measures, typically carried out several times a day for many days, ascertain moods, emotions, and other feelings at random moments in individuals' everyday lives.

Which concept of happiness should be applied depends on the issue in question. The hedonic, objectively oriented concepts are useful for many of the intricate questions posed by some psychologists. The more objective methods reduce the memory biases that affect retrospective reports of experience in global self-reports. Moreover, these approaches have the advantage of being precise in terms of intensities measured. To a large extent, these measures assess an individual's level of affect. The subjectively oriented concepts are necessarily less precise because cognitive processes—which may differ among individuals and over time—play a major role. But precisely because cognitive factors enter into subjective happiness, these concepts are useful for issues connected with happiness, which have a bearing on social aspects. Moreover, physiological and moment-based measures rely on strongly normative judgments in the sense that happiness is assessed according to fixed rules, although our attitude toward particular pleasures and pains is not a priori given. Individual well-being is not an isolated feeling, but strongly depends on the conditions in which the persons concerned live. Thus, social comparisons are of great importance and have to be taken into account. Similarly, individuals do not have a fixed, once and for all given grid for measurement; they adjust to changing circumstances. A case in point is the effect of higher income on happiness. At first, individuals indicate a higher degree of happiness, but after some months, this increase tends to evaporate, and the level of happiness is not much higher than it was before the increase in income. These and related aspects of subjective happiness will be extensively discussed in later chapters of this book.

1.3   WHY IS HAPPINESS IMPORTANT?

Studying happiness, and empirically measuring its distribution among persons and countries, and assessing its development over time is interesting for several reasons.

1.3.1 Getting to Know How Happy People Are

How happy are, for example, low-income people compared to the rich? How happy are the young compared to the old? Women compared to men? Nationals compared to foreigners?

In order to reach some intuitive understanding of these and similar questions, Box 1.1 presents the average happiness scores of "typical" persons in society, using the case of Switzerland.

Box 1.1. Average Satisfaction with Life of Typical People

In a large survey, Swiss residents were asked, "How satisfied are you with your life as a whole these days?" and gave answers on a scale ranging from 1 ("completely dissatisfied") to 10 ("completely satisfied"). The reported satisfaction levels are analyzed by the econometric estimates discussed in detail in the following chapters. These findings lead to the following happiness psychograms.

It is assumed that all of the people live in a small city, and that the degree of democratic participation rights (see Chapter 8) is 4.

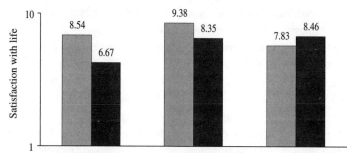

Peter is 33 years old and is married. He had an apprenticeship as an electrician. People such as Peter report, on average, a happiness score of 8.54. He has now lost his job and the equivalence income of the household has shrunk from Sfr. 3,100 to only Sfr. 2,700. In his new situation, people state, on average, a life satsifaction level of 6.67.

Anna is 63 years old. She is widowed and lives with her partner. She has a university degree and works in a PR agency. The equivalence income of the couple is over Sfr. 4,000. For a woman such as Anna a satisfaction score of 9.38 is predicted. Now imagine that Anna is retired and suffers from a serious illness. People such as her then report, on average, a level of satisfaction with life of 8.35.

Tony is 42 years old. He has only minimal formal education and he earns an income of Sfr. 3,600 per month. He is divorced and lives on his own. Men such as Tony report, on average, a happiness level of 7.83. If Tony were married, a level of 8.46 would be predicted.

Data Source: Leu, Burri, and Priester (1997)

We distinguish three "typical" persons who differ greatly with respect to their characteristics. The purpose is to show how certain life circumstances such as losing one's job (Peter), suffering from an illness (Anna), and getting married (Tony) affect self-reported satisfaction with life.

- Peter is happy (a score of 8.54 out of 10), although he has a relatively low income (SFr. 3,100 per month). The loss of his job as an electrician and the concomitant income loss reduce his happiness score substantially, by almost two points, to 6.67.

- Anna is even happier than Peter (9.38 out of 10). She is well educated and earns a reasonable salary (SFr. 4,000 per month). When she retires (without income loss) and becomes seriously ill, her happiness score falls by roughly one point to 8.35.

- Tony has little education, earns a relatively low income (SFr. 3,600 per month), and is the least happy of the three (7.83 out of 10). He finds a marriage partner, which raises his happiness score by more than half a point to 8.46.

The three "typical" people identified here are, of course, only examples. In principle, once the determinants of happiness have been measured, it is feasible to construct such happiness schedules for every conceivable type of person. However, such constructions of happiness psychograms are of little general use. In the following, we will therefore concentrate on single partial effects on happiness induced by various factors of subjective well-being.

It is also interesting to know how happiness has changed over time. Is it true—as cultural pessimists like to argue—that people get more and more unhappy? Or do people get happier all the time, as the optimists claim? Are economists right when they take it as a matter of course that the strong increase in per capita real income over the past decades (and centuries) has made people happier? Figure 1.3 presents the development of life satisfaction and real gross domestic product per capita for Japan from 1958 to 1991.

Japan is probably the country with the most spectacular growth in income since World War II. Between 1958 and 1991, its per capita income rose sixfold. Nevertheless, the Japanese people report a satisfaction with life that remains largely unchanged over this period. This surprising result needs explanation.

Finally, it is interesting to know how rich and poor countries compare with respect to subjective well-being. Is it really true that people in underdeveloped countries are quite happy despite their

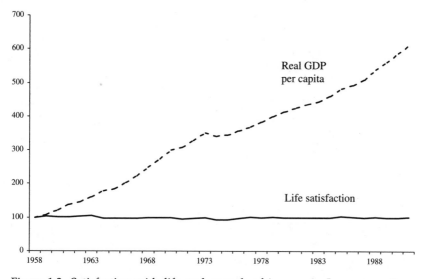

Figure 1.3. Satisfaction with life and growth of income in Japan over time. Data from Penn World Tables and World Database of Happiness.

low real per capita income? Or is this view just a romantic notion that does not take into consideration the hardship imposed by low income? Figure 1.4 exhibits a cross-country comparison of subjective happiness of over 80,000 people in 51 countries worldwide in the 1990s.

Reported satisfaction with life across countries shows a moderate positive correlation with average real income per capita in purchasing power parities. In general, people in rich countries are clearly happier than are those in poor countries. This positive relationship is especially strong with countries below a GNP per capita of U.S. $10,000 (in 1995). There are no rich countries where people's happiness, on average, is low. But, for the rich countries, it does not seem that higher per capita income has any marked effect on happiness. At the lower end of the scale, there are many poor developing and transition countries where residents experience low satisfaction with life. But there are also some exceptional countries with low per capita income that report reasonably high average satisfaction scores. The relationship between happiness and per capita income across countries is thus complex.

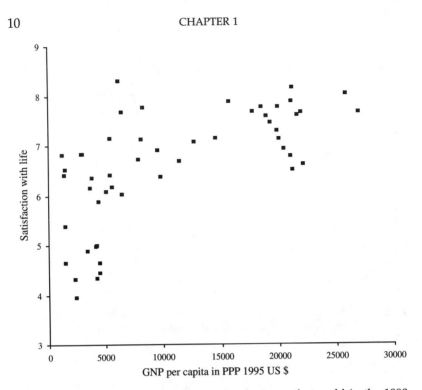

Figure 1.4. Life satisfaction and income levels across the world in the 1990s. The number of observations is 80,556. Data from World Values Survey 1990– 1993/1995–1997 (ICPSR 2790) and World Development Report 1997.

1.3.2   Identifying the Determinants of Happiness

What are the factors that make people happier or unhappier than others? This is a crucial question because it helps us to understand how—and to what extent—the situation can be improved.

It is useful to distinguish five types of determinants:

(a) *Personality factors*, such as self-esteem, personal control, optimism, extraversion, and neuroticism.
(b) *Socio-demographic factors*, such as age, gender, marital status, and education.
(c) *Economic factors*, such as individual and aggregate income, unemployment, and inflation.
(d) *Contextual and situational factors*, such as particular employment and working conditions, the stress involved at the workplace, interpersonal relations with work colleagues, relatives and friends,

and—most importantly—the marriage partner as well as living conditions and health.

(e) *Institutional factors*, such as the extent of political decentralization and citizens' direct political participation rights.

For years, personality, socio-demographic, and contextual factors have been extensively analyzed by psychologists. They have, moreover, studied some economic factors. In recent years, however, economists have also contributed significant research on the effect of economic factors on subjective well-being. In this book, we want to critically survey and interpret the results of past research from an economic point of view. Moreover, we seek to empirically identify as many of the determinants of happiness as possible in a concrete microeconometric happiness function for Switzerland. Being economists, we emphasize the economic determinants, which indeed turn out to be crucial. It is impossible to account for differences in happiness between people without taking into account income, employment, and inflation. Happiness is dependent on material factors and economic prospects.

But we are political economists too. We therefore also direct our attention to how different institutions influence happiness. The kind of society people live in has so far been severely neglected as a source of happiness. This book focuses exactly on that topic. Does a decentralized system, in which many political decisions are taken at the communal or district level, raise citizens' well-being? Do people experience more satisfaction when they have more extended possibilities of directly influencing political decisions via popular initiatives and referenda? We will show empirical evidence in favor of both of these propositions in chapter 8.

1.3.3 Explaining the Psychological Mechanisms Producing Happiness

Subjective well-being is an attitude consisting of the two basic aspects of cognition and affect. "Affect" is the label attached to moods and emotions. Affect represents people's instant evaluation of the events that occur in their lives. The cognitive component refers to the rational or intellectual aspects of subjective well-being. It is usually assessed with measures of satisfaction. It has been shown that pleasant affect, unpleasant affect, and life satisfaction are separable constructs.

The cognitive aspect involves a component of judgment and comparison. Happiness is thus not given and immutable, but is constructed within the person concerned and largely depends on the social environment within which each person has been socialized and within which he or she lives. There are, in particular, four psychological processes that have to be taken into account:

(a) *Adaptation.* People get used to new circumstances and accordingly adjust their subjective level of well-being. Hedonic adaptation thus reduces individuals' responsiveness to repeated or continued stimulus. Adaptation refers to a lot of different mechanisms; in the case of habituation, it is an automatic passive biological process. It has already been pointed out that people get used to a higher level of income, so subjective happiness tends to converge over time to its initial level. People winning the lottery, thereby experiencing a large increase in wealth, not surprisingly feel happy, but get adjusted and, after some time, on average indicate an only moderately higher level of well-being than before they won the lottery.

(b) *Aspiration.* People evaluate their situation with regard to an aspiration level that is formed by their hopes and expectations. If people attain their aspiration levels they are satisfied with their lives. Usually, aspiration levels are closely correlated with current or past attainments as, for example, current income, which is mostly considered satisfactory for one's household.

(c) *Social comparison.* There is no absolute measuring stick with respect to subjective happiness. People compare their positions with those of relevant other persons. This obviously holds for income, as has been shown in a large body of literature on the importance of relative income. But similar processes of comparison take place with respect to unemployment. People out of work are significantly less happy than those with jobs, but their unhappiness is less intense if they live in an environment in which many others are unemployed too.

(d) *Coping.* People have a strong capacity to overcome unfortunate events. Perhaps the most striking examples are paraplegics. Initially, they suffer a huge drop in subjective well-being. But over time, many of them are able to actively adapt to their misfortune. After some time, they indicate a not-much-lower level of personal happiness than before the accident.

1.3.4   Consequences on Behavior

Whether people are happy or unhappy has a large effect on how they live in many respects. For example,

- Happier persons are more successful in the labor market. They find a job more easily than unhappy persons, and they tend to progress more quickly in their careers.
- Happier persons more easily find a partner and are thus less exposed to loneliness.
- Happier people are more cooperative; they are more inclined to help others and to incur a risk in doing so.

As these examples testify, it is extremely difficult in many cases to identify the direction of causation. To take the first example, it is also true that people who are more successful in their job search and career are therefore happier than those who are less successful. The issue of causation will accompany us throughout the whole book.

1.3.5   Raising Happiness: The Individual Level

The results presented here provide important information on what factors tend to raise or lower subjective well-being. This information may allow people to organize themselves in order to attain their idea of the "good life."

The determinants identified are a good, but insufficient, basis for that purpose. There are aspects and circumstances where individuals have limited, and even deficient, faculties in order to lead a life of higher happiness. By way of example, consider the following situations.

- In carefully designed experimental situations, people have proved that they are unable to correctly recall pain suffered in the past. While they were well able to recall the maximum pain and the pain at the end of the period of suffering, they almost completely disregarded the length of time they had to endure the pain. As a result, they tend to make biased decisions if faced with a choice between maximum pain and the pain at the end of the period of suffering on the one hand, and the duration of pain on the other hand.
- People tend to disregard the extent and speed with which they adjust to new situations. This deficient faculty can be observed almost every day. How many people go to great lengths to raise their income, only to detect a short while later that this higher

income has not greatly raised their happiness, if at all. One sometimes wonders why people are not able to take this adaptation to higher income levels into account, but real life shows that it is rarely done.

The results of happiness research collected in this book may help to overcome these and other cognitive biases influencing behavior. Individuals can learn to successfully deal with them by taking a more detached point of view. One may, in particular, resort to self-binding. One thus imposes rules on ones own future behavior in order not to commit specific cognitive errors. An example would be that one does not accept a job that offers a higher salary before having extensively talked to friends and relatives about its likely effect on one's well-being in the long run. Not being themselves involved in receiving the "better" job and the higher income, outsiders are more able to predict the extent of the adjustment of happiness to the higher salary and the effects, for example, of longer working hours on the enjoyment of family life.

Yet this book is not a contribution to self-help. It thus differs fundamentally from the many treatises teaching you how to achieve happiness. But this book helps in avoiding certain pitfalls, and examines the basis from which satisfaction with life emerges. We concentrate on the question "Under *which* conditions do people report *what* with regard to their subjective well-being?" It is useful to know, for instance, that individuals make systematic errors with respect to evaluating pain or predicting the extent to which future income can make one happy. This, in turn, leads to questioning under which conditions people can accurately predict affective or cognitive consequences of their behavior on happiness.

1.3.6 Raising Happiness: The Societal Level

The populations of different countries and in different periods of time reveal marked differences in happiness. An obvious reason for these differences in subjective well-being may be the prevailing economic conditions. Persons living in an economically depressed country, with high unemployment and rampant inflation, are likely to be unhappy. It is one of the major purposes of this book to inquire into the effects of the economy on happiness. Once the determinants are identified, they can serve as goals in the political process. In order for these determinants to be useful, it is important to know their relative impact on happiness, because some economic determinants are often in conflict with each other. This applies in particular to unemployment and inflation. An expansionary economic policy, designed to stimulate the economy and to thereby reduce the number of people unemployed, is likely to raise the inflation rate (at least after some time has passed). Such a policy unequivocally serves to raise the well-being of the population if unemployment drops off considerably and if getting a job raises subjective happiness notably, while inflation rises only a little and the price increases do not have much effect on the feeling of happiness. It is obvious that the conditions just mentioned are not necessarily met, so that an expansionary economic policy may work against happiness.

Happiness may also differ among countries, because their political and social lives are governed by different *institutions*. Institutions fundamentally shape how a society is organized. In most countries, the basic institutions are enshrined in the constitution, which lays down the way decisions are to be made in society. Thus, it assigns a role to politics, to the market, to government bureaucracy, and to organized groups. It also attributes inalienable rights to individuals—in particular, basic human rights and the right to politically participate via elections and/or via popular referenda. Within the area of political decision making, the constitution stipulates the role of the three powers (legislative, executive, and judicial) and determines the responsibilities of the central state and the federal units (say, provinces, regions, and communes or states, counties, and cities).

In this book, we argue strongly and demonstrate empirically that two institutions crucially affect subjective well-being: political decentralization and the possibility of political participation by the citizens. To grant political units the right to decide for themselves as many government policies as possible, and to introduce extensive possibilities for citizens to make their wishes felt directly in the political process, seems to us to be a good way to raise the overall happiness of the population.

But as was the case at an individual level, this book does not offer a blueprint on how to attain a happy country. A nation and its citizens are sovereign, and there is no point in telling them what they should or should not do. Rather, what can be offered is information on how the state of the economy and institutional conditions typically affect subjective well-being. If such information is accepted as reasonable and convincing, individuals will take it up and will try to achieve it in the context of the political process. Such a position differs fundamentally from the one of a benevolent dictator, who knows what is best for the population and radically imposes and enforces the respective policies. History has shown that such benevolent dictatorships soon lapse into tyranny and bring unhappiness upon the populations.

The procedural approach used here also rejects the idea that the happiness scores revealed by individuals can simply be mechanically summed up or aggregated in some other way so as to arrive at a consistent measure of aggregate happiness. It follows that government policy cannot consist of maximizing such an aggregate measure of welfare. Rather, the citizens take into account the information available to them concerning the determinants of happiness. It is the *political process* shaped by the *institutional* (or *constitutional*) *conditions* that forms the aggregation process.

1.4 PROCEDURE

Chapter 2 discusses more deeply how people's subjective well-being is empirically measured and how these measures correlate with other manifestations of happiness, such as smiling, or with unhappiness, such as committing suicide. Chapter 3 studies the effects of personality and demographic factors on happiness. Moreover, the empirical analysis of a concrete microeconometric happiness function is introduced. The corresponding results serve as a grid for the remainder of the book and are discussed in the respective chapters.

The following two parts focus on the central issues with which this book is concerned. Part II shows how economic conditions affect people's well-being. In particular we show that being unemployed makes for unhappiness due to stress and social disapproval, even if the change in income is controlled for. Income also systematically affects happiness, but this impact is mitigated by processes of comparison and adjustments induced. A higher rate of inflation negatively affects subjective well-being. This result is in conflict with economists' idea that people can adjust to (predicted) inflation and that it therefore should not harm them.

Part III discusses the systematic influence of political and social institutions on happiness. The final part (Part IV) summarizes the findings and reflects on the role of happiness in an economy and society as a whole, as well as its role in economics as a social science.

Hints on the Literature

Happiness has always been a central topic in philosophy and ethics. See, for instance,

Sumner, Leonard W. (1996). *Welfare, Happiness, and Ethics*. Oxford: Oxford University Press.

Psychologists have also been dealing with the subject of happiness for a long time. A recent authoritative contribution is from

Kahneman, Daniel, Ed Diener, and Norbert Schwarz (eds.) (1999). *Well-Being: The Foundations of Hedonic Psychology*. New York: Russell Sage Foundation.

Earlier works include

Argyle, Michael (1987). *The Psychology of Happiness*. London: Methuen.
Michalos, Alex C. (1991). *Global Report on Student Well-Being. Volume 1: Life Satisfaction and Happiness*. New York: Springer.
Myers, David G. (1993). *The Pursuit of Happiness: Who Is Happy and Why?* New York: Avon.
Strack, Fritz, Michael Argyle, and Norbert Schwarz (eds.) (1991). *Subjective Well-Being: An Interdisciplinary Perspective*. Oxford: Pergamon Press.

Very useful surveys of the psychological research on happiness include

Diener, Ed, Eunkook M. Suh, Richard E. Lucas, and Heidi L. Smith (1999). Subjective Well-Being: Three Decades of Progress. *Psychological Bulletin* 125(2): 276–303.
Ryan, Richard M., and Edward L. Deci (2000). To Be Happy or to Be Self-Fulfilled: A Review of Research on Hedonic and Eudaimonic Well-Being. Mimeo. University of Rochester, Rochester, NY.

That happiness is not necessarily connected with outcomes, but rather with processes, has been emphasized in the "flow" concept of happiness by

Csikszentmihalyi, Mihaly (1990). *Flow: The Psychology of Optimal Experience*. New York: Harper Perennial.

Sociologists have also made important contributions to happiness research. See, in particular,

Veenhoven, Ruut (1993). *Happiness in Nations: Subjective Appreciation of Life in 56 Nations 1946–1992*. Rotterdam: Erasmus University Press.

Economists are latecomers to the subject, at least as far as empirical work is concerned. A path-breaking contribution is

Easterlin, Richard A. (1974). Does Economic Growth Improve the Human Lot? Some Empirical Evidence. In Paul A. David and Melvin W. Reder (eds.), *Nations and Households in Economic Growth: Essays in Honour of Moses Abramowitz*. New York and London: Academic Press, 89–125.

The economics community has been made aware of the subject, mainly by a small symposium in the *Economic Journal* with papers by

Frank, Robert H. (1997). The Frame of Reference as a Public Good. *Economic Journal* 107(445): 1832–47.

Ng, Yew-Kwang (1997). A Case for Happiness, Cardinalism, and Interpersonal Comparability. *Economic Journal* 107(445): 1848–58.

Oswald, Andrew J. (1997). Happiness and Economic Performance. *Economic Journal* 107(445): 1815–31.

More recent contributions are, for instance,

Di Tella, Rafael, Robert J. MacCulloch, and Andrew J. Oswald (2001). Preferences over Inflation and Unemployment: Evidence from Surveys of Happiness. *American Economic Review* 91(1): 335–41.

Frey, Bruno S., and Alois Stutzer (1999). Measuring Preferences by Subjective Well-Being. *Journal of Institutional and Theoretical Economics* 155(4): 755–78.

Frey, Bruno S., and Alois Stutzer (2000). Happiness, Economy and Institutions. *Economic Journal* 110(466): 918–38.

Much of the literature stemming from the various sciences available up to the late 1990s has been ably documented in the comprehesive survey by

Lane, Robert A. (2000). *The Loss of Happiness in Market Democracies*. New Haven and London: Yale University Press.

Current contributions to the study of happiness appear in various psychological journals, such as *Psychological Bulletin*, and in general economics journals, such as *American Economic Review*, *Economic Journal*, and *Kyklos*. Specialized reviews include

Social Indicators Research (since 1974).

as well as the newly founded

Journal of Happiness Studies (since 2000).

Data on happiness for a great number of countries and periods have been collected by Ruut Veenhoven in the

World Database of Happiness: *http://www.eur.nl/fsw/research/happiness/*.

The following are examples dealing with self-help (a topic not treated in this book):

Foster, Rick, and Greg Hicks (1999). *How We Choose to Be Happy: The 9 Choices of Extremely Happy People: Their Secrets, Their Stories*. New York: Putnam.

Myers, David G. (1993). *The Pursuit of Happiness: Discovering the Pathway to Fulfillment, Well-Being, and Enduring Personal Joy*. New York: Avon.

Niven, David (2000). *The 100 Simple Secrets of Happy People: What Scientists Have Learned and How You Can Use It*. San Franciso: Harper.

Prager, Dennis (1998). *Happiness Is a Serious Problem: A Human Nature Repair Manual*. New York: Regan.

Chapter 2

WELL-BEING AND ECONOMICS

2.1 THE CONVENTIONAL VIEW OF UTILITY IN ECONOMICS

THE 1930s witnessed a revolutionary change in the concept of utility. Economists—in particular, those inspired by the influential Lionel Robbins (1932)—became convinced that utility could not be cardinally measured. Utility should be used to explain the choices made by individuals between various goods. Empirically, utility should be inferred from the choices actually made. It is therefore appropriate to speak of "decision utility" in the sense of a preference index indicating whether good A is preferred to good B.

Since World War II, this so-called *new welfare economics* has become the conventional view enshrined in a myriad of theoretical treatises and textbooks. The idea that utility should be cardinally measured in order to explain individual choices has been given up completely in favor of ordinal utility. In order for utility to be reflected in *revealed behavior*, individuals are required to be well (or even completely) informed, aware of the choices made, and consistent in their wishes. Utility has just become a number without any further substantive meaning whatsoever.

The switch from the idea of measurable cardinal utility to a preference index of ordinal utility—graphically represented by the consumer indifference curves—was successful in economics for two good reasons:

(a) States of minds, such as how much satisfaction or pleasure a good yields, are inherently difficult to measure. Economists endeavoring a scientific approach to their discipline are deeply skeptical about the possibility of being able to measure utility.

(b) Cardinal utility is not necessary for economic theory. Hicks (1934) and Allen (1934) demonstrated early on that demand theory can be entirely grounded on ordinal utility in the form of a preference index. Samuelson (1938) formulated the general behavioristic foundations of standard theory, in which it is axiomatically taken that utility is no more than preference. A definitional chain is established, relating utility exclusively to choice behavior. Observed choice, in turn, is the only basis of empirical knowledge about individuals' utility. But no empirical knowledge of persons' emotional states or opinions about their utility is needed to explain the choices individuals make between goods in markets. Houthakker (1950) and Uzawa (1960) gave revealed preference theory its present form: For any observed demand function satisfying some undisputed conditions of regularity, there exist unique, well-ordered preferences over commodities rationalizing the demand function if, and only if, a set of axioms of revealed preference is satisfied by demand. The preference axioms require consistency, in the sense that choices made by consumers from different budget sets correspond to the choices individuals would have made had they consciously maximized a binary preference relation. Everyone is thus assumed to have pursued their well-defined goals in markets in the best possible way.

Gary Becker (1962) was able to go one step further. He showed that it is possible to derive the most important implication of demand theory—that a price rise induces a fall in demand, all other influences being constant—without using any concept of utility.

Modern economic theory has thus taken a huge step away from a substantive and empirically measurable idea of utility in terms of satisfaction or pleasure. A major exception where cardinal utility is needed is cost-benefit analysis, in which specific projects such as bridges, harbors, or roads are evaluated. But otherwise, especially in prestigious "pure" theory, the arguments adduced in favor of empty preferences still have wide prevalence today.

2.2 A Reconsideration

Another dramatic change has taken place recently: A movement has arisen within economics that claims that utility should be given content in terms of happiness, and that it can, and should, be measured. This turnaround has resulted from four major developments:

(a) More and more evidence has been accumulated suggesting that individual preferences and individual happiness are distinct and

may often diverge. Most importantly, it has become clear that much behavior observed in real life—such as giving to charities or offering volunteer labor—cannot be well explained by solely self-concerned preferences. This applies not only to market behavior, but even more to social activities, such as voting in politics or contributing to public goods. To the extent that such behavior is attributed to altruistic motives, it is no longer possible to establish a direct relationship between observed behavior and individual preferences, as postulated by traditional revealed preference theory. The same holds if the consumers are not as well informed as axiomatically assumed in received theory, or if they discount the future in an excessive and inconsistent way. These failures not only have been observed in real life, but have been isolated in a large number of careful laboratory experiments undertaken by economists.

(b) Utility has been filled with content by various enterprising economists. The most influential has probably been Tibor Scitovsky with his book *The Joyless Economy*, published in 1976. He argued that most of the pleasures in life cannot be bought in markets, are not priced, and are not for sale. Rather, intrinsic work enjoyment and a challenging consumption pattern yield satisfaction.

Several other economists have further undermined the reliance on nonsubstantive utility. The idea that relative income compared to the incomes of friends and neighbors, rather than absolute income, is the crucial determinant of consumption has been peddled for a long time. It has, in particular, been taken up by James Duesenberry (1949), reverting to insights by Thorstein Veblen (1899), and has more recently been popularized by Robert Frank in *Choosing the Right Pond* (1985) and *Luxury Fever* (1999).

(c) Research on the *concept and measurement of happiness* has made great progress in psychology since the 1950s. While there is virtually no direct connection between psychology and theoretical economics, empirically oriented economists have become aware that the fundamental idea cherished in the new welfare economics—that it is impossible to measure utility—is mistaken. The high level of rigor typical for experimental psychology, and the empirical support provided for the concept of happiness, have helped to make the new idea of measurable utility palatable to at least some economists. But it took considerable time before

an economist actually used happiness data and thus reverted to cardinal and interpersonally comparable measure of utility (Easterlin 1974).

(d) Over the past few years, as a by-product of the emergence of economic psychology, theories and empirical evidence have emerged, showing that people are not always able to choose the greatest amount of utility for themselves. Two psychologists, Richard E. Nisbett and Lee Ross (1980, p. 223), even go so far as to claim that "people do not know what makes them happy and what makes them unhappy." This statement is certainly exaggerated, but it makes it clear that the divergence between *substantive utility* (in the sense of subjective well-being) and *preference* go beyond the restrictions noted by economists. It is useful to distinguish three types of reasons:

(1) *Contextual influences,* such as the already mentioned comparison to other persons.

(2) *Biases in cognition,* leading to asymmetries and thus to distorted decisions. Some of them are

- Prospect theory, according to which losses are more heavily valued than gains of the same size. Hence gains and losses of the same magnitude do not result in unchanged utility. This particular effect has been noted by at least some orthodox economists—the results were published by Daniel Kahneman and Amos Tversky (1979) in the prestigious economics journal *Econometrica*. But, on the whole, it has had no impact on pure theory, which has proceeded on the principle of "business as usual." The same holds for all other anomalies of behavior.

- Neglecting the actual duration, which was already mentioned in chapter 1: People focus on two distinct aspects— namely, the most intense pain suffered ("peak") and its ending—while largely disregarding how long they endured the pain (Kahneman and Varey 1991).

- The endowment effect suggesting that people prefer an object simply because it is in their possession over the same, or equivalent, object, that they do not own (Thaler 1980).

- Overoptimism, according to which people in identifiable situations believe that the outcomes of events are better for them than for others. Thus, most persons underestimate the probability of being involved in an accident or contracting

cancer or AIDS. Similarly, most people overestimate their capabilities. Thus, a large majority of motorists believe that they belong to the top 20 percent of drivers, which is, of course, objectively impossible. The same holds for their own evaluation of their work performance (Meyer 1975). The ipsative possibility set (the one they perceive as constraining their own actions) systematically deviates from the objective possibility set, which distorts behavior (Frey and Heggli 1999). Another case is the premarital expectation that one's own romantic marriage will be happy ever after and will not end up in divorce—an expectation that is quite unrealistic in view of divorce rates that are 50 percent and higher (Frey and Eichenberger 2001).

(3) *Limited ability to predict one's future tastes.* An important case, already mentioned on several occasions, is the adaptation to higher income, or rising aspiration levels, that are not sufficiently, taken into account if they are taken into account at all. Even more striking is the inability to predict one's future preferences if one becomes disabled. Most people think it preferable to die in an accident than to lose both legs or both eyes. But studies of quadriplegics show that they are only slightly less happy than healthy persons. After a difficult time of adjustment, the happiness of seriously disabled victims rises again to a level close to the one before the accident. The effect also works in the opposite direction. Studies suggest that lottery winners are very happy after winning, but that their happiness levels revert back near to the original levels after some weeks (Brickman, Coates, and Janoff-Bulman 1978). These prediction errors are not normally corrected by personal experience, partly because most people can only personally experience a few such life events.

The developments sketched here all lead back to the more inclusive views on utility held before the advent of the new welfare economics. Indeed, in the Golden Age of Greek philosophy, Aristotle defined happiness as the supreme good. It is the only value that is final and sufficient; everything else is merely a means to an end, and once happiness is attained, nothing else matters. But the absolute good consists of doing well rather than of actual pleasures. A happy person is a moral person. Individuals are not reasonable judges of their own happiness.

In the Christian Middle Ages, Thomas Aquinas defined the quality of human life in terms of virtue, closeness to God, and other personal qualities. Confucius emphasized the relationship between people and therefore focused on the quality of life in society.

The fathers of economics in the Scottish Enlightenment acknowledged the limits to which material goods and income create utility. Thus, Adam Smith (1776) observed that there is a point beyond which higher income has little or no use. For John Stuart Mill (1863), liberty, not income, was the surest way to the greatest good. He also provided a distinction between more and less valuable activities and pleasures, and thought that everyone should see and accept the link between their own good and the good of society.

The Utilitarians, such as Jeremy Bentham (1789), were quite convinced that utility can be measured. According to them, the total utility experienced during a period is composed of the integral of instant utility, which can be measured by a "hedonometer" (Edgeworth 1881). It is interesting to note that the psychologist Daniel Kahneman (1999) today suggests essentially the same construct—but based on the background of half a century of extensive and careful research in his discipline.

This view assumes happiness to consist of *hedonic* well-being and deals with the experience of pleasure versus displeasure. It includes all judgments on the good and bad aspects of life. Well-being is not reduced to physical hedonism, but also refers to the pleasure reaped from attainment of goals or valued outcomes in various other areas. Most researchers in psychology use assessments of subjective well-being consisting of three parts: life satisfaction, the presence of a positive mood, and the absence of a negative mood. Subjective well-being has been used as the most important index of happiness in psychology.

Another view to consider refuses to take hedonic well-being as such as the major criterion for happiness. According to Aristotle, hedonic well-being is vulgar and causes human beings to follow their desires slavishly. Not all outcomes that a person values yield well-being when actually achieved. They may produce pleasure, but some outcomes are simply not "good" for people. Therefore, hedonic well-being should not be identified with happiness. The *eudaimonic* view of happiness asks people to live according to their "daimon" (true self). Eudaimonia takes place when people act in congruence with deeply held values and are fully engaged. Then people experience what it is to be intensely alive and to be who they really are, which has been called *personal expressiveness* (Waterman 1993). It is closely associated with being challenged and making an effort, with personal growth and development.

Self-determination theory (Ryan and Deci 2000a) seeks to find out what it means to fulfill the self, and how this can be accomplished. It thus inquires into the underlying causes producing well-being. Three fundamental psychological needs are posited: autonomy, competence, and relatedness. Actualizing these needs is crucial for psychological growth (intrinsic motivation in particular), vitality, as well as well-being in the sense of life satisfaction and psychological health. Self-determination theory claims that the satisfaction of these basic psychological needs generally supports hedonic well-being as well as eudaimonic well-being. While hedonic and eudaimonic well-being are distinct, their respective measures are often strongly correlated.

2.3 REPORTED SUBJECTIVE WELL-BEING

Many terms are used to denote substantive utility in the way just discussed: *happiness, subjective* or *reported well-being, satisfaction*. Throughout this book, these terms are employed interchangeably.

How can subjective well-being be captured?

(a) *Physiological and neurobiological indicators.* While great efforts are made at the moment to develop corresponding measuring instruments that, for example, rely on brain waves, there are so far no practically usable indicators available. It is doubtful that there ever will be, because cognitive aspects play such a large role in happiness.

(b) *Observed social behavior.* While some behavioral acts are more frequently observed in happy persons—such as high activity level, outgoing actions, or friendliness—they can also be observed in unhappy persons. They therefore do not lend themselves as indicators of happiness.

(c) *Nonverbal behavior.* There is certainly a relationship between frequent smiling in social interaction or enthusiastic body movements and happiness. But again, such actions are also sometimes undertaken by unhappy persons. An outside observer therefore finds it difficult to judge a person's well-being. This even applies to suicide, which is a most extreme form of non-verbal behavior. It is beyond doubt that most people attempting or committing suicide are unhappy. However, many unhappy persons do not resort to suicide.

In addition, the aspects discussed in the previous subsection are relevant here. All factors driving a wedge between preferences and behavior also need to be taken into account when attempting to infer happiness from revealed behavior.

(d) *Surveys*. Self-reported happiness has turned out to be the best indicator of happiness. Extensive research has shown that people are capable of consistently evaluating their own state of well-being.

This book concentrates on surveys based on subjective well-being. Individuals' happiness may be captured by *single-item* or *multiple-item questions*. Box 2.1 shows a number of such questions used in various approaches.

Box 2.1. Measures of Subjective Well-Being

Subjective well-being has been investigated in a great many ways. Some measures of happiness have been shown to reflect to a large extent affective components of subjective well-being that involve positive emotional aspects. In contrast, measures of satisfaction reflect relatively more aspects of the cognitive component of subjective well-being.

The first standard happiness question has been applied by the University of Michigan's Survey Research Center (SRC) and the National Opinion Research Center (NORC):

Taken all together, how would you say things are these days—would you say that you are very happy, pretty happy, or not too happy?

This three-point item question is very similar to the four-point item one of the *World Value Survey*. This survey is intensively studied in cross-country happiness research. It asks the question,

Taken all together, how happy would you say you are: very happy, quite happy, not very happy, not at all happy?

The affective component of subjective well-being is directly addressed, for example, by the multi-item affect scale from the Midlife Development Inventory (MIDI). Multi-item scales generally have higher validity and reliability than single-item scales because random measurement errors

Continues

Box 2.1. *Continued*

tend to be smaller on average and because of the broader range of components of subjective well-being that are considered explicitly.

MIDI assesses positive and negative affect according to the responses given to the following questions:

During the past 30 days, how much of the time did you feel . . .

Negative Affect	Positive Affect
1. So sad nothing could cheer you up?	1. Cheerful?
2. Nervous?	2. In good spirits?
3. Restless or fidgety?	3. Extremely happy?
4. Hopeless?	4. Calm and peaceful?
5. That everything was an effort?	5. Satisfied?
6. Worthless?	6. Full of life?

The response options for the affect scales are as follows:

1 = None of the time
2 = A little of the time
3 = Some of the time
4 = Most of the time
5 = All of the time

A single-item satisfaction scale is included in the *Eurobarometer Survey*. In Europe, the Eurobarometer Surveys have been collected for many years by the Statistical Office of the (now) European Union; it covers all member countries and therefore provides an excellent data source. This survey asks,

On the whole are you very satisfied, fairly satisfied, not very satisfied, or not at all satisfied with the life you lead?

Among the multiple-item approaches, the *Satisfaction with Life Scale* introduced by Ed Diener and co-workers has become prominent. It is composed of five questions, with answers rated on a 1-to-7 scale ranging from "strongly agree" to "strongly disagree":

1. "In most ways my life is close to ideal."
2. "The conditions of my life are excellent."
3. "I am satisfied with my life."
4. "So far I have gotten the important things I want in life."
5. "If I could live my life over, I would change almost nothing."

Continues

Box 2.1. *Continued*

Many more well-being scales have been constructed. It is, however, futile to discuss in general which of them is the best. Rather, what questions and scales are best suited depends on the purpose for which they are to be employed. For some psychological issues, a very differentiated approach may well be appropriate. As will be shown in the course of this book, quite simple questions and restricted scales work well for the purpose of economic research on happiness.

Source: Andrews and Robinson (1991), Pavot and Diener (1993), Inglehart (1990), and Brim and Featherman (1998).

How many *dimensions* should a happiness index contain? The answer to this question depends on what exactly one wants to analyze. For many issues, a common metric of the "overall evaluation of life" is suitable. Psychological research has shown that most moments of happiness experience can be adequately characterized by such a single summary measure. (See Kahneman 1999, p. 8.) It exhibits considerable intrapersonal stability and interpersonal comparability and therefore can be used without major problems for many purposes.

It is, of course, possible to decompose subjective well-being into finer and finer units. Table 2.1 shows various dimensions of happiness that have been differentiated. The table distinguishes between "pleasant affect," "unpleasant affect," and "life satisfaction." They all cover a wide range. Thus, a pleasant affect may simply be joy or be as intensive as ecstasy; unpleasant affects range from guilt and shame

TABLE 2.1
Dimensions of Happiness

Pleasant Affect	Unpleasant Affect	Life Satisfaction
Joy	Guilt and shame	Desire to change life
Elation	Sadness	Satisfaction with current life
Contentment	Anxiety and worry	Satisfaction with past
Pride	Anger	Satisfaction with future
Affection	Stress	Significant others' views of one's life
Happiness	Depression	
Ecstasy	Envy	

Source: Diener et al. (1999), Table 1.

to anger, stress, depression, and envy. Life satisfaction also has many dimensions, such as the time axis: One may be particularly satisfied with one's present life or the past or have expectations about the future. It may relate to one's own feelings as well as to how significant other persons regard one's life.

Of great importance from the economic point of view are the domains from which subjective well-being is collected. The distinction drawn between the private and the public spheres is of special interest. It has been shown that persons feel more satisfied in the personal than in the public sphere (Glatzer 1992). The most important personal domains are

(a) *Labor market.* Job satisfaction is a crucial area of life for a great many persons and has accordingly been extensively studied. Greater employee well-being is associated with better job performance, lower absenteeism, and reduced job turnover, and is therefore of particular interest to firms and other organizations.

(b) *Consumption.* This domain is obviously important for marketing and advertising, but also goes far beyond that. The material standard of living is regularly mentioned by a majority of respondents as being one of the most important elements of well-being. Consumption has become one of the central activities of modern life.

(c) *Family and companionship.* A happy marriage or partnership, and good relations with children and relatives, are considered to be integral parts of well-being by most persons.

(d) *Leisure.* At least in Europe, the amount of leisure time has increased considerably over the past few decades, both because of a drop in the number of working hours—a 35-hour working week is not far off—and because of early retirement along with longer life. Leisure thus takes on an increasingly important role in life. The situation in the United States is somewhat different: Average working hours seem to have increased, particularly for management positions—hence the book entitled *The Overworked American* by Juliet Schor (1992).

(e) *Health.* People are very much concerned with health. They name good health as one of the major ingredients of happiness.

It may come as a surprise to learn that the public domains relating to international and domestic issues, such as civil unrest, war, political liberty, civil rights, and social equality, are not mentioned by the respondents of happiness surveys as being as important as the issues belonging to the personal domain of everyday life. One reason may be that people take developments in the public domains as a given. Because they see little chance of being able to influence them, they try to abstract from them. (This is the explanation offered by Easterlin 2000a, p. 4.) However, as we shall demonstrate in this book, *political institutions*—in particular, the extent of direct participation rights of the citizens via referenda, as well as the extent of government decentralization—have a systematic influence on people's happiness. As was argued, it does not make sense to decide *in abstracto* whether one should use a one-dimensional or multidimensional indicator of happiness. It all depends on the issue being studied. But it is important to note that a one-dimensional indicator of overall life satisfaction works well: "It is empirically possible for most individuals to evaluate their life as a whole" (van Praag and Frijters 1999, p. 427).

2.4 EVALUATING MEASURES OF HAPPINESS

Measures of subjective well-being are characterized by three aspects:
- They reside within the individual and do not claim or want to be objective.
- They take into account both negative and positive influences on happiness.
- They globally assess happiness over the whole life domain and are not restricted to particular areas, such as job satisfaction or health.

Subjective well-being has a cognitive aspect referring to the extent an individual perceives that his or her aspirations have been met. In addition, there is an affective element referring to the extent that one finds one's life to be enriching and feels satisfied and fulfilled by it. It is therefore not easy to *formalize* subjective well-being. But the following reported well-being function may be helpful (see Blanchflower and Oswald 2000b):

$$W = H[U(Y, t)] + \varepsilon.$$

W denotes the self-reported level of well-being. On a bounded cardinal scale ranging from 1 to 10, it corresponds, for instance, to 1 for "extremely unhappy" or 10 for "extremely happy." The function $U(..)$

represents the respondent's well-being or utility and is observable only by the individual asked. The exact structure is hidden from the interviewer and from other individuals. Y denotes the whole extensive set of determinants of reported subjective well-being. t indicates that the relationship between these determinants Y and well-being may vary over time due to assorted reasons. $H[.]$ is a continuous nondifferentiable function relating actual well-being to reported well-being. The function $H[.]$ rises in steps as U increases. The error term ε serves to capture other hidden factors influencing the connection between actual well-being and reported well-being, such as the inability of human beings to accurately communicate their happiness level.

In some cases, it may be useful to distinguish between *stocks* and *flows* of well-being. The satisfaction or distress arising from life events in a particular time period is the flow of psychic income, while the stable personal characteristics, such as personality traits (extraversion, neuroticism, and openness to new experiences), social background (sex, age, and socio-economic status), and social networks (intimate relationships and friendships), may be taken as the stocks of happiness pertaining to a particular person (Headey and Wearing 1991). The economic concept of stocks and flows may be used in an even more direct way. The stock may be considered to be the aggregate, and suitably discounted, flows of happiness in the past. This is the concept used by Daniel Kahneman (1999) when distinguishing between instant utility (the flow) and total utility (the stock).

Another formulation, borrowing from traditional economic theory, is the social production function developed by Siegwart Lindenberg and his coworkers. (See, e.g., Ormel, Lindenberg, Steverink, and Verbrugge 1999; Lindenberg and Frey 1993.) Well-being is assumed to be the central goal of human activity, which is composed of physical well-being and social well-being. These goals are produced by five main instrumental goals: stimulation, comfort, status, behavioral confirmation, and affection. People are taken to produce their well-being subject to a set of constraints and adaptive strategies, choosing the particular combination that maximizes their individual well-being.

There are four main criteria with which indicators of happiness can be evaluated: reliability, validity, consistency, and comparability across nations.

2.4.1   Reliability

Reliability refers to the extent to which two or more measures intended to tap the same dimension of happiness agree with one another. Reliability may also refer to stability—that is, the property that an individual's responses should stay the same (all other things being equal) when he or she is asked the same questions at a later point of time. The answers should not depend on a fluke or be the result of volatile moods. The following problems may arise:

- *Distorted appraisal.* Respondents use heuristics to make the instant judgments that are the basis of their responses. The "availability heuristic" suggests, for instance, that people are unduly influenced by pieces of information that happen to be readily available. If the interviewer happens to be in a wheelchair, the benefits of good health become salient, and the correlation of happiness ratings to health will be more pronounced.
- *Distorted response.* There may be problems in communicating the feeling of happiness or the particular sequence of questions may influence the results (which should not be the case).

However, studies reveal that reported subjective well-being is moderately stable and appropriately sensitive to changing life circumstances. (See, e.g., Headey and Wearing 1991.) The problems just mentioned can be mitigated or even overcome by a careful survey design. This also suggests that the respondents find the questions meaningful and that they understand them.

2.4.2   Validity

The validity of a measure requires that it reflects the concept it is intended to reflect. Responses to happiness questions should thus reflect true inner feelings. Biases may arise for several reasons:

- *No opinion.* Respondents may not have any clue about how happy they are because they have never thought about this question.
- *Distorted reporting.* Because of ego-defense mechanisms, or because they perceive it as socially desirable, respondents tend to overstate their level of happiness or to understate it, as in the case of the "unhappy artist."

Some of these biases are random and hence do not affect aggregate cross-section analysis. Other distortions can again be mitigated by an appropriate survey research design.

2.4.3   Consistency

Consistency refers to how well the inner feeling of happiness experienced by persons as measured by the index of well-being corresponds to other observations of the same phenomenon. Subjective well-being correlates with a large number of such observations. (See, e.g., Frank 1997, p. 1833.) Compared to the average person, people reporting to be more happy than average

- Are rated to be more happy by spouses, other family members, friends, and associates.
- Are more often smiling during social interactions.
- Are more easily prepared to initiate social contacts.
- Are more ready to help other persons.
- Are less often absent from work.
- Are less involved in quarrels at work.
- Are more optimistic about the future.
- Are strikingly energetic, flexible, and creative.
- Recall more positive than negative life events.
- Have a higher tolerance level of frustration.
- Are less likely to attempt to commit suicide.
- Are more healthy because the body's immune system fights disease more effectively.
- Need less psychological counseling.

2.4.4   Comparability across Nations

It has sometimes been claimed that well-being measures perform badly when used for comparisons between countries. There may indeed be various kinds of cultural bias in reports of happiness. (See, e.g., Diener, Diener, and Diener 1995.) Thus, Americans have a tendency to claim that they are (very) happy because happiness is positively valued in that society. The French may have the opposite bias. Charles de Gaulle is reported to have quipped: "Happy people are idiots." The Japanese are said to be reluctant to profess to being very happy because of the social custom of modesty prevailing in that country.

Table 2.2 lists happiness indices for a number of countries in order to provide an overview. The reported subjective well-being data range from Denmark, where persons are on average happiest (with an average score of 8.16 on a 10-point life satisfaction scale) and Switzerland (8.02) to the Ukraine and Armenia (with scores 3.95 and 4.32, respectively). In general, persons living in the former Soviet Union countries are on average most unhappy (with a score between 3.95 and 5.39). The population of many formerly communist countries in Central Europe is not particularly happy either, especially in Bulgaria (score 4.66). It may come as a surprise that people in Africa, Central and South America, and Asia profess to be quite happy (with scores ranging from 6.08 for South Africa to 7.78 for Argentina). But note that the table does not include some of the poorest countries. The populations of most OECD countries are well off, which is reflected in a quite high satisfaction with life (Austria having the lowest with 6.51, and Denmark having the highest with 8.16).

Researchers on happiness have used various methods to deal with the claimed distortions due to cultural differences. An example is the *social desirability scale* developed by Douglas Crowne and David Marlowe (1964), which serves to isolate the cultural effects.

While cultural differences undoubtedly play a role, they are not so strong that they make cross-cultural comparisons of happiness meaningless. At least some of the problems can be mitigated by appropriate measurement methods.

Reported happiness measures are certainly not ideal. They should always be looked at with a critical eye. Nevertheless, one should at the same time keep in mind the following conditions:

(a) The required precision depends on the usage intended. For many psychological purposes, it is important to have very precise and detailed measures. For the questions posed by economists, pure precision is less import; it is normally more important to have a good representative sample and a sufficiently large volume of data. Unsystematic errors in individual reports of subjective well-being are then dealt with by applying appropriate econometric techniques.

(b) Many of the shortcomings listed may be mitigated by appropriate research designs.

TABLE 2.2
Reported Subjective Well-Being in Various Countries

	Average Satisfaction with Life	Year		Average Satisfaction with Life	Year
Africa			**Former Soviet Union Countries**		
Nigeria	6.82	1995	Azerbaijan	5.39	1996
South Africa	6.08	1996	Estonia	5.00	1996
			Lithuania	4.99	1996
			Latvia	4.90	1996
Central and South America			Georgia	4.65	1996
Argentina	7.78	1995	Russia	4.45	1995
Mexico	7.69	1996	Belarus	4.35	1996
Brazil	7.15	1997	Armenia	4.32	1997
Uruguay	7.13	1996	Ukraine	3.95	1996
Chile	6.92	1996			
Venezuela	6.72	1996			
Peru	6.36	1996	**OECD Countries**		
			Denmark	8.16	1990
			Switzerland	8.02	1989
Asia			Canada	7.89	1990
Taiwan	6.89	1995	Ireland	7.88	1990
Philippines	6.84	1996	Sweden	7.77	1996
China	6.83	1995	Netherlands	7.77	1990
South Korea	6.69	1996	Finland	7.68	1996
India	6.53	1996	U.S.	7.67	1995
Bangladesh	6.41	1996	Norway	7.66	1996
			Belgium	7.60	1990
			Australia	7.58	1995
Central Europe			Britain	7.46	1998
Slovenia	6.46	1995	Italy	7.30	1990
Poland	6.42	1997	Spain	7.15	1995
Czech Republic	6.37	1990	Germany	7.12	1997
Turkey	6.18	1997	Portugal	7.07	1990
Slovakia	6.15	1990	Iceland	6.93	1990
Hungary	6.03	1990	France	6.78	1990
Romania	5.88	1993	Japan	6.61	1995
Bulgaria	4.66	1997	Austria	6.51	1990

Source: World Values Survey 1990–1993/1995–1997 (ICPSR 2790).

(c) The quality of the happiness data should be compared to alternative concepts of measuring people's level of living and well-being. It is to these that we now turn our attention.

2.5 ALTERNATIVE CONCEPTS OF WELL-BEING

There is a long history of attempts to capture people's well-being using various kinds of measures. Here we discuss some of the most important endeavors.

2.5.1 National Product

Measuring human welfare by constructing an overall measure of economic activity is still the most widely used method. Today, gross national product (GNP) is *the* measure of economic development. It is used to compare standards of living across countries as well as the rate of growth over time. In 1948, the underlying System of National Accounts was adopted by the United Nations in order to make the standards of living and the developments of different economies comparable worldwide.

Using the GNP has one great advantage over subsequent efforts to provide an overall measure of well-being: It is based on a theory analyzing the relationships between individuals and firms involved in creating goods and services. The basic idea is that the value of the goods and services produced is given by the marginal utility for the consumer. In equilibrium—which is assumed to obtain—marginal utility is equal to the market price. The aggregate value of a bundle of goods and services therefore corresponds to the monetary expenditures made by the consumers. This is an ingenious device for solving the evaluation problem.

The national product is, however, faced with serious problems if used as an indicator for well-being:

(a) While at the margin, utility corresponds to price, this does not hold for the consumption of earlier (intramarginal) units. These produce a higher marginal utility than the equilibrium price. The value of the aggregate bundle of goods and services is thus seriously underestimated.

Moreover, the microeconomic foundations of national product are less firm than they appear. (See Slesnick 1998 for a survey.)

In particular, it is in general not possible to aggregate from the level of consumers to the level of the economy as a whole, mainly because of distributional considerations. Indeed, the concept of individual real income or expenditure only translates into real national income if the nation is taken to be a person—which, of course, it is not. Therefore, even in a narrowly utilitarian sense, a higher level of GNP does not necessarily deliver more aggregate welfare (Sen 1979).

(b) The national product considers marketed goods and services. It thus excludes a large part—if not the major part—of social activities. Thus, the services produced in private households, as well as all other interpersonal relationships not based on money, are not measured.

There is one major exception to this market principle. National product includes government activities occurring outside the market. However, the production of the public sector is captured by its cost, which means that the productivity of government activity is fixed and does not increase over time.

(c) The destruction of utility is partly measured as output and thus raises national product. An example is road accidents, which are reflected in expenditures for the rescue teams, hospital care, and the car repairs induced. Other examples of such "regrettables" are commuting, police protection, sanitation, road maintenance, defense, and the disamenities of urban life.

(d) Aspects of income distribution and its change are neglected, though it is known that relative income matters greatly for well-being.

These and other shortcomings of national product are generally known, but the concept is still the center of political, economic, and media attention. This is to a great extent deserved. Consider an economy that has grown in the past and then suffers a marked recession. It is most probable that the people's well-being suffers badly as a result. Few economies have reached such a high level of abundance that a lower level of GNP would not reduce welfare. But, at the same time, the grievous limitations of national product should not be forgotten. There is plenty of room for further measures of human well-being.

2.5.2   Extensions of National Product

Many different efforts have been undertaken to overcome the weaknesses of GNP and to move closer to measuring human welfare. A first step is to delete the 'regrettables' from the accounts. But more important has been to derive welfare measures for nonmarket activities. Household production typically amounts from one-quarter to one-half of conventionally measured national income. The imputed value of leisure is even larger and reaches about the same size as GNP. Taken together, these additional welfare components add about 150 percent to the conventional measure. (See Offer 2001, p. 7.) The *Measure of Economic Welfare* designed by William Nordhaus and James Tobin in 1972 is the best known extension of the national product following this tradition.

More recently, the concept of *sustainability* of welfare has received special attention. The concept defines an aggregate utility level, which can be maintained over an infinite period of time. It has been theoretically shown that the national product net of asset depletion also describes the discounted sustainable productive potential of an economy (Weitzman 1976). Asset depletion, which is generally thought to be important, is caused by the use of nonrenewable natural resources. Other nonmarket factors to be taken into account are the various kinds of pollution such as air, water, ground, and noise pollution. A further step is to include the cost of social detriments such as crime and divorce. The *Economic Aspects of Welfare*, constructed by Xenophon Zolotas in 1981, makes an effort at integrating all these factors into an overall measure.

The *Index of Sustainable Economic Welfare*, devised by Herman E. Daly and John B. Cobb in 1989, in addition takes into account income distribution. As we have stated repeatedly, concerns about income distribution have a marked effect on individual happiness. Over the past few years, there is strong evidence that the distribution of income (even after tax) has become even more unequal. The most glaringly obvious aspect of this is top managers earning millions, sometimes even hundreds of millions of dollars per year from stock options and other bonuses. It is therefore important to take the changes in income distribution into account.

The national product can also be extended if measurement problems are overcome. Individual utilities are certainly influenced by the existence and development of a *shadow* or *underground economy*. Shadow activities (though unregistered) contribute a large and increasing proportion of goods and services to the gross national product. In order to measure its size, there are a large number of sometimes refined approaches available:

(a) Surveys where representative participants in the economic process are asked about their involvement in the nonofficial economy.
(b) Questionnaires addressed to persons with specific knowledge of unofficial activities, such as trade unionists and entrepreneurs.
(c) Data provided by the tax authorities on the amount of tax evasion.
(d) The currency-demand approach, which is based on the idea that unofficial activities are paid in cash in order to leave behind no traces.
(e) The energy approach, assuming that there is a stable relationship between observable energy inputs and both official and unofficial production. In many countries, especially of the Third World or transition economies, it is quite easy to measure electricity input, for instance, and to thereby estimate the size of the shadow economy.
(f) The hidden variables approach, which looks at both the inputs and possible consequences of the existence of the shadow sector. One of the relevant consequences is, for instance, a fall in official work participation rates, suggesting that people take up work outside the conventionally measured economy.

Table 2.3 lists estimates of the size of the shadow economy in various countries. Its size ranges up to 75 percent of gross national product in some African countries such as Nigeria and Egypt. It is also large in some countries of Central and South America and Asia—in several countries (for example, Mexico, Peru, and Thailand) reaching more than 40 percent of GNP. Moreover, it is sizable in some European countries, such as Hungary and Poland, and also in some countries belonging to the European Union. (It is estimated to be up to 30 percent in Greece, Italy, Spain, Portugal and Belgium.) The smallest shadow economies are reported in the small countries of Switzerland and Austria, as well as in the large countries of Japan and the United States.

Another sector left out of GNP is the so-called *voluntary sector*. There is little doubt that its activities produce substantial utility to the beneficiaries. In addition, the persons engaged in the voluntary sector reap utility because they perform meaningful work.

CHAPTER 2

TABLE 2.3
Size of the Shadow Economy as % of GDP, Average over 1990–93.
(Calculations Based on Physical Input (Electricity) and Currency
Demand Approaches)

Africa		OECD Countries	
Nigeria	} 68–75	Greece	
Egypt		Italy	
Tunisia	} 39–45	Spain	} 24–30
Morocco		Portugal	
		Belgium	
Central and South America			
Mexico	} 40–60	Norway	
Peru		Denmark	
Chile		Ireland	
Venezuela	} 25–35	France	} 13–23
Brazil		Netherlands	
		Germany	
		Great Britain	
Asia			
Thailand	} 70	Japan	
Philippines		United States	
Malaysia	} 35–50	Austria	} 8–10
South Korea		Switzerland	
Singapore	} 13		
Central Europe			
Hungary	} 20–28		
Poland			
Romania	} 9–16		
Czech Republic			

Source: Schneider and Enste (2000), Table 2.

Figure 2.1 provides estimates of the size of the voluntary sector in various countries. The largest voluntary sectors in terms of
the percentage of volunteers in the population are reported for the
Netherlands, the United States, the United Kingdom, and France.
In contrast, in Central and South American countries, the voluntary
sector seems to be very small. The same holds for Hungary.

2.5.3 Social Indicators

The fundamental idea behind social indicators is that the availability
and access to particular goods and services constitute a precondition

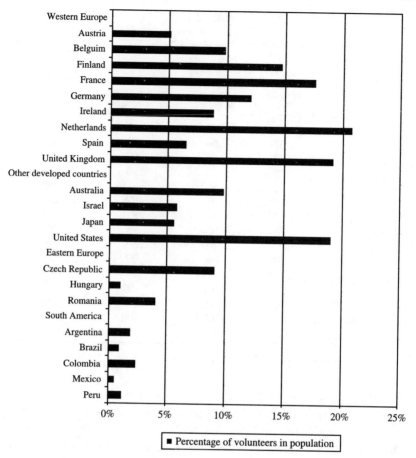

Figure 2.1. Size of the voluntary sector in various countries. Data from Salamon and Anheier (1997).

for welfare or happiness. Typical goods with this property are nutrition, housing, health, education, and the quality of the environment. Crime, poverty, social inequality, and racial and other types of segregation make for unhappiness. In contrast to the extensions of national income, social indicators are not measured in terms of money. One of the most obvious problems therefore is that it is difficult to assess their relative importance for well-being.

Table 2.4 provides examples of widely used social indicators. Three "classical" social indicators are listed: life expectancy, school enrollment, and access to fresh water. The fourth 'indicator' is GNP per capita, which is made comparable by using purchasing power pari-

TABLE 2.4
Social Indicators

	Life Ex-pectancy at Birth, 1998 (Years)	Participation in Secondary Education, 1997 (Net Enroll-ment Ratio)	Access to Safe Water, 1990–96 (% of Population)	GNP per Capita at PPP, 1999 (International $)
Argentina	73	77	65	11324
Brazil	67	66	72	6317
Canada	79	95	99	23725
China	70	70	90	3291
France	78	99	100	21897
Germany	77	95	NA	22404
India	63	60	81	2149
Japan	81	100	96	24041
Kenya	51	61	53	975
Nigeria	53	NA	39	744
South Africa	63	95	70	8318
Switzerland	79	84	100	27486
Thailand	72	48	89	5599
United Kingdom	77	92	100	20883
United States	77	96	NA	30600

Source: World Development Indicators 2000.

ties (PPP). According to the first three indicators, Japan, France, and the United Kingdom excel, though the United States has a higher per capita income. Kenya and Nigeria have low life expectancy (some-what more than 50 years at birth, compared to almost 80 years in rich countries), and low access to safe water (53 percent and 39 percent, respectively, compared to almost 100 percent in rich countries). On the whole, the three classical social indicators exhibit a strong positive correlation with per capita income. But there are exceptions. A strik-ing case is China, where people have long lives (on average 70 years), 70 percent have secondary education, and 90 percent have access to fresh water.

In some cases, only one indicator is considered. An example is *quality-adjusted life years*, which looks at the number of years remain-ing until death, corrected for the quality of health (Zeckhauser and Shepard 1976). Economic historians have looked at a person's height as an indirect welfare index (Fogel 1993, Komlos 1994).

Most social indicators take several subindices together, often giv-ing them the same weight. The *Physical Quality of Life Index* consists of infant mortality, literacy, and life expectancy at age one. The best-known indicator now also used by the World Bank, the *Human Development Index*, is made up of income per head, life expectancy at birth, and education. There are also approaches comprising a much larger set of indicators such as, the *Index of Social Progress* developed by Richard Estes in 1988 with 36 indicators in 10 subgroups.

A related approach is due to Amartya Sen, who first presented it in his 1980 Tanner lecture. It is based on two notions:

(a) *Functionings*, referring to the state of a person—that is, the various things that an individual manages to do or be in the course of leading his or her life.

(b) *Capabilities*, reflecting the alternative combinations of functionings the person can achieve, and from which he or she can make a collection.

Well-being is seen as a combination of various "doings" and "beings." The quality of life is assessed in terms of the capability to reach valued functionings.

2.6 CONCLUSIONS

The classical economists were convinced that utility has content and can be measured. The well-being of persons was seen to consist of subjective happiness. The new welfare economics—which was new in the 1930s—changed this view in a revolutionary way: Utility was deprived of all content and was reduced to a preference index reflecting revealed behavior. There was no way to scientifically measure cardinal utility. Moreover, ordinal utility suffices to derive the relevant theorems of economic theory.

At present, we are witnessing another revolution in viewing utility. Supported by new insights from psychology as well as by the identification of a significant number of behavioral anomalies, utility has been filled with content again: Utility can and should be cardinally measured in the form of subjective well-being. Individual preferences and happiness turn out to be distinctive concepts; they may deviate systematically and noticeably from each other.

Individual subjective well-being may be measured in many ways, ranging from physiological and neurobiological indicators and observed social and nonverbal behavior to surveys. Depending on the issue to be studied, many different dimensions and domains of happiness may usefully be distinguished. The subjective well-being measures based on surveys do not claim to be objective, but attempt a global assessment of the whole sphere of life. Relevant criteria for assessing their usefulness are reliability (is the appraisal of respondents' well-being and their responses undistorted?), validity (does the measure reflect true inner feelings?), consistency (does the measure correspond to other observations normally connected with happiness?), and comparability across nations.

The happiness measures certainly do not fully meet these criteria in an ideal way, but some of the shortcomings are of little or no relevance for the purpose at hand. Thus, for example, the criterion of international comparability is irrelevant for the analysis presented on the effect of institutions on happiness (chapters 8 and 9) because the happiness data only refer to one country. It should, moreover, be remembered that all social science measures are imperfect. Examples are the gross national product as well as its extensions (such as the Index of Sustainable Economic Welfare) and social indicators (such as the Human Development Index). The discussion of these alternative measures shows that they are no substitute for happiness indicators. But they can certainly amend reported subjective well-being by pointing to otherwise possibly neglected aspects.

Hints on the Literature

Excellent discussions on the new welfare economics and the position of conventional economics with respect to cardinal and ordinal utility are provided in

Holländer, Heinz (2001). On the Validity of Utility Statements. *Journal of Economic Behavior and Organization* 45(3): 227–49.

Ng, Yew-Kwang (1997). A Case for Happiness, Cardinalism, and Interpersonal Comparability. *Economic Journal* 107(445): 1848–58.

Van Praag, Bernard M. S., and Paul Frijters (1999). The Measurement of Welfare and Well-Being: The Leyden Approach. In Daniel Kahneman, Ed Diener, and Norbert. Schwarz (eds.), *Well-Being: The Foundations of Hedonic Psychology*. New York: Russell Sage Foundation, 413–33.

A major step beyond conventional welfare economics has been undertaken by

Scitovsky, Tibor (1976). *The Joyless Economy: An Inquiry into Human Satisfaction and Dissatisfaction*. Oxford: Oxford University Press.

Similarly radical positions are taken by

Frank, Robert H. (1985). *Choosing the Right Pond*. New York: Oxford University Press.

———(1999). *Luxury Fever: Why Money Fails to Satisfy in an Era of Excess*. New York: Free Press.

Multinational studies of subjective well-being were started in the late 1970s with the work of

Cantril, Hadley (1976). *The Pattern of Human Concerns*. New Brunswick, N.J.: Rutgers University Press.

Gallup, George H. (1976). Human Needs and Satisfactions: A Global Survey. *The Public Opinion Quarterly* 41: 459–67.

A comprehensive but short survey of the present state of the concept and measurement of happiness appears in

Easterlin, Richard A. (2000). Income and Happiness: Towards a Unified Theory. Mimeo. University of Southern California, Los Angeles.

Biases in cognition are extensively discussed in

Schwarz, Norbert, and Fritz Strack (1999). Reports of Subjective Well-Being: Judgmental Processes and Their Methodological Implications. In Daniel Kahneman, Ed Diener, and Norbert Schwarz (eds.), *Well-Being: The Foundations of Hedonic Psychology*. New York: Russell Sage Foundation, 61–84.

For the special case of overoptimism, see

Weinstein, Neil D. (1981). Unrealistic Optimism about Future Life Events. *Journal of Personality and Social Psychology* 39(5): 806–20.

The concept has been generalized and introduced into economics as *ipsative theory* by

Frey, Bruno S., and Beat Heggli (1999). An Ipsative Theory of Human Behavior. In Bruno S. Frey, *Economics as a Science of Human Behavior*. Boston: Kluwer Academic Publishers, 195–211.

The limited capacity to predict future tastes is the subject of

Loewenstein, George, and David Schkade (1999). *Wouldn't It Be Nice? Predicting Future Feelings*. In Daniel Kahneman, Ed Diener, and Norbert Schwarz (eds.) *Well-Being: The Foundations of Hedonic Psychology*. New York: Russell Sage Foundation, 85–105.

The role of emotions in economics has been discussed by

Elster, Jon (1998). Emotions and Economic Theory. *Journal of Economic Literature* 36(1): 47–74.

A broad discussion of reported subjective well-being can be found in the surveys cited in the hints on the literature in chapter 1 as well as in

Veenhoven, Ruut (1991b). Questions on Happiness: Classical Topics, Modern Answers, Blind Spots. In Fritz Strack, Michael Argyle, and Norbert Schwarz (eds.), *Subjective Well-Being: An Interdisciplinary Perspective*. Oxford: Pergamon Press, 7–26.

———(1997). Progres dans la comprehension du bonheur. *Revue Quebecoise de Psychologie* 18: 29–74.

Diener, Ed, Eunkook M. Suh, Richard E. Lucas, and Heidi L. Smith (1999). Subjective Well-Being: Three Decades of Progress. *Psychological Bulletin* 125(2): 276–303.

This last paper also discusses the various decompositions of happiness into areas and domains. Job satisfaction is extensively discussed in

Warr, Peter (1999). Well-Being and the Workplace. In Daniel Kahneman, Ed Diener, and Norbert Schwarz (eds.), *Well-Being: The Foundations of Hedonic Psychology.* New York: Russell Sage Foundation, 392–412.

For a formalization of well-being and its integration into the economic context, see

Blanchflower, Daniel G., and Andrew J. Oswald (2000). Well-Being over Time in Britain and the USA. NBER Working Paper No. 7487. Cambridge, Mass.: National Bureau of Economic Research.

Reliability and validity of happiness indicators are discussed in the paper just quoted by Veenhoven (1997).

For the correlation of happiness measures with other observations (that is, consistency), see, for example,

Myers, David G. (1993). *The Pursuit of Happiness: Who Is Happy and Why?* New York: Avon.

Comparability across nations is discussed, for instance, by

Diener, Ed, Eunkook M. Suh, Heidi Smith, and Liang Shao (1995). National Differences in Reported Subjective Well-Being: Why Do They Occur? *Social Indicators Research* 34(1): 7–32.

Diener, Ed and Eunkook M. Suh (eds.) (2000). *Culture and Subjective Well-Being.* Cambridge, Mass.: MIT Press.

Alternative approaches to measuring human well-being are discussed in

Offer, Avner (2001). On Economic Welfare Measurement and Human Well-Being over the Long Run. In Paul A. David, Peter Solar, and Mark Thomas (eds.), *The Economic Future in Historical Perspective.* London: British Academy.

The microeconomic bases of conventional measurements are surveyed by

Slesnick, Daniel T. (1998). Empirical Approaches to the Measurement of Welfare. *Journal of Economic Literature* 36(4): 2108–65.

The various possibilities of measuring the size and development of the shadow economy are surveyed and estimates are provided in

Schneider, Friedrich, and Dominik Enste (2000). Increasing Shadow Economy All over the World—Fiction or Reality? *Journal of Economic Literature* 38(1): 77–114.

A survey and estimates of the voluntary or "third sector" are given by

Roy, Kakoli, and Susanne Ziemek (2000). On the Economics of Volunteering. Discussion Papers on Development Policy No. 31. Center for Development Research. University of Bonn, Germany.

The capabilities approach is due to

Sen, Amartya K. (1993). Capability and Well-Being. In Amartya Sen and Martha Nussbaum (eds.), *The Quality of Life*. Oxford: Oxford University Press, 30–53.

Chapter 3

PERSONALITY AND SOCIO-DEMOGRAPHIC INFLUENCES ON HAPPINESS

3.1 The Economic Perspective

PSYCHOLOGISTS AND SOCIOLOGISTS rightly focus on the possible influence of personality factors (such as optimism, self-esteem, and perceived personal control) and demographic factors (such as age and gender) when studying why people are happy or unhappy. These factors play a large role in their respective field and therefore psychologists and sociologists have a lot of factual knowledge about them. They are also well aware of possible pitfalls when using these concepts. Moreover, simple observation based on real-life experience suggests there are people who are intrinsically "happy" and others who are intrinsically unhappy. The same applies to demographic factors. Many people are convinced that old people become increasingly less happy "by nature," not only because their physical and cognitive capacities deteriorate, but also because of psychological factors such as depression.

From the economic point of view, personality and demographic factors are not of primary importance. They are influenced partly by economic conditions. The extent of a person's optimism is likely to be higher when the economy is booming than when it is depressed. Similarly, personal control is perceived to be higher when an economy prospers than when economic conditions are bad. Demographic factors, such as age and gender, do not depend on the state of the economy. But marital status to some extent does: Getting married (or getting a divorce) at times depends to some degree on economic conditions.

To the extent that personality and demographic factors depend on economic conditions, their influence on happiness is captured by directly analyzing the effect of economic factors on happiness. If, however, these factors exert an independent influence on subjective well-being, they have to be taken into account in order to correctly specify the relationship between the various determining factors and happiness. Thus, even if one concentrates on economic and institutional factors—as economists rightly do—personality and demographic factors should be integrated into the analysis (that is, into a multiple regression equation) in order not to fall prey to an estimation bias. In the empirical study presented later in this chapter and book, these factors are used as "controls" to the extent that corresponding variables are available. As personality and demographic factors as such are of limited interest for the reasons just given, what follows is only a short survey of the findings reached by other social scientists. For an in-depth discussion of the many different, and sometimes inconsistent, results, the reader is referred to the specialized literature listed at the end of this chapter. The survey provided here concentrates on robust and major results. Section 3.2 discusses the personality factors and section 3.3 the demographic factors influencing happiness. Section 3.4 introduces our own empirical analysis of a microeconometric happiness function for Switzerland. For socio-demographic factors it is demonstrated how survey data on subjective well-being can be empirically studied. Section 3.5 draws some conclusions.

3.2   PERSONALITY FACTORS

In many studies, personality has turned out to be a strong predictor of subjective well-being. Above all, two different sets of factors pertaining to an individual's personality structure significantly influence subjective well-being.

3.2.1   Temperamental Predisposition

Some people have a genetic predisposition to be happy or unhappy, which can be attributed to inborn individual differences in the nervous system. If one focuses on happiness over the long run, heritability may have a substantial influence on happiness, but the respective impact very much depends on the environment. The relationship between personality and happiness may be described by a dynamic equilibrium theory (Headey and Wearing 1989), according to which the fundamental levels of subjective well-being are determined by the genetically given capacity to be happy or unhappy. Events, such as higher income, move people above (or below) this baseline, but in time they will return to this stable level.

That people indeed have different genetic capacities to feel happy or unhappy is supported by the empirical observation that there is consistency across different domains of life. A person who is happy at work also tends to be happy in his leisure time or at home with his family.

3.2.2 Traits and Cognitive Dispositions

Persons expecting favorable outcomes in their lives will work hard to achieve the goals they have set for themselves. In contrast, people expecting failure will tend to disengage from the goals they have set themselves. This type of behavior leads to more successful achievement of goals by optimists than by pessimists (Scheier and Carver 1985). As a result, optimists tend to be happier.

A related trait is *perceived control*. It has, for instance, been found that persons with low income are less unhappy when they have strong control beliefs (Lachman and Weaver 1998). They do not take low income as immutable, but are convinced that they can change the situation. As a consequence, such low-income recipients are less unhappy than are pessimists who find themselves in the same situation. But it is difficult to disentangle whether optimism and perceived control are the cause or the result of higher happiness. Happy people recall more good events because they initially encode more of the events occurring in their lives in a positive way (Seidlitz and Diener 1993). In contrast, people who ruminate on the negative events in their lives tend to have lower subjective well-being.

It is interesting to note that *unrealistic optimism* and *unrealistic control perceptions* also contribute to happiness (Taylor and Brown 1988). Persons with these traits are better able to successfully adjust to unfavorable circumstances, including extremely adverse ones.

Many studies find that *extroversion* contributes to happiness whereas *neuroticism* can lead to unhappiness. This relationship is strong and consistent. A major reason may be that extroverted persons are more sensitive to rewards and therefore experience a larger positive affect when they are exposed to rewarding stimuli (Lucas et al. 2001). As many situations in the company of others are more pleasant than staying alone, extroverts more actively seek social situations than do introverted persons, which in turn raises the extroverts' subjective well-being. Extroverts' greater happiness may thus partly be explained by spending a greater amount of time in positive interactions with other people. But they also tend to respond more positively to the same stimuli and events than other people do. Extroverts are happier than introverts, even when they live alone, work in jobs with few social contacts, or live in rural, isolated areas (Diener et al. 1992).

Self-esteem is another trait positively and strongly related to happiness. Indeed, people employ many diverse cognitive strategies to maintain their self-esteem—for instance, by ignoring evidence that might undermine this belief (e.g., Dunning, Leuenberger, and Sherman 1995). This relationship is not universal, but holds mainly for Western cultures centering on the individual. In more collectivist cultures valuing the family and group relationship above everything else, harmony rather than self-esteem is strongly correlated with life satisfaction. (See Kwan, Bond, and Singelis 1997 for a comparison of this correlation in the United States and Hong Kong.)

3.3 Socio-Demographic Factors

The early studies on happiness assumed that factors such as age, gender, and marital status are the major determinants of happiness. Individual differences in well-being were attributed to socio-economic groups defined, for example, by age, sex, and marital status, and individual differences in happiness were thought to be by-products of these group differences. The socio-demographic approach therefore differs basically from the approach discussed in the previous section, where differences in well-being were attributed to personality factors unique to a particular person.

This section discusses three demographic factors—age, gender, and ethnicity (race)—and four more strongly socially determined sets of factors—in particular, for health. It stands to reason that the happiness of old persons strongly depends on whether they are in reasonably good health. Controlling for health and other factors (for example, in Great Britain), it has been found that happiness is lowest around age 40 (for men, age 43; for women, age 40). People seem to be happier when they are younger as well as when they are older. This decline and rise in self-professed well-being may be attributed to an adaptation to conditions. By midlife, people may give up some of their aspirations and therefore enjoy life more fully.

For several reasons it is difficult to capture the influence of age on well-being:

- The term *happiness* may change its meaning with age.
- The interpretation of the response scale on which well-being is reported may change due to semantic conventions or reference groups.
- The age effect may interfere with a cohort effect. The change in happiness observed may be due to the time that has elapsed and not to age as such. Thus, old people today are on average less healthy than their counterparts in the future will be. A study of young Americans and Europeans (Blanchflower and Oswald 2000a) suggests indeed that they are getting happier over time.
- Even causation is not as clear as it seems to be at first sight. Happy people live a little longer than unhappy people, which contributes to a positive correlation between age and happiness.

Because of these problems, much care should be taken when claiming that old age leads to unhappiness, or that the old are happier than the young. It should be noted that the economic studies just referred to reach a more differentiated conclusion—namely, that the young and the old are happier than the middle-aged.

3.3.2 *Gender*

Women exhibit higher self-reported happiness than men, but the difference is rather small (e.g., Inglehart 1990, White 1992). That there are gender differences in well-being is also reflected in angry moods, aggressive behavior, sadness, fear and anxiety, antisocial personality disorder, conduct disorder, and substance abuse and dependence (Nolen-Hoeksema and Rusting 1999). But the higher professed happiness of women seems to be at odds with the many studies of mental disorders, revealing higher rates for women than men for all mood and anxiety disorders (with the exception of manic episodes, see Kessler et al. 1994). What also distinguishes women from men is that women on average experience *both* more extreme positive emotions and more extreme negative emotions than men do. Women have a higher tendency to report being very happy and also a somewhat higher tendency to report being very unhappy. Women and men differ mainly in the intensity of feelings, which may explain the overall observation of "happier" women. This difference may in turn be due to the gender roles, deriving from the association between gender and social roles in society. Women are allowed and even taught to be more emotional than men, especially when it comes to intimate relationships (Wood, Rhodes, and Whelan 1989).

Women's higher subjective well-being may also be explained by a higher genetic capacity to experience happiness or by lower aspiration levels. Women may just be happier than men because they are expecting less in life or have been taught to be satisfied with less.

In consonance with research by psychologists, the studies of happiness undertaken by economists have generally found that women profess to be happier than men do. According to one study (Blanchflower and Oswald 2000b), American women have, however, experienced a decline in reported well-being from the early 1970s to the late 1990s, while men have not. This comes as a surprise because these decades have witnessed a reduction in the discrimination against women and their fuller integration into working life. However, increased equality may have raised women's aspirations so that they are less satisfied with the same life circumstances than earlier. While aspiration levels are difficult to empirically assess independent of reported happiness, it is crucial to control for other influences when analyzing whether women are genetically more or less happy than men. It is well known, for instance, that women receive lower income, even for the same type of work. This particular factor would make women less happy than men.

3.3.3 Ethnicity

That blacks are less happy than whites is the finding of all psychological and sociological studies on that topic for the United States (e.g., Campbell, Converse, and Rodgers 1976). But it also holds

3.3.5   Close Relationships and Marriage

Aristotle referred to man as a "social animal" to emphasize how important interpersonal relationships are. To have an enduring, intimate relationship is one of the major goals of most persons. To have friends, companions, and relatives and to be part of a group, be it co-workers or fellow church members, contribute to happiness. The importance of "belonging" is reflected by the experimental finding that even trivial definitions of groups—for instance, persons who favor one abstract painter over another—lead to group identification and affect the dividing up of money (Tajfel 1981).

Without any doubt, the most important interpersonal relationship is marriage and the family. Marriage indeed raises happiness, as has been found in a large number of studies for different countries and periods (e.g., Diener et al. 2000). Married persons report greater subjective well-being than persons who have never married, divorced, separated, or been widowed. Married women are happier than unmarried women, and married men are happier than unmarried men. Married women and married men report similar levels of subjective well-being; that is, marriage does not benefit one gender more than the other.

These results go well with the observation that marriage brings marked advantages in terms of mortality, morbidity, and mental health (Lee, Seccombe, and Shehan 1991). Couples also positively affect each other's well-being (Sullivan 1996). The positive relationship between marriage and happiness persists, even when the influence of variables such as income, age, and education is controlled for.

Does marriage cause happiness or does happiness promote marriage? A selection effect cannot be ruled out. It seems reasonable to say that dissatisfied and introverted people find it more difficult to find a partner. It is more fun to be with extroverted, trusting, and compassionate persons. Happy and confident people are more likely to marry and to stay married (Veenhoven 1989). But careful research has led to the conclusion that this selection effect is not strong and that the positive association of marriage and happiness is mainly due to the beneficial effects of marriage (Mastekaasa 1995).

There are two main reasons why marriage contributes to well-being (Argyle 1999):

- Marriage provides additional sources of self-esteem—for instance, by providing an escape from stress in other parts of one's life (in particular, one's job). It is advantageous for one's personal identity to have several legs to stand on.

- Married people have a better chance to benefit from an enduring and supportive intimate relationship, and they suffer less from loneliness.

Among the nonmarried, persons who cohabit with a partner are significantly happier than those who live alone. But this effect depends on the culture one lives in. It turns out that people living together in individualistic societies report higher life satisfaction than single, and sometimes even married, people. The opposite holds for collectivist societies.

The difference in happiness between married and never-married persons has fallen in recent years. The "happiness gap" has decreased both because the never-married have experienced increasing happiness and because the married have experienced decreasing happiness (Lee, Seccombe, and Shehan 1991). This finding is consistent with people marrying later, divorcing more often, and marrying less, as well as with the increasing number of unmarried partners, even where there are children.

Economic research on happiness has also found that marriage and happiness are very positively connected, holding other influences constant. Somewhat surprisingly, second, third, and fourth marriages turn out to be less happy than first marriages (Blanchflower and Oswald 2000b). With respect to marriage partners, and perhaps marriage as an institution, people do not seem to learn much. Therefore, marriage has been counted among the "behavioral anomalies" (Frey and Eichenberger 2001).

3.3.6 Intelligence and Education

General and President Charles de Gaulle of France is reported to have said that only fools are happy. This corresponds to the picture of an intelligentsia afflicted with self-doubt and even mental illness, of which Friedrich Nietzsche is a typical example.

The presumed negative relationship between intelligence and subjective well-being has been refuted by empirical research. The two appear to be essentially unrelated. Whether particularly intelligent persons are happy depends on how successful they are in their lives, and whether their higher aspirations are counterbalanced by corresponding achievements.

The level of education, as such, bears little relationship to happiness. Education is highly correlated with income, whose effect on subjective well-being will be discussed in chapter 4. Education may indirectly contribute to happiness by allowing a better adaptation to changing environments. But it also tends to raise aspiration levels. It has, for instance, been found that the highly educated are more distressed than the less well educated when they are hit by unemployment (Clark and Oswald 1994).

3.3.7 Religion

Believing in God and happiness are positively related, but the effect is not large. The effect holds even after controlling for demographic influences, such as marital status, income, and, especially, age. Thus Marx may have been right when he proclaimed that religion is an "opiate for the masses" leading to higher feelings of well-being.

There are various reasons why religion raises happiness:

- Church attendance is an important source of social support. Particularly for people who have lost other kinds of support, such as older people and widows, religious activities and the sense of communion experienced provide an effective substitute.
- Religion offers an "interpretative framework" (Ellison 1991), which can instill life with meaning and purpose. The feeling of being close to God and the belief in an afterlife provide existential certainty and are a source of happiness.
- Religious people are better able to cope with adverse circumstances. A bad event can better be overcome if it is attributed to the will of God.
- Church members are on average of better health, mainly because they behave correspondingly: They drink and smoke less and are sexually less promiscuous. They therefore live longer (Jarvis and Northcott 1987).

There may also be reverse causality: Happier people are more religious. This is particularly so in societies in which religion plays a prominent social role and where participation in church is positively regarded. There are also many open questions awaiting research.

The survey did not collect any information on personality factors, but included a number of socio-demographic and socio-economic characteristics of the respondents: The age, gender, citizenship, health, extent of formal education, marital status, employment status, and household income. The household income situation is measured in terms of an equivalence income: Total household income after taxes, social security expenditure, interest on debts, and maintenance is adjusted for the number of persons living in the household.

3.4.2 Estimation Methods and Estimation Results

Table 3.1 presents the detailed results of the econometric estimation of the demographic correlates of happiness for Switzerland in 1992–94. But it should be noted that a *complete* happiness function, including socio-economic and institutional factors, is used in order to avoid a biased estimate. Thus, only the results for the demographic correlates are listed. (The full set of estimated coefficients is presented in Appendix A of this book.)

The first column of data in Table 3.1 gives the descriptive statistics— that is, the *mean value of life satisfaction* (ranging from 1 to 10) of the respective factor. Persons aged between 20 and 29 (first row), for example, report a satisfaction score of 8.19; those between 30 and 39 a satisfaction score of 8.03, and so on. These averages allow for the assessment of the total effect of certain socio-demographic characteristics, such as the age categories just mentioned. Compared with means for other categories of the same demographic dimension, they offer rough information about simple correlations. If you take the age factor, there is neither a positive nor a negative simple correlation with life satisfaction in the raw data. Persons between 50 and 59 years of age are less happy (score 7.97) than younger as well as older age groups. These descriptive results are an amalgam of various effects on happiness taken into consideration for different age categories. For example, life satisfaction may be reduced for older people because of severe illness being more frequent, although age itself may have no negative effect on happiness. Thus, satisfaction with life depend not only on one determinant—age—but on many other factors.

In order to account for the many factors of happiness, two multiple regressions are conducted. These regressions help to disentangle the effects of different socio-demographic, as well as socio-economic and

TABLE 3.1 (Part 1)
Socio-Demographic Factors of Satisfaction with Life in Switzerland, 1992–94

	Descriptive Statistics	Weighted Least Squares	Weighted Ordered Probit	
	Mean (1)	Coefficient (t-Value) (2)	Coefficient (t-Value) (3)	Marginal Effect for a Score of 10 (4)
Age 20–29	8.19		Reference group	
Age 30–39	8.03	−0.142 (−1.06)	−0.084 (−0.96)	−0.028
Age 40–49	8.22	−0.001 (−0.01)	0.001 (0.01)	−0.3 − e3
Age 50–59	7.97	−0.053 (−0.61)	−0.012 (−0.20)	−0.004
Age 60–69	8.45	0.449 (4.53)	0.313 (4.60)	0.112
Age 70–79	8.41	0.557 (4.48)	0.387 (4.66)	0.141
Age 80 and older	8.22	0.435 (2.73)	0.332 (3.01)	0.121
Male	8.22		Reference group	
Female	8.22	−0.011 (−0.25)	0.006 (0.19)	0.002
Swiss	8.30		Reference group	
Foreigner	7.62	−0.489 (−5.10)	−0.31 (−5.14)	−0.098
Good health	8.31		Reference group	
Bad health	7.48	−0.74 (−8.18)	−0.438 (−7.71)	−0.133
Low education	7.97		Reference group	
Middle education	8.31	0.219 (4.18)	0.091 (2.50)	0.031
High education	8.41	0.209 (2.85)	0.069 (1.58)	0.024
Married	8.36		Reference group	
Separated, no partner	6.62	−0.948 (−1.92)	−0.570 (−2.32)	−0.159
Separated, with partner	6.33	−1.32 (−1.78)	−0.762 (−2.14)	−0.195

TABLE 3.1 (Part 2)
Socio-Demographic Factors of Satisfaction with Life, Switzerland in 1992–94

	Descriptive Statistics	Weighted Least Squares	Weighted Ordered Probit	
	Mean (1)	Coefficient (t-Value) (2)	Coefficient (t-Value) (3)	Marginal Effect for a Score of 10 (4)
Widowed, no partner	8.16	−0.264 (−3.35)	−0.201 (−3.98)	−0.065
Widowed, with partner	8.35	0.104 (0.58)	0.047 (0.32)	−0.016
Divorced, no partner	7.43	−0.633 (−4.66)	−0.354 (−4.11)	−0.109
Divorced, with partner	7.90	−0.179 (−0.91)	−0.083 (−0.66)	−0.028
Single, no partner	8.01	−0.262 (−2.91)	−0.171 (−2.63)	−0.056
Single, with partner	8.17	−0.097 (−1.11)	−0.08 (−1.29)	−0.027
Socio-economic factors		Included	Included	
Institutional factor		Included	Included	
Observations		6,137	6,137	

Source of data: Leu, Burri, and Priester (1997).
Notes: Dependent variable: level of satisfaction on a 10-point scale. White estimator for variance; t-values are in parentheses. Standard errors are adjusted to clustering in 26 cantons. Additional control variables (not shown) for size of community (five variables) and type of community (seven variables).

institutional, factors from each other: They show the correlation of every single factor with life satisfaction, all other factors being constant. Staying with the example of age and illness, the correlation between age and happiness is independent of whether older people suffer more often from severe illness than younger people.

In Table 3.1, the second column presents the *coefficients* of a basic multiple regression analysis—namely, a *linear weighted least squares estimate*. The t-values are in parentheses below the respective coefficients. A t-value indicates statistical significance if it is, in absolute value, larger than 2. Statistical significance of a positive (negative) coefficient means that we can expect a positive (negative) coefficient with a probability of 95 percent if we estimate a second equation from a second random sample chosen from the same total population.

As we have put the socio-demographic characteristics into several categories, we always compare them with a reference category. For age, the 20–29 age group is taken as the reference. The coefficients can now be interpreted. The coefficient of the 60–69 age group, for example, indicates that persons in the 60–69 age group are, on average, and keeping all other influences constant, 0.449 points more satisfied with life than persons in the 20–29 age group. This difference is statistically significant. (The t-value is 4.53 and clearly exceeds the threshold value of 2.) This effect is quite sizable. As can also be seen in Table 3.1, persons in the 70–79 age group are even 0.557 points happier, on average, than those between ages 20 and 29, again an effect that is statistically significant (t-value 4.48). The weighted least squares coefficients provide a consistent picture: 30–59 age groups are (ceteris paribus) less happy than the young ones (20–29 age group). Beginning with age groups from 60 up to age 80 and older, people are, on average, happier again. Our estimate thus reflects the U-shaped curve of the (marginal) effects of age on happiness identified for other countries.

Columns (3) and (4) of Table 3.1 list the results of the *weighted order probit estimate*, which takes into account that the happiness variable is not continuous, but that each respondent to the survey can state only whether she considers herself to have a life satisfaction score of 1, or 2, or 3, and so on. Moreover, the happiness variable to be explained by the econometric estimate is bounded above (it cannot exceed 10) and below (it cannot fall below 1). Due to the nonlinear form of the estimation equation, only the sign, but not the size, of a coefficient can be directly interpreted. The coefficient of −0.084 pertaining to the 30–39 age group shows that this age group is—all other factors kept constant—less happy than the people in the reference group (age 20–29). This effect in not statistically significantly different from 0 (the t-value being −0.96). The signs of the coefficients mirror those of the weighted least square estimate: The age groups above 30 seem to be slightly less happy than the young ones. (These effects are small and not statistically significant.) Those above 60 are happier, and this effect is statistically significant.

The quantitative effect of age on happiness—again keeping all other influences on happiness constant—can best be represented by the *marginal effect* for a score of 10 shown in column (4). The marginal effect of −0.028 pertaining to the 30–39 age group indicates that the proportion of persons of age 30–39 who report to be completely satisfied with life (score 10) is 2.8 percentage points lower than for the reference age group 20–29. The marginal effect of −0.028 can also be interpreted to indicate that the probability that a person between 30 and 39 reports himself to be completely satisfied (score 10) is 2.8 percentage points lower than for a person of the reference group. Inspection of the marginal effects of age reveals that the age groups above 60 report a much higher satisfaction with life than the younger age groups. Compared to the reference group (20–29 years of age), the 60–69-year-olds report a 11.2–percentage-point, the 70–79-year-olds a 14.1–percentage-point, and those above 80 a 12.1–percentage-point higher probability of being completely satisfied with life.

The lower parts of Table 3.1 exhibit the effect on life satisfaction of other socio-demographic factors. In the following, only large effects (which are statistically significant) are discussed:

- Foreigners report themselves to be less happy than Swiss nationals. Keeping other influences constant, the difference amounts to 9.8 percentage points.
- Persons in bad health report a 13.3–percentage-points lower probability of being completely satisfied than those in good health (ceteris paribus).
- Persons with middle and higher education are 3.1 percentage points and 2.4 percentage points, respectively, more likely to be very happy than those with a low amount of education.
- The proportions of people reporting the highest happiness score who have no partner and are separated, widowed, or divorced are 15.9, 6.5, and 10.9 percentage points, respectively, lower than for married persons.

3.5 Conclusions

The discussion of the previous work and our own estimates with recent data for Switzerland yield remarkable insights into the influence of personality and, above all, socio-demographic factors on happiness. These influences are of considerable interest for anyone who wants to know the correlates of subjective well-being. But, as has been pointed out at the beginning of this chapter, from the economic point of view these factors also serve as controls in order to well capture the influence of economic and institutional factors on happiness.

The following socio-economic variables have the most consistent and strongest correlation with subjective well-being:

- *Age*: Getting older does not make for unhappiness. Rather, the young and the old are happier than the middle-aged.
- *Gender*: Women report being happier than men, but the difference is not large and has tended to disappear in recent decades.
- *Health*: Good health is an important factor in individual well-being.
- *Close relationships and marriage*: Single women and single men are less happy than married couples, but this difference has tended to decrease in recent years.
- *Education*: A good scholastic background is no guarantee for happiness but may help people to cope better with life, thus raising satisfaction.
- *Nationality*: Foreigners are less happy than nationals.

Our discussion has emphasized that these conclusions must be carefully considered. They are subject to three major problems:

(a) The relationships identified are partly due to a selection effect, such as happy people are more likely to be married than unhappy ones. It is therefore always necessary to check to what degree the selection effect is relevant in a particular case. In the case of marriage, it has been found that the selection effect is minor and that, for several reasons, marriage contributes to subjective well-being.

(b) The causality does not necessarily go from the factors just mentioned to happiness, but may run in the opposite direction. Thus, good health does not only cause happiness, but happy people also tend to be in better health. As with the selection effect, it is necessary to collect additional evidence in order to ascertain the direction of causation.

(c) The effects identified are conditional on a great number of other influences. Thus, the effect of gender on happiness strongly depends on the economic situation. In order to control for such influences, the influences of all factors on happiness have to be simultaneously considered. This has been done in the econometric estimates presented for Switzerland, where socio-demographic, socio-economic, and institutional factors are taken as simultaneous influences on happiness.

Hints on the Literature

The discussion in sections 3.2 and 3.3 of this chapter has greatly benefited from comprehensive surveys by

Argyle, Michael (1999). Causes and Correlates of Happiness. In Daniel Kahneman, Ed Diener, and Norbert Schwarz (eds.), *Well-Being: The Foundations of Hedonic Psychology*. New York: Russell Sage Foundation, 353–73.

Diener, Ed, Eunkook M. Suh, Richard E. Lucas, and Heidi L. Smith (1999). Subjective Well-Being: Three Decades of Progress. *Psychological Bulletin* 125(2): 276–303.

Veenhoven, Ruut (1997). Progres dans la comprehension du bonheur. *Revue Quebecoise de Psychologie* 18: 29–74.

These works contain extensive references to the literature.

The influence of personality on happiness is further discussed, for instance, in

Diener, Ed, and Richard E. Lucas (1999). Personality and Subjective Well-Being. In Daniel Kahneman, Ed Diener, and Norbert Schwarz (eds.), *Well-Being: The Foundations of Hedonic Psychology*. New York: Russell Sage Foundation, 213–29.

DeNeve, Kristina M., and Harris Cooper (1998). The Happy Personality: A Meta-Analysis of 137 Personality Traits and Subjective Well-Being. *Psychological Bulletin* 124(2): 197–229.

The relationship between age and happiness is the topic of

Diener, Ed, and Eunkook M. Suh (1997). Subjective Well-Being and Age: An International Analysis. *Annual Review of Gerontology and Geriatrics* 17: 304–24.

Horley, James, and John J. Lavery (1995). Subjective Well-Being and Age. *Social Indicators Research* 34: 283–86.

Mroczek, Daniel K., and Christian M. Kolarz (1998). The Effect of Age on Positive and Negative Affect: A Developmental Perspective on Happiness. *Journal of Personality and Social Psychology* 75(5): 1333–49.

The question of whether, and why, women are happier than men is discussed in

Nolen-Hoeksema, Susan, and Cheryl L. Rusting (1999). Gender Differences in Well-Being. In Daniel Kahneman, Ed Diener, and Norbert Schwarz (eds.), *Well-Being: The Foundations of Hedonic Psychology*. New York: Russell Sage Foundation, 330–50.

Close relationships and marriage as determinants of happiness are treated in

Lee, Gary R., Karen Seccombe, and Constance L. Shehan (1991). Marital Status and Personal Happiness: An Analysis of Trend Data. *Journal of Marriage and the Family* 53 (November): 839–44.

Myers, David G. (1999). Close Relationship and Quality of Life. In Daniel Kahneman, Ed Diener, and Norbert Schwarz (eds.), *Well-Being: The Foundations of Hedonic Psychology*. New York: Russell Sage Foundation, 374–91.

Sullivan, Oriel (1996). The Enjoyment of Activities: Do Couples Affect Each Others' Well-Being? *Social Indicators Research* 38(1): 81–102.

Economists who have captured the influence on happiness of demographic factors include

Blanchflower, Daniel G., and Andrew J. Oswald (2000). Well-Being over Time in Britain and the USA. NBER Working Paper no. 7487. Cambridge, Mass.: National Bureau of Economic Research.

Clark, Andrew E., and Andrew J. Oswald (1994). Unhappiness and Unemployment. *Economic Journal* 104(424): 648–59.

Graham, Carol, and Stefano Pettinato (2000). Happiness, Markets, and Democracy: Latin America in Comparative Perspective. Working Paper no. 13. Washington D.C.: Center on Social and Economic Dynamics, Brookings Institution.

The empirical data that are extensively analyzed in this book are from a survey conducted by

Leu, Robert E., Stefan Burri, and Tom Priester (1997). *Lebensqualität und Armut in der Schweiz*. Bern: Haupt.

A deeper understanding of the applied econometric estimation techniques is provided by

Greene, William H. (1997). *Econometric Analysis*, 3rd ed. Upper Saddle River, N.J.: Prentice Hall.

PART II

Economic Effects on Happiness

WITHIN THE ECONOMY, there are three major influences on happiness:
- Income.
- Unemployment.
- Inflation.

These are the central variables of macroeconomic theories, and they have also proved to be the major determinants of the citizens' satisfaction with their government, as captured by election and popularity functions. Income, unemployment, and inflation are directly relevant to an economic analysis of happiness for the following reasons:
- Material conditions and prospects are two major concerns for most people when they are asked about life satisfaction.
- The three macroeconomic variables can be influenced by economic policy. Economists have accumulated a great deal of knowledge about the possibilities and limits of bringing about changes in income, employment, and prices. They thus have a comparative advantage, which is not the case for personality factors or some socio-demographic factors.

Chapter 4 discusses the relationship between income and happiness, taking three different aspects into consideration. First, comparisons are made between countries as a whole: Are people in the richest countries necessarily the happiest? Or do people in developing countries enjoy life more? Second, comparisons are examined over time: Does growth in income lead to more happiness? Third, comparisons are drawn between individuals: Are the rich happier than the poor?

Chapter 5 analyzes the impact of unemployment on happiness. Are some hard-nosed economists correct in saying that all unemployment is voluntary? If so, then not being employed does not cause any hardship. Or are other scholars who consider unemployment a heavy blow to the individuals concerned nearer to the truth—even when the unemployed do not suffer a loss in income due to being on social security?

Chapter 6 deals with the role of inflation in happiness. Economists tend to argue that predicted inflation does not cause any hardship, because the contracts (in particular, the wages) can be fully adjusted by the individuals to the expected price increases. Only unexpected inflation reduces happiness. According to this view, which is shared by a large number of scholars, expected inflation should not affect happiness (except in a minor way due to the small transactions costs involved). Or is it possible that inflation nevertheless reduces life satisfaction?

These three chapters not only show the available evidence from other scholars, but also present our own research results for Switzerland in the early 1990s.

Chapter 4

INCOME

MOST ECONOMISTS take it as a matter of course that higher income leads to higher happiness. And why not? A higher income expands individuals' and countries' opportunity set; that is, more goods and services can be consumed. The few people not interested in more commodities need not consume them; they have the freedom to dispose of any unwanted surplus free of charge. It therefore seems obvious that income and happiness go together (provided, of course, that the two are correctly measured). Consequently, economics textbooks do not even make an effort to come up with a reason, but simply state that utility U is raised by income Y: $U = U(Y)$, with $U' > 0$.

Psychologists are more subtle in this respect. They are not so confident that higher income always leads to more satisfaction. They may be influenced by studies such as those made on the winners of large sums of money in the state lottery (Brickman et al. 1978). The winners had won within the previous year and reported only slightly higher levels of life satisfaction than a control group (4.0 versus 3.8 on a five-point scale), and were significantly less pleased with everyday events. Smith and Razzell (1975) found that the increased wealth also entailed significant costs for winners of the British football pools. A large percentage of the winners quit their jobs, thereby losing relationships and a sense of accomplishment. Moreover, tensions with other people tended to increase because the winners were often expected to provide financial assistance to relatives and friends. The analysis of lottery winners therefore finds that, after a period of adaptation, the winners' average utility is not significantly higher than it was before the event.

But some economists do not subscribe to the idea that higher income produces higher happiness. One of them is John Kenneth

Galbraith who, in his famous book, *The Affluent Society* (1958), pointed out the limited use of higher private income while the public sector is starving. The first economist to seriously study the data on happiness, Richard Easterlin (1974), concluded that "money does not buy happiness." Another author claiming that the most cherished values cannot be bought in markets is Tibor Scitovsky with his *Joyless Economy: The Psychology of Human Satisfaction* (1976). Scitovsky even argues that a high level of wealth brings continuous comforts and thereby prevents the pleasure that results from incomplete and intermittent satisfaction of desires. More recently, Robert Frank in *Luxury Fever* (1999) emphasizes that ever-increasing income and consumption have nothing to do with happiness.

In the following, three different aspects of the relationship between income and happiness are discussed:

- Are persons in rich countries happier than those in poor countries? (Section 4.2)
- Does an increase in income over time raise happiness? (Section 4.3)
- Are the people with high income in a country happier than those with low income? (Section 4.4).

Section 4.4 also provides our own estimates of the relationship between income and happiness for data for Switzerland. The chapter ends with conclusions drawn from the large amount of available evidence.

4.2 INCOME AND HAPPINESS BETWEEN COUNTRIES

Various studies provide convincing evidence that, on average, persons living in rich countries are happier than those living in poor countries. This result, which conforms to conventional economic beliefs, has, for instance, been established in an extensive study covering 55 nations (Diener, Diener, and Diener 1995). The differences in income between the countries was measured by using exchange rates as well as purchasing power parities in order to control for the international differences in the cost of living. The data on happiness are from the World Value Survey, which is the best source for international comparisons of life satisfaction over such a large number of countries. Veenhoven (1991a) and Inglehart (1990) found the same positive association between income and happiness comparing a somewhat different set of countries. An examination of eight cross-national studies, employing 10 indicators of happiness (and controlling for different occupations), concludes that there is "a strong indication ... that personal satisfaction rises with the level of economic development of the nation" (Inkeles and Diamond 1986, p. 94).

Figure 1.4 in chapter 1 graphically illustrates the relationship between average per capita income in a country (on the horizontal axis) and average life satisfaction (on the vertical axis). The figure shows that reported subjective well-being indeed rises with income. Some authors identify a curvilinear relationship: Income provides happiness at low levels of development, but once a certain threshold has been passed, income has little or no effect on happiness. This refined relationship also holds for Figure 1.4, where there is no sizable correlation between wealth and satisfaction with life above an average income level of U.S. $10,000.

A visual inspection of the relationship between income and happiness across countries is, however, of limited value. The positive correlation may be produced by other factors than income as such. In particular, countries with higher per capita incomes tend to have more stable democracies than poor countries have. So it may well be that the seemingly observed positive association between income and happiness is in reality due to the more developed democratic conditions. In chapter 8, it will indeed be demonstrated that the more developed democratic institutions are, the more satisfied the citizens are.

In addition to democracy, there are many other conditions going with income that may produce the observed positive correlation between income and happiness. Just to mention three more, the higher the income, then the more secure human rights are, the better average health is, and the more equal the distribution of income is. Thus, human rights, health, and distributional equality may seemingly make happiness rise with income.

Another aspect to consider is whether causality runs from income to well-being, as has been implicitly assumed so far. It could, in principle, be the case that there is an inverse causation. It might, for instance, be argued that the more satisfied the population is with life, the more it is inclined to work hard, and the higher therefore is the per capita income. Or, happy people may be more creative and enterprising, leading again to higher income. (For similar arguments, see Kenny 1999.) But there is substantial evidence that it is indeed income that produces subjective well-being, at least for countries below a certain threshold of wealth. It has been established that essentially all social indicators are more positive in nations of higher income: Richer countries enjoy more and better-quality food, cleaner drinking water, better and more widely spread education, better health services, higher longevity, more parity between the sexes, and more respect for human rights. (See, e.g., Easterly 1999.)

The available evidence allows us to conclude that, across nations, income and happiness go together and that higher income increases people's subjective well-being in poor countries. The notion that people in poor countries are happier because they live under more "natural" and less stressful conditions can be considered a myth. Economists, beginning with Jeremy Bentham, have correctly seen that higher income offers welcome opportunities and options to the population that the poorer people must forgo—at least up to a certain treshold.

The causal factors that relate wealth to happiness, however, are not yet fully understood. Future research with time series will have to disentangle the effects on subjective well-being of income and factors such as political stability.

4.3   Income and Happiness over Time

Several scholars (e.g., Blanchflower and Oswald 2000b, Lane 1998, p. 462, and Myers 2000, p. 61) have identified a striking and curious relationship: Per capita income in the United States has risen sharply in recent decades, but the proportion of persons considering themselves to be "very happy" has fallen over the same period. Graphically, the development of income and happiness deviates in the manner of a scissor. Consider, for instance, Figure 4.1.

Between 1946 and 1991, income per capita in the United States rose from about $11,000 to $27,000 in 1996 dollars—that is, rose by a factor of 2.5 or by 150 percent. This is a tremendous rise in average purchasing power. The rise was reflected in almost all households having an indoor toilet, a washing machine, telephone, and color television as well as a car. (See Easterlin 2000b or Lebergott 1993.) The figure also shows, however, that this tremendous rise in material well-being was accompanied by a modest *decrease* in average happiness. In 1946, average happiness rated on a three-point scale was close to 2.4. In 1991, after 45 years of affluence, average happiness dropped to 2.2.

Figure 4.1. Happiness and income per capita in the United States, 1946–91. Data from World Database of Happiness, Bureau of Economic Analysis of the U.S. Department of Commerce and U.S. Bureau of the Census.

This result is surprising because it is contradictory to the results presented in the previous section that people in richer countries report being happier. There are, of course, many possibilities to explain this odd finding. One would be that these are only raw data and that a positive correlation between wealth and happiness is hidden due to changes in the composition of the population. Another is that the meaning of happiness may have changed over time. Perhaps 55 years ago, people were more inclined to state that they were "very happy" though in a deeper sense their subjective well-being has not changed much or is even higher now than it was in 1946. If these explanations are correct, Figure 4.1 is simply misleading and there is no reason to ponder it.

Quite a different reaction is to take the figure as an indication that "money does not buy happiness" or that there is more to subjective well-being than just income. One of the most important processes is that people adjust to past experiences.

4.3.1   *Changing Aspiration Level*

Human beings are unable and unwilling to make absolute judgments. Rather, they are constantly drawing comparisons from the past or from their expectations of the future. Thus, we notice and react to deviations from *aspiration levels* that depend on our own, or other people's, experiences in the past. A rise in our income initially provides a surge of satisfaction, but after some time we get accustomed to it and are not happier than before. This is especially relevant if income serves to buy consumer goods. Take, for instance, television sets. Earlier, we were perfectly happy to receive one or two channels in black and white. Today, we expect, as a matter of course, to receive dozens of channels in color. We have quickly adjusted our expectations to technical progress.

Additional material goods and services initially provide extra pleasure, but it is always only transitory. Higher happiness with material things wears off. Satisfaction depends on change and disappears with continued consumption. This process or mechanism that reduces the hedonic effects of a constant or repeated stimulus is called adaptation. It is this process of hedonic adaptation that makes people strive for ever higher aspirations.

Four important consequences follow:

(a) The upward adjustment of expectations induces human beings to accomplish more and more. They are never satisfied. Once they have achieved something, they want to achieve ever more. The concept of "rising aspiration levels" thus does not only hold for material goods and services but also for many immaterial achievements. Receiving the Nobel prize or a gold medal at the Olympic Games, for instance, certainly elates the winners, but after some time they start to compare themselves to people who are even better—for example, to Marie Curie, who won two Nobel prizes, or to Mark Spitz, who won seven gold medals in the Munich Olympic Games in 1972. On a more pedestrian level, a promotion makes for temporary happiness, but at the same time raises the expectation and aspiration for further promotions.

(b) Wants are insatiable. The more one gets, the more one wants. As long as one has a yearly income of \$50,000, an income of \$100,000 seems a lot. But as soon as one has achieved it, one craves

$200,000. The expected marginal utility of income does not seem
to decrease much if at all.

(c) Greater opportunities (provided by higher income) do not always
raise happiness. Opportunities may well generate higher aspirations, thereby lowering subjective well-being. As a result, people
who are trapped in a situation are not necessarily more unhappy
than those with many opportunities.

(d) Most people think that they felt less happy in the past, but expect
to be more happy in the future (Easterlin 2000a). This asymmetry
can be explained by changing aspirations, as will be illustrated
shortly.

The effects of changes in income affecting aspiration levels are
shown in Figure 4.2. Initially, people have a certain aspiration level A_1
so that income Y_1 produces happiness H_1. Rising income—say, from
Y_1 to Y_2—raises happiness from H_1 to H_2. If it rises further—say, to
Y_3—happiness is further increased to H_3. The points a, b, and c trace
a curve with decreasing marginal utility of income, as is normally
assumed in economic theory. This curve holds for a particular point in
time. It suggests that a higher income indeed makes people happier.

But, over time, aspiration adjusts to the higher income level. The
aspiration level curve A_1 shifts downward to A_m. Ex post, the income
rise from Y_1 to Y_2 does not produce any increase in happiness if the
aspiration curve indeed shifts as much downward as is assumed in
the graph. If the increase in income jacks up aspirations even higher—
say, to aspiration curve A_h—income Y_2 even produces lower happi-

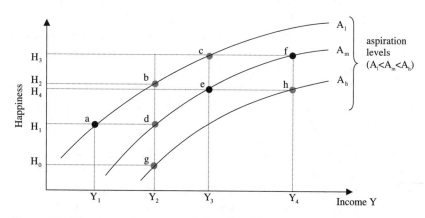

Figure 4.2. Happiness, income, and the role of the aspiration level.

ness than the lower income Y_1. This corresponds to Figure 4.1, with the average happiness level shown on the vertical axis.

Aspiration level theory suggests that increases in income and aspiration levels are intimately connected. The increase in happiness expected on the basis of a given aspiration curve—for example, along the points a, b, and c on aspiration curve A_1—does not materialize. Rather, an increase in income is accompanied by a downward shift in the aspiration curve. In equilibrium, one may, for example, observe that the sequence of points a, e, and f materializes. As the curves are drawn, higher income goes with higher happiness, but an increase in income produces a much smaller increase in happiness than with given aspiration levels.

As just indicated, the figure helps to explain the asymmetry in evaluations of happiness referring to the past and to the future. People with income Y_3 judge their past happiness on the basis of the *current* aspiration level A_m. As income has risen—say, from Y_2 to Y_3—the previous income is evaluated to have produced happiness H_1 at point d, which is lower than today's happiness level H_4, as given at point e. Current happiness is thus taken to be higher than in the past. In actual fact, when the individuals *actually* received income Y_2, they had a lower aspiration level and therefore that income actually produced happiness H_2 in the past, which in our figure is even higher than today's happiness H_4.

Future income is also evaluated on the basis of the *current* aspiration level. Let's assume a person situated at point e with income Y_3 and happiness H_4. She anticipates that an income increase from Y_3 to Y_4 produces a well-being along curve A_m, so that happiness H_3 at point f is expected. But the person does not take into account that the aspiration level also rises and that the aspiration curve will therefore shift downward—say, to curve A_h. In actual fact, therefore, when the higher income Y_4 is indeed reached, the level of happiness is only H_4 at point h, and not H_3 as it would be if the aspiration level stayed constant at point f. The actual happiness of the increase in income is thus systematically lower than expected beforehand. (In Figure 4.2, happiness even stays constant.)

Adaptation level theory is well grounded in psychology (in particular, Helson 1964, Brickman and Campbell 1971, Parducci, 1995, and, for a modern discussion, Frederick and Loewenstein 1999), as is the concept of aspiration levels (Irwin 1944). According to aspiration level theory, happiness is determined by the gap between aspiration and achievement (Michalos 1991, Inglehart 1990, ch. 7). In economics, the theories of preference change have concentrated on habit formation (e.g., Marshall 1890, Duesenberry 1949, Modigliani 1949, Pollak 1970, and, more recently, Carroll and Weil 1994). These theories are strongly supported by modern research on happiness.

4.4 INCOME BETWEEN PERSONS

The effects on happiness of income can also be assessed by comparing people with different incomes at a particular point in time who live in the same country. At first sight, people with higher income have more opportunities to achieve whatever they desire: They can buy more material goods and services. Moreover, they have a higher status in society. Higher income yields higher utility. Conversely, the poor are unhappy. After all, if someone does not like a high income and believes that poverty makes one happy, he is free to dispose of his high income at no cost. These considerations are rather compelling, and it has therefore been a truism in traditional economics that higher income is associated with higher utility.

In contrast, the research on happiness has looked at the relationship between income and subjective well-being in a much more differentiated way. There are many reasons why income does not buy happiness. Perhaps the most fundamental one is that it may be impossible to reach happiness by earning and spending income: "[P]eople are really seeking nonmaterial goals such as personal fulfillment or the meaning of life and are disappointed when material things fail to provide them" (Dittmar 1992 in Argyle 1999, p. 358). Happiness is in this sense "priceless"; that is, it cannot be achieved by material factors.

4.4.1 Empirical Evidence

The relationship between income and happiness at a particular point in time and in a particular location (country) has been the subject of a large empirical literature. After running many regressions with all kinds of data, the general result seems to be that happiness and income are indeed positively related. But differences in income only explain a rather low proportion of the differences in happiness among people. Other factors are more important to explain why some people are more happy than others.

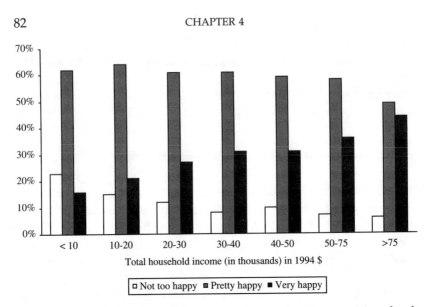

Figure 4.3. Population distribution of happiness according to various levels of income, United States, 1994. Data from National Opinion Research Center (1999) presented in Easterlin (2000a).

But there is a noticeable effect of income on happiness within nations. Consider, for example, Figure 4.3 showing the U.S. population's 1994 percentage distribution of happiness taking seven levels of income into account.

The proportion of persons rating themselves to be "very happy" rises from 16 percent for those with incomes below $10,000 to 44 percent for those with incomes above $75,000. Conversely, the proportion of persons considering themselves to be "not too happy" falls from 23 to 6 percent. The "mean happiness" rating rises from 1.8 for those with incomes below $10,000 to 2.8 for those with incomes above $75,000. However, a simple correlation between happiness and income is only 0.20.

Data for Europe from the Euro-Barometer Survey Series (1975–91) reveal a similar picture. There is a correlation between happiness and income. For example, 88 percent of those people located in the upper quartile of income rate themselves to be "fairly satisfied" or "very satisfied," while only 66 percent of those in the lowest income quartile do likewise. (See the data presented in Di Tella, MacCulloch, and Oswald 1999.)

More refined regressions, taking into account a large number of factors independent of income that influence happiness—such as age,

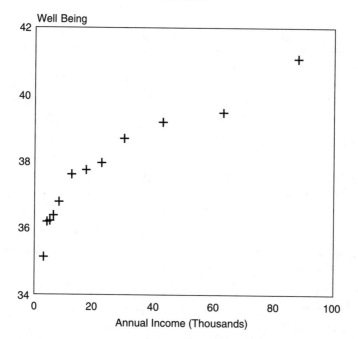

Figure 4.4. Income and well-being in the United States, 1981–84. Data from Diener et al. (1993), figure 2. Reprinted with the kind permission of Kluwer Academic Publishers, Dordrecht.

gender, education, and health—also find a positive effect on happiness, but the effect is smaller. Other economic factors (in particular, unemployment and inflation) and noneconomic factors (in particular, health) often exert a greater influence.

The effect of income on happiness is usually captured in a single correlation or with a single coefficient in regression models. However, several scholars assume that the relationship between income and happiness is curvilinear. Figure 4.4 provides such a picture for the United States for 1981–84.

At low levels of income, a rise in income strongly raises well-being. But once an annual income of about U.S. $15,000 has been reached, a rise in income level has a smaller effect on happiness. Higher income is still experienced as raising well-being, but at a lower rate.

For Switzerland, in contrast, the highest income recipients even report somewhat lower well-being than does the income group immediately below. Table 4.1 presents the partial results, referring to the effect of income in a multiple regression, taking into account a large

TABLE 4.1
Income and Satisfaction with Life in Switzerland, 1992–94

	Descriptive Statistics	Weighted Least Squares	Weighted Ordered Probit	
	Mean	Coefficient (t-Value)	Coefficient (t-Value)	Marginal Effect for Score of 10
Equiv. income less than SFr. 2,000	7.98	Reference group		
Equiv. income SFr. 2,000–3,000	8.17	0.155 (2.49)	0.079 (2.05)	0.027
Equiv. income SFr. 3,000–4,000	8.24	0.259 (3.51)	0.149 (3.15)	0.052
Equiv. income SFr. 4,000–5,000	8.49	0.423 (4.91)	0.273 (4.87)	0.098
Equiv. income SFr. 5,000 and more	8.45	0.332 (4.80)	0.208 (4.07)	0.074
Socio-demographic factors		Included	Included	
Other socio-economic factors		Included	Included	
Institutional factors		Included	Included	
Observations		6,137	6,137	

Source of data: Leu, Burri, and Priester (1997).

Notes: Dependent variable: level of satisfaction on a 10-point scale. White estimator for variance; *t*-values are in parentheses. Standard errors are adjusted to clustering in 26 cantons. Additional control variables (not shown) for size of community (five variables) and type of community (seven variables).

number of control variables. (The complete estimation equation is reported in Appendix A.)

In order to detect any nonlinear relationship between income and satisfaction with life, five income categories are specified in the estimation equation. The reference group includes people with an equivalence household income per month lower than SFr. 2,000. Average life satisfaction on a 10-point scale steadily increases with higher income, from 7.98 up to a level of 8.49 for incomes between SFr. 4,000 and SFr. 5,000. However, for the 12 percent of the people constituting the top income earners, average satisfaction with life falls back to an average score of 8.45. These descriptive results are confirmed in the multiple regression analysis. People in the second top income category report, with a statistically significant higher probability of 9.8 percentage points, being completely satisfied compared to people with an income below SFr. 2,000. For the top category, this marginal effect is only 7.4 percentage points.

What has been said so far refers to rich countries. In contrast to the findings reported for Switzerland, especially in poor countries, the effect of income on subjective well-being certainly does not stop after physical needs have been fulfilled. Rather, there is a stronger influence of income on happiness (Veenhoven 1991a). The strongest correlation between income and life satisfaction measured so far is 0.45; it has been observed in the poor areas of Calcutta (Biswas-Diener and Diener 2000). But also interviews with some of the richest people in the United States reveal a "moderately higher" level of well-being than is found in a comparison group (Diener, Horwitz, and Emmons 1985).

4.4.2 Relative Income

As pointed out, there may be many reasons why higher income does not simply translate into higher happiness. Without doubt, one of the most important ones is that people compare themselves to other persons. It is not the absolute level of income that matters most, but rather one's position relative to other people. This dimension of social comparison has not been considered in this chapter so far. The ideas focusing on preference changes due to comparison with, for example, one's past consumption level or expected future income are supplemented with concepts of interdependent preferences due to comparisons with relevant others. (See, e.g., Becker 1974, Frank 1985b, Pollak 1976.)

In section 4.3.1 of this chapter, we discussed the concept of aspiration levels suggesting that people take into account their own past experiences. Here we now focus on comparisons with relevant other people. In economics, Easterlin (1974, 1995) used the concept of aspirations as a frame of reference to explain happiness. He acknowledges that people with higher income are, on average, happier, but raising everybody's income does not increase everybody's happiness, because, in comparison to others, income has not improved.

Many economists in the past have noted that individuals compare themselves to significant others with respect to income, consumption, status, or utility. One of the earliest was Thorstein Veblen (1899). He coined the term *conspicuous consumption* to describe the state of wanting to impress other people. The relative income hypothesis has been formulated and econometrically tested by James Duesenberry (1949), who posits an asymmetric structure of externalities. People look *upward* when making comparisons. The philosopher Bertrand Russell (1930, pp. 68–69) described this human proclivity in the following way:

> Napoleon envied Caesar, Caesar envied Alexander, and Alexander, I daresay, envied Hercules, who never existed. You cannot, therefore, get away from envy by means of success alone, for there will always be in history or legend some person even more successful than you are.

Aspirations thus tend to be above the level actually reached. The wealthier people impose a negative external effect on the poorer people, but not vice versa. As a result, savings rates depend on the percentile position in the income distribution, and not solely on the income level, as in a traditional savings function. (See, e.g., Kapteyn 2000 or Kosicki 1987.)

A major line of research has been begun by Bernard van Praag and Arie Kapteyn (1973) and associates (e.g., Kapteyn and Wansbeek 1982, 1985, van Praag and Frijters 1999). They construct an econometrically estimated individual welfare function with a "preference shift" parameter that captures the tendency of material wants to increase as income increases. They find that increases in income shift aspirations upward but that individual satisfaction nevertheless increases. The preference shift "destroys" about 60 to 80 percent of the welfare effect of an increase in income; that is, somewhat less than a third remains.

Fred Hirsch (1976), in his book *Social Limits to Growth*, emphasizes the role of relative social status by calling attention to "positional goods," which, by definition, cannot be augmented because they solely rely on not being available to others. For instance, only the rich will ever be able to afford servants. This theme was taken up by Robert Frank (1985a,b, 1999), who argues that the production of positional goods in the form of luxuries, such as exceedingly expensive watches or yachts, is a waste of productive resources, as overall happiness is thereby decreased rather than increased.

4.4.3 Treadmills

Some scholars have concluded that we are on a "hedonic treadmill" (Brickman and Campbell 1971): People adapt to improving economic conditions to the point that no real benefit in terms of higher happiness is attained. Instead of building on adaptation level theory (Helson 1964), a different version uses the notion of a homeostatic process that tends to restore a similar level of happiness under varying circumstances (Headey and Wearing 1992). People subjected to life-altering events ultimately return to a level of well-being that is characteristic of their respective personalities. Each person's ability to experience satisfaction is mainly inherited. Thus, each person may be on an individual treadmill that tends to restore happiness to a predetermined point after each change of conditions.

In contrast, the "satisfaction treadmill" is based on induced changes in aspiration levels (instead of changes in hedonic experiences as in the case of the hedonic treadmill; Kahneman 2000). However, empirical evidence suggests that the two concepts of treadmill effects cannot be easily disentangled. Moreover, empirical evidence does not support the strong implications of any treadmill taken at face value. Even if accident victims report higher levels of life satisfaction than expected by outside observers (Brickman, Coates, and Janoff-Bulman 1978), their level is lower than that of a control group and it sometimes only adapts after a relatively long time period. The same holds for noise adaptation with high variability as with highway or aircraft noise. In panel interviews, Weinstein (1982) finds that residents became increasingly pessimistic about their ability to adjust to the noise of a newly opened highway. In a longitudinal and cross-sectional analysis, Cohen et al. (1981) observe that children in noisy schools do less well on a cognitive task than children in the control group and that adaptation to aircraft noise among them is low. Further evidence for slow or weak adaptation comes from studies of people with chronic or progressive diseases (see Frederick and Loewenstein 1999 for a survey) or of people who lost a child or a spouse (see Stroebe, and Stroebe 1987, Stroebe, Stroebe, and Hansen 1993). In a panel analysis for Germany between 1984 and 1994, it has been shown that life changes explain 30 percent of the initial variance in life satisfaction and that stable factors, such as personal capabilities and social relations, account for a fraction of similar size (Ehrhardt, Saris, and Veenhoren 2000). The rest of the variance is assigned to errors. This is evidence of considerable mobility on the happiness ladder in a society far from full adaptation and fast changes of aspiration levels. This leads us back to the empirical evidence that a higher position in the income distribution does raise happiness—but the amount is small, especially compared to increases due to other influences on happiness.

4.4.4   What Comparison?

There is no doubt that people compare themselves to other people and do not use absolute judgments. But it is crucial to know with which other people such a comparison is undertaken. In a study of 10,000 British workers, two economists (Clark and Oswald 1996) identified the reference group to be people with the same personal characteristics—for example, gender, education, and job. They conclude in agreement with many other studies that the absolute income level has little effect on happiness. In contrast, relative income matters: The lower the income of the group one compares oneself with, the more satisfied people are. If one's spouse or another household member earns more, satisfaction is lower. (See also Neumark and Postlewaite 1998.)

A more simple and obvious way to study income comparisons is to look at gender differences. As women are paid less than men are, even for the same work, meaning that there is gender discrimination, women should be less happy than men are. However, this is contradicted by the empirical findings. Women report to be equally happy or even happier than men are, even controlling for all sorts of other influences on happiness.

This result is indeed paradoxical. Why do women report being happier than men even though they are discriminated against? One answer might be that women feel an obligation to (falsely) indicate that they are happy even if they are not. In view of the high validity of the data on happiness (see chapter 2), this explanation is not very convincing.

A better explanation might be that women compare themselves to other women and then feel entitled to less pay than men. With the emancipation of women, this comparison is likely to have shifted. Increasingly, women compare themselves to men, especially if they perform the same work. Then they are dissatisfied with what they earn and report lower happiness.

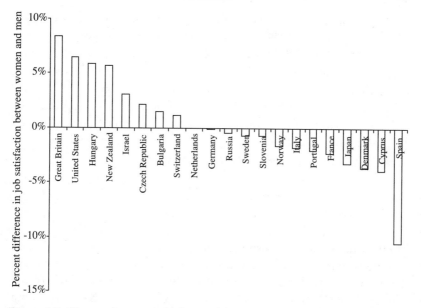

Figure 4.5. The gender gap of job satisfaction. The values indicate the percentage difference between women and men. A positive value thus indicates that females are more satisfied with their jobs than men. Data from Sousa-Poza and Sousa-Poza (2000), Figure 2. Reprinted with the kind permission of Helbing and Lichtenhahn, Basel/Geneva/Munich.

Indeed, young, better-educated professional women and those in male-dominated workplaces report no higher work satisfaction than men do (Clark 1997).

Moreover, the paradox of the happy yet lowly paid woman seems to be a purely Anglo-Saxon phenomenon (Sousa-Poza and Sousa-Poza 2000). It is prevalent only in the United States, Great Britain, New Zealand (and Hungary). In other countries, such as Spain, Denmark, Japan, France, and Norway, the reverse happens: Men report higher job satisfaction than women do, which correlates with their higher wages. This is shown in Figure 4.5.

Figure 4.5 indicates the gender gap of work satisfaction for 21 countries. It is measured as the difference between the percentages of females and males who report above-average satisfaction with their main jobs (on a seven-point scale). In all the countries considered, the share of satisfied male and female workers is above 60 percent except in Hungary and Russia. (See also chapter 5.) The ranking of the gender difference in job satisfaction shows that the satisfaction gap in women's favor is largest in Great Britain. Over 8 percentage points more women report to be satisfied with their jobs than men. At the other end of the scale, significantly fewer women in Spain report that they are satisfied with their jobs than men do. Overall, there are more countries in the sample in which women are less satisfied than men are. Thus, a close look at the gender gap reveals that it is not a general phenomenon. Whereas it obviously holds for the Anglo-Saxon world, there is no such paradoxical relationship between relative income and satisfaction in many other countries.

4.5 CONCLUSIONS

Traditional economics assumes, as a matter of course, that higher income produces more utility and individual well-being. Models take for granted the relationship between utility U and income Y of the form $U = U(Y)$, with $U' > 0$ and $U'' < 0$—that is, the diminishing marginal utility of income. This approach has the advantage of simplicity. It is taken to hold for all relationships between income and well-being, be it across countries, over time, or between individuals within a country at a given point of time.

The results of happiness research change this picture. They provide a more refined view by introducing additional aspects that can no longer be disregarded if one wants to deal with empirical realities. It is important to see that happiness research does not simply introduce new variables, but completely alters the structure of the relationship between income and utility. Happiness research makes clear that traditional economics' claim that the basic relationship between income and happiness holds irrespective of whether one compares countries, time, or persons is unfounded.

Nevertheless, the propositions of accepted economics can be upheld for particular conditions. Comparing across countries, it is true that income and happiness are positively related and that the marginal utility falls with higher income. Higher income clearly raises happiness in developing countries, while the effect is only small, if it exists at all, in rich countries. Economists are right when they reject the notion of "poor but happy countries" sometimes advanced by romantics.

The situation is completely different for the relationship between income and happiness over time: Increasing per capita income has not raised individual well-being in the long run. Empirical evidence thus is inconsistent with positive marginal utility of income. The empirical evidence can well be explained by introducing an additional theoretical concept alien to traditional economics (but noted by nonorthodox scholars a long time ago): Aspiration levels adjust to the rise in income. People get used to their higher income level, which then produces less happiness for them than they would enjoy if no such adjustment had taken place.

A second important theoretical concept that is useful for explaining the empirical evidence where income and happiness levels between people are concerned is *relative income*. Individuals do not value absolute income, but compare it to the income of relevant others. This opens up the issue of what persons or groups one compares oneself with. The discussion of the particular case of women suggests that the comparison group does not necessarily stay constant, but may change as the result of change in income experienced. Taking comparisons of income into account immediately shows that higher income does not simply produce higher utility. However, within nations a positive effect prevails, and in poor countries the evidence points to an even larger effect of a higher relative income level on happiness between persons. Happiness research thus produces new insights into the very old and central relationship between income and well-being. On the whole, the ideas on the part of heterodox researchers of introducing changing aspiration levels and income comparisons between people are borne out. But until now they relied to a large extent on hunches. For the first time, happiness research has adduced convincing empirical evidence using advanced econometric methods.

Hints on the Literature

The general relationship between income and happiness is discussed in the surveys referred to in the previous chapters and in

Ahuvia, Aaron C., and Douglas C. Friedman (1998). Income, Consumption, and Subjective Well-Being: Towards a Composite Macromarketing Model. *Journal of Macromarketing* 18(2): 153–68.

Diener, Ed, and Robert Biswas-Diener (2000). Will Money Increase Subjective Well-Being? A Literature Review and Guide to Needed Research. Mimeo. University of Illinois.

Furnham, Adrian, and Michael Argyle (1998). *The Psychology of Money*. London and New York: Routledge.

Income and happiness between countries (section 4.2) are treated in, for instance,

Diener, Ed, and Eunkook Mark Suh (1999). National Differences in Subjective Well-Being. In Daniel Kahneman, Ed Diener, and Norbert Schwarz (eds.), *Well-Being: The Foundations of Hedonic Psychology*. New York: Russell Sage Foundation, 434–50.

Diener, Ed, Marissa Diener, and Carol Diener (1995). Factors Predicting the Subjective Well-Being of Nations. *Journal of Personality and Social Psychology* 69(5): 851–64.

Inglehart, Ronald (1990). *Culture Shift in Advanced Industrial Society*. Princeton, N.J.: Princeton University Press.

Inglehart, Ronald, and Hans-Dieter Klingemann (2000). Genes, Culture, Democracy, and Happiness. In Ed Diener and Eunkook M. Suh (eds.), *Culture and Subjective Well-Being*. Cambridge, Mass.: MIT Press, 165–83.

Veenhoven, Ruut (1991). Is Happiness Relative? *Social Indicators Research* 24(1): 1–34.

For the effect of income on happiness over time (section 4.3) see

Blanchflower, Daniel G., and Andrew J. Oswald (2000). Well-Being over Time in Britain and the USA. NBER Working Paper no. 7487. Cambridge, Mass.: National Bureau of Economic Research.

Diener, Ed, and Shigehiro Oishi (2000). Money and Happiness: Income and Subjective Well-Being across Nations. In Ed Diener and Eunkook M. Suh (eds.), *Culture and Subjective Well-Being*. Cambridge, Mass.: MIT Press: 185–218.

Easterlin, Richard A. (2000). Income and Happiness: Towards a Unified Theory. Mimeo. Los Angeles: University of Southern California.

The relationship between income and happiness between persons (section 4.4) is the subject of previously mentioned studies as well as

Argyle, Michael (1999). Causes and Correlates of Happiness. In Daniel Kahneman, Ed Diener, and Norbert Schwarz (eds.), *Well-Being: The Foundations of Hedonic Psychology*. New York: Russell Sage Foundation, 353–73.

Diener, Ed, Ed Sandvik, Larry Seidlitz, and Marissa Diener (1993). The Relationship between Income and Subjective Well-Being: Relative or Absolute? *Social Indicators Research* 28: 195–223.

Gardner, Jonathan, and Andrew J. Oswald (2001). Does Money Buy Happiness? A Longitudinal Study Using Data on Windfalls. Mimeo. Warwick, U.K.: Warwick University.

Myers, David G. (1993). *The Pursuit of Happiness: Who Is Happy and Why?* New York: Avon.

Schyns, Peggy (2000). The Relationship between Income, Changes in Income and Life Satisfaction in West Germany and the Russian Federation: Relative, Absolute, or a Combination of Both? In Ed Diener and D. R. Rahtz (eds.), *Advances in Quality of Life Theory and Research*, Vol. 1. Dordrecht: Kluwer, 83–109.

Veenhoven, Ruut (1995). Satisfaction and Social Position: Within Nation Differences, Compared across Nations. In W. E. Saris, R. Veenhoven,

A. C. Scherpenzeel, and B. Bunting (eds.), *A Comparative Study of Satisfaction with Life in Europe*. Budapest: Eotvos University Press, 254–62.

Economists' particularly important contributions not mentioned yet include

Clark, Andrew E., and Andrew J. Oswald (1996). Satisfaction and Comparison Income. *Journal of Public Economics* 61(3): 359–81.

Di Tella, Rafael, Robert J. MacCulloch, and Andrew J. Oswald (1999). How Do Macroeconomic Fluctuations Affect Happiness? Mimeo. Boston: Harvard Business School.

Easterlin, Richard A. (1995). Will Raising the Incomes of All Increase the Happiness of All? *Journal of Economic Behaviour and Organization* 27(1): 35–48.

A useful survey of the various kinds of social comparisons is provided by

Antonides, Gerrit, and W. Fred Van Raaij (1998). *Consumer Behaviour: A European Perspective*. West Sussex, U.K.: John Wiley & Sons, ch. 14.

Chapter 5

EMPLOYMENT

5.1 INTRODUCTION

MOST ECONOMISTS see unemployment as an unfortunate event to be avoided as much as possible. To become unemployed is considered to be costly and, above all, involuntary. Government should intervene in order to raise the aggregate demand for goods. To produce the additional goods, more labor would be required and unemployment would fall. This view is behind Keynesian theory, which dominated the field in the 50s and 60s and is now experiencing a comeback.

But there are also economists who hold quite a different view. According to the "new classical macroeconomics," unemployment is voluntary. People choose to leave employment because they find the burden of work and the wage paid unattractive compared to being unemployed and getting unemployment benefits and leisure. Involuntary unemployment is a disequilibrium phenomenon and is relatively short-term, until individuals and firms have adjusted. Government interventions to jack up demand result in higher future inflation and should therefore be avoided. As people choose to be unemployed, because they expect to be better off, it should not affect their happiness.

Few politicians, social scientists, or laypeople subscribe to this view. It is taken to be cynical, as it seems obvious that workers are dismissed and that unemployment is an unfortunate state to be in. However, by analyzing the unemployed as having made a choice between alternatives, the economists of the new classical persuasion have drawn attention to certain aspects that are hard to dispute:

(a) There are certainly some workers who prefer not to work and to enjoy the benefits of a social security system, which in some countries almost totally compensates for the loss of income.

(b) Much unemployment is transitory. The unemployed soon find work again, often in a more productive sector, and earn higher wages than before. Dismissing workers as a reaction to demand and cost considerations also means that people will be hired again. When workers cannot be laid off for legal reasons, firms are also reluctant to hire them.

(c) Many people who are officially unemployed are in fact working in the shadow economy where they are not burdened by taxes and social security contributions. In recent years, this part of the economy has reached a considerable size in many countries. In Belgium, Greece, Italy, Norway, Portugal, Spain, and Sweden it is around, and sometimes much above, 20 percent of official GDP for the period 1996–97. (See Table 2.3 in chapter 2.)

In all three cases, it is not unreasonable to assume that the unemployed do not suffer, and that some of them are even quite satisfied with their situation.

The issue of whether, and to what extent, the unemployed are dissatisfied remains unresolved. For that reason, happiness research on unemployment is of particular interest and importance.

In this chapter, four questions and their ramifications will be discussed in sections 5.2 through 5.5:

- What is the level of happiness of an unemployed person?
- How does general unemployment in an economy affect happiness?
- What influences work satisfaction?
- How much happiness does leisure provide?

5.2   PERSONAL UNEMPLOYMENT

How particular people are affected when they become unemployed needs to be analyzed with the help of a microanalysis that looks at individual data. Such a study (Di Tella, MacCulloch, & Oswald 2001) was undertaken for 12 European countries over the period 1975–91, employing Euro-Barometer data. In a cross-section sample, the "classical" life satisfaction question was asked: "On the whole, are you very satisfied, fairly satisfied, not very satisfied, or not at all satisfied with the life you lead?" The analysis—which controls for a great number of other determinants of happiness, such as income and education—finds that the self-proclaimed happiness of those people being unemployed is much lower than that of employed persons with otherwise similar characteristics. The loss of happiness experienced by unemployment amounts to 0.33 units in the previously mentioned happiness scale, ranging from 1 ("not at all satisfied") to 4 ("very satisfied").

Our study for Switzerland comes to a very similar result. The results in Table 5.1 show that unemployed people report, on average, a satisfaction level of 6.56 on a 10-point scale, compared to an average score of 8.21 for employed people. Using the ordered probit estimate of the happiness function fully reproduced in Appendix A, the marginal effect of being unemployed, rather than being employed, can be calculated, holding other factors such as income constant. The share of unemployed people stating to be "completely satisfied" (satisfaction score of 10) is 20.6 percentage points lower than in the group of employed persons. Equivalently, the probability of having an unemployed person stating the highest satisfaction level is 20.6 percentage point lower than the probability for an employed one. This compares to other marginal effects of, for example, 3.1 percentage points between people with low and middle education, and 13.3 percentage points between healthy and unhealthy people. Unemployment thus has a substantial negative effect on the happiness of the people experiencing it.

Table 5.1 shows, moreover, the satisfaction with life that is connected with different kinds of employment status. There is no sizable difference in mean satisfaction between the seven categories of employment, except for people being unemployed. If it is controlled for correlated effects, housewives are happier, and retired people are less happy than employed people. Even if a lot of working people cannot wait to be retired, for some people the fundamental change in their way of living is bound up with reduced well-being, maybe due to a loss of meaningful activities.

A number of other studies (see Darity & Goldsmith 1996 for a survey) for many different countries and time periods have also found that personally experiencing unemployment makes people very unhappy. In their path-breaking study for Britain, Clark and Oswald (1994, p. 655) summarize their results as "Joblessness depressed well-being more than any other single characteristic including important negative ones such as divorce and separation." Korpi (1997, p. 125) in his study for young Swedes goes so far as stating, "Unemployment has an unambiguously negative effect on well-being."

It is important to note that all these results refer to the "pure" effect of being unemployed. The lower income level as well as other indirect

TABLE 5.1
Employment Status and Satisfaction with Life in Switzerland, 1992–94

	Descriptive Statistics	Weighted Least Squares	Weighted Ordered Probit	
	Mean	Coefficient (t-Value)	Coefficient (t-Value)	Marginal Effect for Score of 10
Employed	8.21		Reference group	
Self-employed	8.31	0.013 (0.18)	0.051 (0.94)	0.018
Unemployed	6.56	−1.615 (−4.84)	−0.815 (−4.93)	−0.206
Student	8.16	0.031 (0.22)	−0.001 (−0.01)	−0.001
Housewife	8.38	0.158 (1.87)	0.13 (2.30)	0.045
Retired	8.23	−0.294 (−2.84)	−0.164 (−2.65)	−0.055
Other employment status	8.37	0.127 (0.65)	0.119 (0.89)	0.042
Demographic factors		Included	Included	
Income level		Included	Included	
Institutional factor		Included	Included	
Observations		6,137	6,137	

Source of data: Leu, Burri, and Priester (1997).

Notes: Dependent variable: level of satisfaction on a 10-point scale. White estimator for variance; t-values are in parentheses. Standard errors are adjusted to clustering in 26 cantons. Additional control variables (not shown) for size of community (five variables) and type of community (seven variables).

effects that may, but need not, go with personally being unemployed are kept constant. They can, of course, be added, depending on the problem one wants to analyze. Consider, for example, the loss in income due to being unemployed. In some countries it is—after tax—close to zero; that is, spending power is not noticeably affected and no adjustment is needed. In other countries (for example, Italy and Spain), the unemployed do indeed suffer a substantial loss in income. In Switzerland, to give a concrete example, depending on previous wage and on circumstances (for example, whether one has children or is disabled), unemployment benefits make up either 70 or 80 percent of the past income. With an income level of 70 or 80 percent compared to previous paid employment, the probability that an unemployed person states that he is "completely satisfied" is 20.6 percentage points lower due to the "pure" unemployment effect. If the income level is not controlled for, the overall effect on happiness of becoming unemployed is estimated. In the sample for Switzerland this effect is minus 21.5 percentage points (not reported in Appendix A). If the "pure" effect of being unemployed is subtracted from the overall effect, an approximation of the long-term effect due to a lower income level is revealed. This partial effect amounts to minus 0.9 percentage points only in our sample. However, the long-term effect of a lower income level does not capture the financial shock resulting from unemployment. According to the concept of loss-aversion (Kahneman & Tversky 1979), unemployed people suffer from the loss in income in the short run. If unemployed people are compared with other people who suffer from a worse financial situation than in the previous year, one-third of the reduced well-being can be attributed to the income shock (Frey & Stutzer 1999, p. 764). Thus, two-thirds of the overall negative effect of unemployment on happiness still remain and can only be explained by nonpecuniary costs.

The insights gained definitively suggest that unemployed persons suffer substantial cost as a result of their fate. The drop in happiness may, to a large extent, be attributed to psychological and social factors (see the survey by Feather 1990):

(a) *Psychic cost*. Unemployment produces depression and anxiety, and results in a loss of self-esteem. Especially for people very involved in their work, not having a job is a heavy blow. It has been established in numerous studies (see Argyle 1989) that the unemployed are in worse mental (and physical) health than people with work. As a result, they are subject to a higher death rate, more often commit suicide, and are more prone to consuming large quantities of alcohol. Their personal relationships are also more strained. As work is generally more central for men, unemployment makes men more unhappy than women (Argyll 1999, p. 364). Persons younger than 30 years of age suffer less, probably because they know that they will have less trouble getting a new job and can adjust more easily to new circumstances (Clark & Oswald 1994). Indeed, men between 30 and 49 years of age are most distressed, and women over 50 years of age are least distressed from being unemployed (Gerlach & Stephan 1996). Distress is highest for the well educated. This can be explained by the opportunity cost of the higher income forgone. The psychic cost is considerably higher for those being made redundant for the first time. In contrast, persons who have been unemployed more often in the past suffer less—to some extent they get used to being unemployed (Clark, Georgellis, & Sanfey 1999).

(b) *Social cost.* Being unemployed has a stigma attached to it, particularly in a world in which one's work essentially defines one's position in life. This aspect will be further discussed in section 5.3 of this chapter.

The empirical research based on estimating happiness functions contrasts strongly with the views held by the new classical macroeconomists. For those affected, being made redundant is considered to be a most unfortunate event, creating major unhappiness.

It could be argued that what has been found may be interpreted quite differently. While the negative correlation between unemployment and happiness is well established, it may well be that the causation is contrary to what has been implied so far: Unhappy people do not perform well and therefore are laid off. Happy persons are more fitted to work life, which makes it less likely for them to lose their job. The question of reverse causation, due to a selection bias, has been analyzed in many studies with longitudinal data, before and after particular workers lost their jobs—for example, due to the closure of a plant. There is evidence that unhappy people are indeed not performing well in the labor market, but the main causation clearly runs from unemployment to happiness. (See, e.g., Winkelmann & Winkelmann 1998 for German data or Marks & Fleming 1999 for Australian data, the latter considering in detail various effects on mental health.)

5.3 General Unemployment

People may be unhappy about unemployment even if they are not themselves made redundant. They may fear being hit by unemployment, and they may feel bad about the unfortunate fate of those unemployed. They may also feel repercussions on the economy and society as a whole. They may dislike the increase in unemployment contributions and taxes that is likely to happen in the future, they may fear that crime and social unease will increase, and they may even see the threat of violent protests and uprisings.

The previously mentioned study of 12 European countries over the period 1975–91 (Di Tella, MacCulloch, & Oswald 2001) finds that—keeping all other influences constant—a one–percentage-point increase in the general rate of unemployment from 9 percent (the European mean) to 10 percent reduces stated life satisfaction by 0.028 units on the four-point scale applied. This effect is of considerable size. This small rise in unemployment is equivalent to shifting more than 2 percent of the population downward from one life-satisfaction category to another—for example, from "not very satisfied" to "not at all satisfied."

The overall effect of unemployment on social well-being can be calculated by adding the loss experienced by those persons being unemployed to the overall effect of unemployment. Consider again a one–percentage-point increase in unemployment. In section 5.2, it was shown that the unemployed experience a fall of 0.33 in their happiness scale. This figure must be multiplied by the 1 percent of the population who have been unlucky enough actually to become unemployed: $0.33 \times 0.01 = 0.0033$. Added to the general effect of a one–percentage-point unemployment increase of 0.028, it leads to a total decrease of 0.0313 (Di Tella, MacCulloch, & Oswald 2001).

This calculation must be taken with a grain of salt. It is at best able to gauge the effects of unemployment on happiness in an approximate way. One reason for having to be careful is that there may be various interactions between personal and more general unemployment, which may in turn affect the evaluation of happiness.

An important interaction refers to reference groups. As is the case for income, individuals tend to evaluate their own situation relative to other persons. For most persons, unemployment lowers their happiness less if they are not alone with this particular fate. When unemployment is seen to hit many persons one knows or hears of, both the psychic and the social effects are mitigated. Self-esteem is better preserved because it becomes obvious that being out of a job is less due to one's own fault and more due to general developments in the economy. Stigma and social disapproval are less prevalent if unemployment hits many other people at the same time.

In order to empirically test the effect of reference groups on reported well-being, happiness scores are regressed on three types of explanatory variables:

- Personal unemployment.
- Unemployment among a reference group.
- An interaction variable combining personal and reference group unemployment.

Using as a reference group the employment state of one's partner or, alternatively, the region an individual lives in, such a happiness function has been estimated for British data over the period 1991–96, again keeping all other influences constant (Clark 2000). As in virtually all previous studies, the unemployed are much more dissatisfied than people with a job, and the general level of unemployment lowers happiness. In contrast, the unemployed indeed suffer less when a larger proportion of partners, or other people living in their region, are also out of work. The same result is reached when general unemployment in the economy is taken as the point of reference (Kelvin & Jarrett 1985).

Unemployed people's well-being, moreover, depends on the strength of the social norm to work. Social interaction of unemployed people with other community members, their forced reference group, has the effect of showing them how they are expected to behave, and norm-conforming behavior is enforced through social sanctions. In an estimation across Swiss communities, it has been shown that the stronger the social norm to live off one's own income, the lower is unemployed people's reported satisfaction with life (Stutzer & Lalive 2000).

Reference groups are certainly of major importance for showing the extent to which people are distressed by their own unemployment. However, what group one refers to is not given, but can to some extent be chosen (Falk & Knell 2000). People out of work tend to associate with other people without work, partly because they have time to do so and/or partly because they retreat from community life. It is also known that marriages and partnerships have a high risk of breaking down when one of the partners is unemployed. In all these cases, the definition of the reference group adjusts to one's labor market status. Causation then does not run unambiguously from the reference group to the evaluation of unemployment in terms of happiness.

5.4 EMPLOYMENT AND WORK SATISFACTION

Work or job satisfaction is one particular domain of overall well-being. Other domains are, for example, satisfaction with housing, with health, and with the natural environment. Overall satisfaction with life as a whole is strongly correlated with the various domain satisfactions. It has even been claimed (Van Praag, Frijters, & Ferrer-i-Carbonell 2000) that life satisfaction is a total of the satisfactions gained in the various domains. But, again, mutual interaction must be taken into account, and causation may go in both directions. People with, say, high job satisfaction also tend to be happy with their life in general; people who are generally happy also tend to be satisfied with their work. Research (Judge & Watanabe 1993, Judge & Locke 1993) suggests that the effect of life satisfaction on job satisfaction is somewhat stronger than the other way around.

In view of the central role work plays in today's society (see, e.g., Lane 1991, Wilson 1996, Hochschild 1997), job satisfaction is of great interest in itself. The respective question in nationwide surveys is "All in all, how satisfied are you with your job?" Figure 5.1 shows that, in 1997, in many countries, among them Denmark, Switzerland, Spain, the Netherlands, and the United States, at least 50 percent of the workers reported that they feel "very satisfied" or even "completely satisfied" with their jobs. Workers in East European countries, including East Germany, as well as Britain, Italy and France, were somewhat less satisfied with their jobs, but even there, well over one-third are either "completely" or "very satisfied." The highest level of persons indicating that they are "dissatisfied" with their jobs was in Japan (15 percent), followed by Russia (14 percent), Britain, and France (11 and 10 percent, respectively).

These and other data have been analyzed in hundreds of studies. (See Warr 1999 for a survey.) It is important to distinguish two quite different aspects related to a job:

(a) *Intrinsic features.* They relate to the conduct of work itself. Examples are
   - The opportunity for personal control.
   - The possibility of utilizing one's skills.
   - The variety of work tasks.
   - Supportive or controlling supervision.
   - Opportunities for personal contacts.

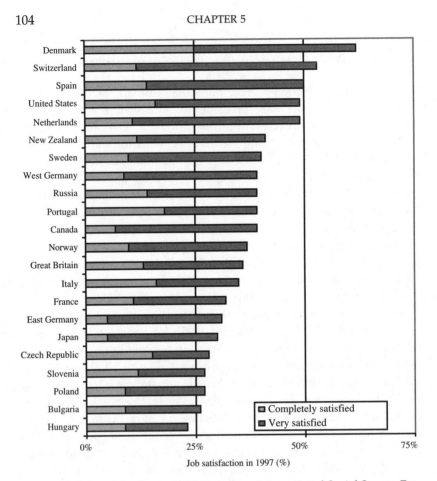

Figure 5.1. Job satisfaction in 1997. Data from International Social Survey Program 1997.

(b) *Extrinsic features*. They refer to the background of the work conditions. Examples are

- Pay, including fringe benefits.
- Working conditions.
- Job security.
- Physical security at work.
- Social status—for example, social rank or occupational prestige.

The two features of job satisfaction are often positively related, but the extent varies greatly according to the specific context. Some researchers argue that intrinsic features satisfy more effectively innate needs than extrinsic features and thus contribute more to individual subjective well-being (Ryan et al. 1996). However, more importantly, intrinsic and extrinsic job satisfaction are related due to systematic motivational dependence. Crowding theory (see Frey 1997b, building on Deci & Ryan 1985) suggests that external intervention, especially in the form of monetary rewards and orders being given undermines intrinsic motivation and satisfaction when the intervention is felt to be controlling by the job holder. In contrast, if the external intervention is taken to be supportive, the job holder's intrinsic motivation and satisfaction are raised. Crowding-out and crowding-in have been identified in hundreds of laboratory experiments and also real-life settings, including within firms. (See Frey & Jegen 2001.)

For economics, the consequences of job satisfaction are of vital importance. In particular, for firms and other organizations, it is crucial to know whether happy employees are also productive employees. In general, overall job satisfaction and performance are positively related. (For a meta-analysis, see Iaffeldano & Muchinsky 1985.) It stands to reason that dissatisfied people do not work well, impose high costs on the employers by being more often absent from the job, and change jobs more frequently than other people. Employees experiencing little satisfaction from their work and having low intrinsic motivation cannot be expected to engage themselves in the organization and be creative and innovative (Amabile 1996, 1998). This is very important because, in most jobs, the employers can monitor their employees only very partially (the so-called multiple task problem; see Holmström & Milgrom 1991); it is therefore necessary to rely, at least partly, on the workers' intrinsic motivation. Dissatisfied employees also have little incentive to think seriously about whether the tasks they perform are sensible for the goals of the organization they work in (the so-called fuzzy task problem; see Frey & Osterloh 2000, p. 36). People with high job satisfaction are prepared to undertake pro-social activities or engage in extra role behavior; that is, they conform to what is expected in terms of "organizational citizenship" behavior.

Work is certainly not only undertaken because it is paid (as many economic models assume). Rather, it provides intrinsic satisfaction, which is revealed by the fact that many people are prepared to undertake unpaid work. For many people, volunteer and charity work is a source of intense satisfaction. Table 5.2 documents the various benefits provided by volunteer work. Volunteer work satisfies innate needs

TABLE 5.2
The Benefits of Doing Volunteer Work in the United Kingdom

	Very Important (%)	Fairly Important (%)	Not Very Important (%)	Not Important at All (%)	Don't Know (%)
I meet people and make friends through it.	48	37	11	4	0
It's the satisfaction of seeing the results.	67	26	5	2	1
It makes me feel less selfish as a person.	29	33	24	13	2
I really enjoy it.	72	21	6	2	—
It's part of my religious belief or philosophy of life to give help.	44	22	9	23	2
It gives me a sense of personal achievement.	47	31	16	6	—
It gives me the chance to get a recognized qualification.	3	7	15	74	1

Source: Lynn and Smith (1991) in Argyle (1999), Table 18.2.

because it provides positive intrinsic work features. The survey results in Table 5.2 reveal that volunteers appreciate the work as such as well as the opportunity to see its results, and that gives them a sense of personal achievement. Whereas internal opportunities for personal contacts are important, the collection of externally relevant qualifications is not.

But having satisfied workers is not necessarily a blessing for a firm. Evidence suggests that, beyond a certain level, very high job satisfaction is no longer conducive to the firm's goals. The employees enjoy themselves at work, but do not necessarily do the hard work also required. As in the case of other relationships, the causation between job satisfaction and work performance is less clear than it might look at first sight. Reverse causation also matters: High performers feel happy with their jobs and with life in general. In contrast, those who are less productive than others tend to be easier dissatisfied with their work and lives.

5.5 LEISURE

We have advanced a lot of evidence that, in general, work is often experienced and reported as being highly satisfying. At the same time, leisure is also positively correlated with happiness (Argyll 1996). Economic theory seems to have drawn the wrong distinction between work creating disutility and leisure providing utility. Rather, people want to be adequately challenged (that is, they wish to perform), but they do not wish to be overtaxed. Thus economics should concentrate on distinguishing between the two.

Among the leisure activities that have been analyzed as providing particular satisfaction are sports activities, which reduce depression and anxiety, as well as various group activities such as being a member of a social club, a musical or theatrical group, or a sports team. The most popular leisure activity nowadays is watching television. In moderation, it can contribute to satisfaction. But too much watching television is correlated with unhappiness. The causation is open (as with all the leisure activities mentioned) because those persons tending to spend the most time in front of a television set do not know what else to do (Argyle 1996).

5.6 CONCLUSIONS

Happiness research comes up with clear results with respect to the effects of unemployment on well-being. The findings are in marked contrast with the notion cherished by some economists that unemployment is voluntary so no utility loss is to be expected from being unemployed. All studies using happiness data find that unemployment causes major unhappiness for the persons affected. The costs arising are both psychological and social in nature. The latter has to do with the fact that one's work defines one's position in life. Not having work leads to isolation, which makes it difficult or impossible to lead a satisfactory life. For those in employment, job satisfaction is a crucial part of life satisfaction. The marked fall in happiness caused by unemployment is not solely due to loss of income. Indeed, the distress occurs even if one compensates for the reduction in income as well as for other factors that may indirectly be connected with unemployment.

Happiness research suggests an even more basic change in outlook compared to the traditional economic approach. The notion that work produces disutility, implicit and often explicit in economic models, is rejected. Rather, the opposite is true: Having work increases happiness, while not having work makes for unhappiness. Happiness research thus opens up a more realistic and, at the same time, more humane view of work as a central activity in life. Economists should start from this basis and only then consider under what conditions work is perceived to be a burden.

The findings reported here help us to obtain a more refined view of the role work plays in the economy and in society. Two aspects are particularly important:

- Unemployment has two conceptually different effects: It lowers the happiness of those persons who actually lose their jobs and, for various reasons, also causes distress to employed persons because they feel threatened, fear social unrest, or are sorry for the unfortunate people out of work.
- Unemployment needs to be seen in a wider context than normally considered in economics. How unhappy the unemployed are partly depends on their surroundings. The fate of being unemployed is less depressing when one compares oneself with others who are also out of work. But as was the case for income, the reference group is not given, but depends on one's own unemployment history. In contrast, being unemployed is a heavier burden in a social setting in which having a job is a strong social norm.

Hints on the Literature

The effect of personal unemployment on happiness is considered in economics by

Clark, Andrew E., and Andrew J. Oswald (1994). Unhappiness and Unemployment. *Economic Journal* 104(424): 648–59.

Winkelmann, Liliana, and Rainer Winkelmann (1998). Why Are the Unemployed So Unhappy? Evidence from Panel Data. *Economica* 65(257): 1–15.

For surveys on the nonpecuniary stress of unemployment, see, from the psychological perspective,

Feather, Norman T. (1990). *The Psychological Impact of Unemployment.* New York: Springer.

Murphy, Gregory C., and James A. Athanasou (1999). The Effect of Unemployment on Mental Health. *Journal of Occupational and Organizational Psychology* 72(1): 83–99.

From the economic perspective,

Darity, William, and Arthur H. Goldsmith (1996). Social Psychology, Unemployment and Macroeconomics. *Journal of Economic Perspectives* 10(1): 121–40.

The relationship between subjective well-being and general unemployment is discussed in

Di Tella, Rafael, Robert J. MacCulloch, and Andrew J. Oswald (2001). Preferences over Inflation and Unemployment: Evidence from Surveys of Happiness. *American Economic Review* 91(1): 335–41.

Recent empirical research and surveys on work satisfaction are found in

Blanchflower, David G., and Andrew J. Oswald (1999). Well-Being, Insecurity and the Decline of American Job Satisfaction. Mimeo. Warwick, U.K.: University of Warwick.

Hamermesh, Daniel S. (1999). The Changing Distribution of Job Satisfaction. NBER Working Paper no. 7332. Cambridge, Mass.: National Bureau of Economic Research.

Spector, Paul E. (1997). *Job Satisfaction: Application, Assessment, Causes, and Consequences*. Thousand Oaks, Calif.: Sage.

Warr, Peter (1999). Well-Being and the Workplace. In Daniel Kahneman, Ed Diener, and Norbert Schwarz (eds.), *Well-Being: The Foundations of Hedonic Psychology*. New York: Russell Sage Foundation, 392–412.

The psychological view on subjective well-being and leisure is provided in

Argyle, Michael (1996). *The Social Psychology of Leisure*. London: Penguin.

Chapter 6

INFLATION

6.1 Introduction

An increase in the general price level—inflation—is disliked by the population. But a lot depends on what kind of inflation takes place. When the price increase is anticipated, individuals can adjust to it. They can make contracts that take into account that prices will be higher in the future. In particular, they will ask for a wage increase in the future in order to compensate for the loss in purchasing power of money. In contrast, if inflation is not anticipated or comes as a shock, such adjustment is not possible. Wage earners, as well as owners of nominal assets such as cash or bonds, risk being the losers.

Economics starts with this distinction between anticipated and unanticipated inflation when analyzing how inflation affects individuals. Adjustment is the more costly, the higher is the *variability* in aggregate inflation and in relative prices caused by an increase in inflation. People then must invest a lot of effort in informing themselves about, and insulating themselves from, the expected price increases. They may make various errors, such as underestimating the extent of future inflation or how a particular price changes compared to other prices.

The costs of inflation have been divided into assorted categories (Fischer and Modigliani 1978):

(a) Costs that would persist even in an economy in which all prices are indexed (i.e., in which no relative price changes and no real income losses exist). They consist of "shoe-leather" or "trips to the bank" costs when people try to save on currency, and in "menu" costs when suppliers have to change their prices and then print new price lists.

(b) Costs due to running government and private institutions established to deal with changing prices.

(c) Costs produced by the inability to change contracts specified in nominal terms.

(d) Costs due to the effects of uncertainty about future inflation.

(e) Costs caused by government in its efforts to control and suppress inflation. These may consist, for instance, of the imposition of price controls by the state, leading to distortions in relative prices and hampering economic growth. Even more important, heavy costs may be incurred as a result of restrictive fiscal and monetary policy, causing unemployment and real income losses.

Depending on a number of rather restrictive assumptions, the welfare costs of rising prices can be captured by computing the appropriate area under the money demand curve, the basic idea being that economizing on the use of currency imposes costs in terms of well-being. They are reflected indirectly by the demand-for-money curve. Based on this method, the cost of a 10 percent annual inflation has been calculated to be between 0.3 percent and 0.45 percent of national income (Fischer 1981, Lucas 1981). This is very little and suggests that an anti-inflationary policy is rarely worth the cost it entails in terms of additional unemployment and real income loss.

But many economists would strongly disagree with this conclusion. They point out that stable prices are a crucial prerequisite for a sound economy in which suppliers and demanders can rationally act. High inflation is seen to be the result of high government budget deficits, frequently caused by wars or internal political instability. A state's capacity to finance the budget deficit by floating debt is limited, as the costs in terms of interest to be paid soar, and, finally, nobody is prepared to buy the public bonds any longer. Neither is it endlessly possible to finance the budget deficit by printing money, because the population switches from the internal currency—which is constantly, and ever more rapidly, losing value—to a stable foreign currency (in South America often the U.S. dollar; in Europe, before the introduction of the Euro, the German Mark), or people use goods (such as cigarettes) to perform transactions. As a consequence, high inflation invariably leads to restrictive fiscal and monetary policies with their own high costs.

Most economists take an intermediate position, not least because the empirical evidence on the costs of inflation is far from clear. There is no convincing evidence that a higher rate of anticipated inflation leads to a higher variability in aggregate inflation or in relative prices.

Neither is there strong econometric evidence that higher unanticipated inflation makes inflation more unpredictable or that it causes higher price variability. (See the survey in Drifill, Mizon, and Ulph 1990.) The commonly held opinion of academic economists is that rampant inflation is very dangerous for the economy, while a constant and, hence, predictable but low inflation (say, 1 to 5 percent per year) is not thought to cause any major problems.

The population seems to be of a different opinion. A careful and extensive survey in the United States, Germany, and Brazil (Shiller 1997) finds that people are concerned with quite different issues in connection with inflation than economists are. "If you ask people in conversation why they think that people dislike inflation, everybody says it is because of the increase in the cost of living, the fall in real income" (p. 17). People disregard the fact that inflation very probably also raises their own nominal income. They obviously concentrate on the possible harm, but not on the possible benefits, of inflation to their standard of living. Experiments (Shafir, Diamond, and Tversky 1997) also suggest that people derive satisfaction mainly from the size of their nominal income rather than real income, which is a form of "money illusion." In addition to this psychic effect of inflation, the survey identified other concerns generally neglected by economists. One is that inflation allows opportunists to exploit others in an unfair and dishonest way; another is that inflation undermines the moral basis of society. Many fear that inflation produces political and economic chaos and a loss in national prestige due to the falling exchange rate. These concerns do not appear in the preceding list composed by economists, but they should nonetheless be taken seriously.

6.2 Happiness Studies

An analysis of happiness data allows us to go beyond the a priori notions of theoretical economics. Happiness studies also have a decisive advantage over surveys where people are directly asked how they feel about inflation. It may well be that the corresponding questions trigger reactions that people might not have otherwise. Happiness data are collected independently and are only afterwards linked to actual inflation experiences.

Most happiness data are based on cross-sections. The corresponding analyses between countries find no relationship between average happiness and inflation rates (Veenhoven 1993).

More relevant are combined time series cross-section studies, where the development of inflation in several countries over the course of time can be analyzed. Of most interest is the study of 12 European countries over the period 1975–91 (Di Tella, MacCulloch, and Oswald 1999). The mean rate of inflation was 7.5 percent per year. Based on an econometric estimate, which keeps all other influences including income and unemployment constant, an increase in the inflation rate by one percentage point—say, from the mean rate of 8 to 9 percent per year—is calculated to reduce average happiness by 0.01 "units" of satisfaction—from an average level in the sample of 3.02 to 3.01. (Average satisfaction is calculated from a cardinal interpretation of the four-item scale that gives "not at all satisfied" a value of 1, "not very satisfied" a value of 2, etc.) Correspondingly, an increase in the inflation rate by five percentage points (which historically is a quite likely event) reduces subjective well-being by five percentage points. This is a substantial effect. It means that 5 percent of the population is shifted downward from one life satisfaction category to the next lower one—e.g., from being "very satisfied" to "fairly satisfied."

It is also possible to calculate the dollar cost of inflation if the effect on well-being of inflation is compared to the effect of aggregate income per capita. As a higher GDP per capita of $1,000 increases average satisfaction by 0.06, an inflation rate five percentage points higher would have to be compensated by about $850 in additional income per year (in 1985 U.S. dollars) (Di Tella, MacCulloch, and Oswald 1999, p. 9).

6.2.1   Trade-Off between Inflation and Unemployment

The results reported in the previous chapter on the effect of unemployment on happiness, and the results of inflation just discussed, can now be combined (Di Tella, MacCulloch, and Oswald 2001). The question is by how much, on average, must a country reduce its inflation in order to tolerate a rise of one percentage point in unemployment? Over the relevant range, happiness is assumed to depend linearly on the two economic factors, and the estimate controls for country fixed effects, year effects, and country-specific time trends. It is calculated that a one percentage-point increase in the unemployment rate is compensated for by a 1.7–percentage-point decrease in inflation. Thus, if unemployment rises by five percentage points (say, from 3 to 8 percent), the inflation rate must decrease by 8.5 percentage points (say, from 10 to 1.5 percent per year) to keep the population equally satisfied. The so-called 'Misery Index,' which simply adds the rate of unemployment to the rate of inflation, distorts the picture by attributing too little weight to the effect of unemployment, relative to inflation, on self-reported happiness.

The results of the trade-off between inflation and unemployment based on happiness data are consistent with previous results based on survey data. Research on popularity and election functions (presented in the next chapter) has found that inflation and unemployment are the 'big two' macroeconomic variables that negatively affect voters' satisfaction with the governing party.

6.3 Conclusions

Inflation has a marked effect on people's happiness. The notion held in theoretical economics that inflation per se does not really affect individuals, but that at best unanticipated price rises do, does not hold with the insights gained from happiness research. The respective studies suggest that inflation harms people, quite irrespective of whether it is predicted or not. Obviously, people resent inflation, not least because they fear a lowering in their (future) standard of living, a worsening in the distribution of income (in particular, that some people are exploited), the moral effects on the cement of society, and the political and economic unrest produced, as well as concerns about a loss of national prestige.

Hints on the Literature

The costs of inflation, from the traditional economic point of view, are discussed in

Fischer, Stanley, and Franco Modigliani (1978). Towards an Understanding of the Real Effects and Costs of Inflation. *Weltwirtschaftliches Archiv* 114(4): 810–33.

An extensive review of the theoretical and empirical findings is given by

Drifill, John, Grayham E. Mizon, and Alistair Ulph (1990). Costs of Inflation. In Benjamin M. Friedman and Frank H. Hahn (eds.), *Handbook of
Monetary Economics*. Amsterdam: North-Holland, ch. 19, 1014–66.

A survey of how people feel about inflation is found in

Shiller, Robert J. (1997). Why Do People Dislike Inflation? In Christina D.
Romer and David H. Romer (eds.), *Reducing Inflation: Motivation and
Strategy*. Chicago and London: University of Chicago Press, 13–65.

The happiness function for 12 European countries, 1975–91, has been estimated by

Di Tella, Rafael, Robert J. MacCulloch, and Andrew J. Oswald (2001). Preferences over Inflation and Unemployment: Evidence from Surveys of
Happiness. *American Economic Review* 91(1): 335–41.

Political Effects on Happiness

HAPPINESS IS A COMPLEX PHENOMENON dependent on many factors. In part I, we discussed personality and socio-demographic factors and, in part II, the economic factors of income, unemployment, and inflation.

This third part considers yet another but highly important sphere—namely, politics. Two quite different levels of politics can be distinguished:

Chapter 7 looks at how politics within given constitutional conditions influence people's happiness. The basic framework of the polity is taken as given, and we analyze how ordinary citizens and politicians act within these confines, and how such behavior affects happiness. We take a look at such aspects as how citizens' trust in government evolves over time, to what extent specific government policies (for example, welfare expenditures) affect people's self-reported well-being, and how happiness is affected by the ideological orientation of the government.

Chapter 8 analyzes how different institutional settings influence people's happiness. The various institutional choices are encapsulated in a country's constitution. Most important are how the political system is constructed (is it a democratic, an authoritarian, or a dictatorial system?) and whether political power is concentrated in the capital or spread over regions and municipalities. This chapter focuses first on ways to set up a democracy. It shows that happiness is raised, the more extensive are the political participation rights of the population via initiatives and referenda. Second, it finds that a federalist (that is, a decentralized) political structure giving decision rights to lower levels of government raises people's happiness.

Chapter 9 addresses the effect of the decision-making process itself on happiness. The institution of direct democracy raises happiness for two quite different reasons. The political decisions conform better to the wishes of the population, and the government's activity proceeds in a more efficient manner. But, in addition, we are able to show that the existence of direct political participation rights raises citizens' happiness because they derive procedural utility. This utility is not reaped by foreigners, who are excluded from political participation (e.g., voting) in their host country.

Chapter 7

THE CURRENT
POLITICO-ECONOMIC PROCESS

7.1 INTRODUCTION

USUALLY POLITICS TAKES PLACE within the rules laid down by the constitution. Political actors, such as the government, the voters, interest groups, and public bureaucracy, take the "rules of the game" specified in the constitution as given, and pursue their interests within these confines. Thus, for example, the political parties in a representative democracy proceed from the assumptions that the parliament decides which parties are able to form the government, and that the parliamentary majority promulgates the laws. Therefore, in order to come to power, a political party must endeavor to get as high as possible a share of the citizens' votes. The voters in turn know that once they have voted in the parliamentary elections, they have no constitutionally established direct say in political decision making. This chapter takes the basic framework of the political system—the constitution—as given. It looks at how the behavior of political actors in the current politico-economic process affects people's happiness.

In the literature, the effect of the politico-economic process on citizens' well-being has so far only been evaluated indirectly. Either it has been inferred from existing political conditions, such as the functioning of party competition, or it has been measured by looking at individuals' reactions. The investigation of individuals' reaction to, and therewith evaluation of, political outcomes has concentrated on the influence of macroeconomic variables. At least five approaches can be distinguished (see Frey 1991 for a more detailed description):

- Popularity and election functions.
- Political reaction functions derived from the behavior of governments and central banks.

- Retreat from society or at least from the official economy—for example, by working in the shadow sector.
- Nonconventional political participation ranging from demonstrations to publicly motivated strikes.
- Use of force—that is, all sorts of revolutions and coups d'état.

Section 7.2 compares the results of the first two approaches—popularity, election, and reaction functions—to assess citizens' well-being with results from happiness research. Section 7.3 reports more general evidence on political satisfaction and on the trust put in the government by the population; section 7.4 discusses how specific government policies affect happiness; and section 7.5 looks at how happiness differs among the parts of the population with different political orientations.

7.2 INDIVIDUAL EVALUATION OF CURRENT POLICY

In many democracies, citizens' voting for a certain party is the strongest instrument they can use to show approval or disapproval of past policy or proposed political programs. It reflects the citizens' evaluation of the policy outcome, based on either past experience or future expectation. Thus, a government's or party's popularity, as measured in regular surveys or its reelection, signals the satisfaction of the population. This idea lies behind the empirical analysis of so-called election and popularity functions. As the political agents have an incentive to pursue citizens' wishes in a democracy, their behavior reflects the desires of the electorate. Observed policy thus offers information on what is valued by the voters. Empirically, this relationship is captured by *reaction functions*. In both approaches—popularity and election functions as well as reaction functions—citizens' satisfaction is linked to economic conditions.

7.2.1 *Election and Popularity Functions*

The evaluation of economic conditions by the voters and their reaction in the voting booth or in regular political surveys are the subjects of an immense literature (for example, Paldam 1981, Schneider and

Frey 1988; Nannestad and Paldam 1994). While these reactions can be attributed to various models of individual behavior, the "responsibility hypothesis" has fared best in empirical analyses. Voters are taken to express a general dissatisfaction when the economy is in a bad state and hold the government responsible. Citizens thus tend to vote in a sociotropic way—that is, based on their perception of the state of the macroeconomy rather than on their own economic experience. They also tend to vote retrospectively.

Election and popularity functions have been estimated for a large number of countries and periods. While the sizes of the effects of the various macroeconomic variables differ, of course, it is nevertheless possible to indicate broad magnitudes. The influence of changes in the unemployment rate and in the inflation rate, in the share of votes cast, and in the popularity attributed to government are of similar sizes. A one–percentage-point increase in the unemployment rate lowers the voting or popularity share of the government by between 0.4 and 0.8 percentage points. The same holds for a one–percentage-point increase in the inflation rate.

In contrast, a change in the growth rate of per capita real income often has no statistically significant effect on vote and popularity shares, though the coefficient is usually positive. For those studies that have found statistically significant positive effects, the coefficient tends to be smaller than the respective changes in unemployment and inflation. Thus, for example, a coefficient of 0.02 has been estimated for France (1969–78), 0.4 for Germany (1971–82), and 0.8 for the United Kingdom and 0.5 for the United States (1953–76) (Hibbs 1981, Kirchgässner 1985, Frey and Schneider 1978a,b). Other studies do not identify any systematic (statistically significant) effect of income growth on government votes or popularity.

These results from popularity and election functions are consistent with empirical evidence of the effect of per capita income, unemployment, and inflation on happiness as discussed in the three previous chapters. Unemployment and inflation affect satisfaction with life as well as satisfaction with the government much more than a higher average income level. However, the greater weight of unemployment in the unemployment/inflation trade-off (see chapter 6, section 6.2.1) is not a stylized result of popularity and election functions.

7.2.2   Reaction Functions

The reaction function approach reverses the quantitative theory of economic policy (Tinbergen 1956, Theil 1964). Instead of deriving the optimal use of policy instruments by maximizing the social welfare function, it is assumed that the actual use of policy instruments reflects the maximization of social welfare and, hence, the weights of its components. This approach allows for the determination of the weights policymakers attribute to various macroeconomic goals. The more the policymakers depend on the evaluation of the voters, the more closely the empirically derived weights reflect individual preferences. Reaction functions are to be looked at as revealed preference functions of the citizens, provided the policymakers know the structure of the economy—that is, provided they do not commit any systematic mistakes when using the instruments at their disposal.

Reaction functions have been econometrically estimated for a large number of countries and periods. (For evaluative surveys, see, for example, Wood 1967, Makin 1976.) Most of the studies have been devoted to the behavior of central banks to determine the implied weights of macroeconomic variables. If the preference weights derived are to be interpreted as reflecting the utility of the citizens or social welfare, it has to be assumed that central bankers pursue the citizens' or the population's interests for intrinsic reasons, as most central banks are shielded from direct political influence. The studies yield quite different results not only according to the country and period studied, but also because central bank behavior is dependent on political influences. In the United States, for example, it has been shown that the weights attributed to the various goals depend on the administration in power. Under the Eisenhower administration (1953–61), the unemployment rate and the level of economic activity influenced Federal Reserve behavior, while under the Kennedy and Johnson administrations (1961–69), the inflation rate also exerted a significant influence. Under Nixon (1969–74), the Federal Reserve systematically responded to the unemployment rate, the level of economic activity, and the balance of payments (Froyen 1974).

Some studies have estimated reaction functions for governments. In the United States, for instance, the administrations of Eisenhower, Kennedy, and Johnson emphasized price stability and a favorable balance of payments more strongly than full employment (Friedlaender

1973). A reaction function for the British government and the period 1955–68 suggests that the government dislikes an increase of unemployment by one percentage point as much as an increase in the price level of 0.26 percentage points (Pissarides 1972).

Reaction functions offer a much less clear picture of the effect of macroeconomic variables on people's well-being and are therefore difficult to compare with happiness functions. However, it is revealed that politicians behave differently, depending on what particular ideology they pursue. This makes sense, provided the citizens who vote for them differ in the evaluation of macroeconomic outcomes compared to citizens who vote for other parties. This issue is directly addressed in section 7.5.

Election, popularity, and reaction functions analyze the effect of economic conditions on voters as well as on government and other political decision makers. The following sections take a different perspective—a perspective that directly considers the amount of happiness gained by citizens from the political process.

7.3   INDIVIDUAL SATISFACTION AND GOVERNMENT

The general level of happiness is without any doubt seriously affected by major political events. Typically, such an event could be the assassination of a dictator, the overthrow of a constitutional government, or also the deep uncertainty created by not having any firmly established government. A good example is the Dominican Republic in 1962, where, after President Trujillo's murder, the political situation was very unsettled and political chaos was a real threat. The level of life satisfaction recorded in that country was the lowest ever recorded—namely, 1.6 on the normal 0-to-10 scale. By way of contrast, in politically stable democracies such as Switzerland, Norway, and Denmark, the population expresses high life satisfaction. The corresponding values in the 1990s were, for example, 8.16 for Denmark, 8.02 for Switzerland, and 7.66 for Norway. Thus, happiness and political stability seem to be closely related.

The causation may, however, run in both directions. While it seems obvious that political unrest is dissatisfying to people, it also stands to reason that a dissatisfied population resorts to demonstrations, strikes, and even revolts and revolutions, and thus creates political instability. But it would be a romantic view (see Tullock 1987) to assume that revolutions are normally caused by people's unhappiness with existing political conditions. Most coups d'état and even revolutions are undertaken by competing political clans or parties or the military. There is an exchange of rulers within the "class politique" itself that is only partially fueled by the population's unhappiness with their rulers. The people's dissatisfaction is often merely an excuse to seize power. (See Galetovic and Sanhueza 2000, Weede and Muller 1998, Wintrobe 1998.)

The population may also experience unhappiness during periods of national stress caused by unfavorable foreign policy developments. In Israel, for example, in the period between June 1967 and August 1979, lower levels of well-being were reported by large segments of the population, in particular women, the less educated, the elderly, the more religious, and those of Eastern origin (Landau, Beit-Hallahami, and Levy 1998).

There has recently been much concern about declining trust by citizens in government (the best-known examples being found in Putnam 1993, Fukuyama 1995). Figure 7.1 shows that Americans have indeed lost considerable confidence in the government, and that an increasing percentage of the population believes that it can trust the government only "some of the time."

The proportion of the American population that trusts the government "always" or "most of the time" has decreased from above 70 percent in the early 60s to below 40 percent in the 90s. The lowest proportion was measured in 1994—namely, 21 percent. "Trust in government" has been interpreted as a manifestation of political satisfaction or as one of several determinants of it. Decreasing trust in government not only may signal that the voters are unhappy with the party in power, but may reflect a deeper dissatisfaction with how politics is undertaken by any party—that is, with politicians in general. Decreasing confidence in government has been observed not only in the United States, but also in Europe (but only since 1991). In Japan, as much as 67 percent of the respondents in a national poll reported either hostility to the then reigning cabinet or no interest whatsoever in the government (Lane 2000, p. 201).

Many reasons may be adduced to account for increasing political dissatisfaction. An important one is a sense of political inefficacy. Citizens feel that they have no influence on political decisions and that the professional politicians do whatever they like. Another reason is the

Figure 7.1. Declining trust in the U.S. government, 1958–98. Respondents were asked, "How much of the time do you think you can trust the government in Washington to do what is right: just about always, most of the time, or only some of the time?" The figure traces the percentage who said that they trust the government "always" or "most of the time." Data Source: American National Election Studies, 1958–98, University of Michigan.

impression that the government is run in the interest of special groups but not in the interest of the population as a whole. Psychologists point to a sense of alienation caused by individuals' perceived powerlessness, helplessness, and meaninglessness with respect to politics. Empirically, the relationship between these negative political feelings and satisfaction with life is rather weak. In a cross-national study covering nations with widely different per capita incomes, there is no statistically significant relationship between political distrust and average happiness. In Europe, however, the correlation is rather high (Veenhoven 1993). In poor, developing countries, most governments are authoritarian and the population has little or no say. Therefore, the citizens expect little from the government anyway so they do not relate their satisfaction with life to the political sphere, except in times of major unrest. In contrast, European citizens live in generally well-functioning democracies and they expect governments to act in their interest. When they feel less confident that this is indeed the case, their life satisfaction is reduced.

7.4 Specific Government Policies

Expenditures on social insurance—for medical care, child benefits, payments in case of illness, and disability as well as for unemployment and old age—seem to raise satisfaction with life. A study based on the World Value Surveys for 1980 and 1990 covering between 27 and 38 countries (depending on data availability) found a positive relationship between expenditures on social insurance and happiness. Taking into account differences in per capita income (using purchasing power parities), the partial correlation between social expenditures and happiness even turns around and becomes negative. In both cases, the relationship is statistically insignificant (Veenhoven 2000b). Another study (Di Tella, MacCulloch, and Oswald 1999) considers only part of social insurance—namely, collective unemployment insurance—for 11 countries of the European Union and uses a large number of control variables. It turns out that higher unemployment benefits systematically raise the average happiness in these nations.

7.5 Partisan Political Happiness

Depending on their ideological orientation, citizens respond differently to economic events and the corresponding government policies. Based on Euro-Barometer Survey data for over a quarter of a million persons residing in 10 Western European countries (Belgium, Britain, Denmark, France, Germany, Greece, Italy, the Netherlands, Portugal, and Spain) and for the period 1975–92, both unemployment and inflation have been found to negatively affect individual well-being, controlling for personal characteristics of the respondents, year, and country fixed effects and country-specific time trends (Di Tella and MacCulloch 1999). This result is in line with the findings presented in chapter 5 on unemployment and in chapter 6 on inflation. But individuals with a self-professed left-wing orientation care more about unemployment than about inflation. Politically right-wing individuals, in contrast, experience a bigger drop in their happiness with rising inflation than with rising unemployment. The two groups thus reveal different trade-offs between unemployment and inflation. Left-wing people maintain their levels of satisfaction if a one–percentage-point increase in unemployment is compensated by a rate of inflation 1.8 percentage points lower. A right-wing person is less concerned with unemployment and is therefore equally happy if a one–percentage-point rise in unemployment is compensated by only a 0.9–percentage-points lower inflation rate (Di Tella and MacCulloch 1999, p. 22).

But happiness differs not only with respect to the impact of economic variables but also with respect to the ideological orientation of the government. A government leaning to the ideological right raises the happiness of right-wing individuals (keeping all other influences constant), while left-wing individuals declare themselves to be less satisfied with their lives. Insofar as citizens at least partly tend to vote on ideological grounds rather than on the basis of outcomes attributed to the government, government policy is affected. The partisan models in political business cycle theory (Hibbs 1977,1987, Alesina 1987) are based on this asymmetry, in contrast to the vote-maximizing models (Downs 1957, Nordhaus 1975) where governments consider the aggregate vote outcome. Other models analyzing the mutual interdependence of the economy and polity (Frey and Schneider 1978a,b,1979) combine the two aspects. They assume that governments are forced to pursue a vote-maximizing policy when their reelection is uncertain, but that they can engage in ideological policies when they are confident about being reelected.

The considerations just discussed further suggest that the citizens are not interested only in what governments do but also in who undertakes a specific policy. Citizens not only value outcomes but also processes, a subject that will be further explored in chapter 9.

7.6 CONCLUSIONS

The impact of the behavior of political actors on people's welfare has so far mainly been studied indirectly. For the most part, this has been done by considering the political evaluation of policy outcomes by the citizens. Election functions most importantly capture the effect of macroeconomic conditions on election results, and popularity functions do so by using regular surveys. In democracies, the political decision makers have an incentive to pursue the wishes of the citizens. The extent to which they are willing and able to do so indirectly reflects how happy the electorate is with current politics.

The results of both election and popularity functions indicate a similar magnitude for the effect of unemployment and inflation. In contrast, growth of real income has little if any positive effect on popularity and elections. The results are thus remarkably similar to the ones found in happiness studies.

A different approach is used when one considers the reactions by policymakers to changes in economic conditions. Such actions indirectly reflect the wishes of the electorate, because in a democracy the policymakers are forced, to a considerable extent, to follow citizens' preferences in order to stay in power. These studies reveal a rather opaque picture; the results depend much on the country and period studied, on the particular institutional conditions, and on the ideology of the government in power.

An important line of inquiry focuses on the citizens' trust in government. In the United States, scholars have found a marked loss of confidence in government. This may more generally reflect a dissatisfaction with politics in general. Reasons may be political inefficacy and a perceived lack of influence, as well as an alienation by the citizens. It has been found that in the well-functioning democracies of Europe, trust in government is closely related to happiness. But, in other continents and in less developed countries, this is not the case. No consistent effect of particular government expenditures on happiness has been found, except in particular areas, such as that of unemployment benefits.

Research on partisan political happiness points to the importance of citizens' ideology. Left-wing people care more about unemployment than about inflation; right-wing people have the opposite evaluation. But there is also an effect of government ideology. Right-wing governments (all other things being equal) tend to raise the happiness of right-wing citizens, which points to the importance of procedural utility, an aspect that is taken up in a later chapter.

HINTS ON THE LITERATURE

The difference between the current politico-economic process and the constitutional level is expounded in

Buchanan, James M. (1991). *Constitutional Economics*. Oxford: Blackwell.

Frey, Bruno S. (1983). *Democratic Economic Policy*. Oxford: Blackwell.

Mueller, Dennis C. (1996). *Constitutional Democracy*. New York: Oxford University Press.

The relationship between democracy and happiness is explored from many different angles by

Lane, Robert E. (2000). *The Loss of Happiness in Market Democracies*. New Haven and London: Yale University Press, ch. 11–15.

That an unhappy population rarely initiates a revolution has been discussed in

Tullock, Gordon (1987). *Autocracy*. Dordrecht: Kluwer.

A comprehensive survey of the causes of revolutions is provided in

Opp, Karl-Dieter, Peter Voss, and Christiane Gern (1995). *The Origins of a Spontaneous Revolution: East Germany 1989*. Ann Arbor: University of Michigan Press.

The concept of social capital or civic virtue is discussed in

Putnam, Robert D., with Robert Leonardi and Raffaella Y. Nanetti (1993). *Making Democracy Work: Civic Tradition in Modern Italy*. Princeton, N.J.: Princeton University Press.

Fukuyama, Francis (1995). *Trust: The Social Virtues and the Creation of Prosperity*. New York: The Free Press.

A broad discussion of trust in government is provided in

Nye, Joseph S., Philip D. Zelikow, and David C. King (eds.) (1997). *Why People Don't Trust Government*. Cambridge, Mass., and London: Harvard University Press.

Studies on the effects of specific government policies on happiness are found in

Di Tella, Rafael, Robert J. MacCulloch, and Andrew J. Oswald (1999). How Do Macroeconomic Fluctuations Affect Happiness? Mimeo. Boston: Harvard Business School.

Veenhoven, Ruut (2000). Well-Being in the Welfare State: Level Not Higher, Distribution Not More Equitable. *Journal of Comparative Policy Analysis* 2: 91–125.

Results on partisan political happiness are examined in

Di Tella, Rafael, and Robert MacCulloch (1999). Partisan Political Happiness. Mimeo. Boston: Harvard Business School.

Respective studies in the context of political business cycles appear in

Alesina, Alberto (1988). Macroeconomics and Politics. In Stanley Fischer (ed.), *NBER Macroeconomic Annual*, Vol. 3. Cambridge, Mass.: MIT Press, 13–52.

Hibbs, Douglas (1987). *The American Political Economy: Macroeconomics and Electoral Politics*. Cambridge, Mass.: Harvard University Press.

A collection of articles is found in

Frey, Bruno S. (ed.) (1997). *Political Business Cycles*. Cheltenham, U.K.: Edward Elgar.

Chapter 8

CONSTITUTION: POPULAR REFERENDA AND FEDERALISM

8.1 INTRODUCTION

PEOPLE'S HAPPINESS is influenced by the kind of political system they live in. It is to be expected that people in constitutional democracies are happier because the politicians are motivated to rule according to their citizenry's interests. If they disregard the wishes of the population, the politicians and parties in a democracy fail to be reelected and lose their power. Democratic institutions—in particular, the right to participate in elections and vote on issues—thus contribute to citizens' happiness via a favorable outcome of the political process.

Section 8.2 of this chapter discusses various relationships between democratic systems and subjective reported well-being. Section 8.3 focuses on a quantitative analysis of the effects on happiness of two particular constitutional devices: direct political participation of the citizens via popular referenda and federalist decentralization. Section 8.4 offers conclusions.

8.2 CONSTITUTIONAL DEMOCRACY AND HAPPINESS

A constitution lays down the basic rules or fundamental institutions according to which the political system is supposed to be run. Examples are
- The extents of human rights and property rights.
- The extent to which the state is centralized or decentralized.
- The way the citizens' votes determine the people and parties elected into parliament (for example, proportional versus majority voting).

- Whether the government is directly elected by the voters or depends on the will of the parliament.
- The extent to which the citizens have a direct say on particular issues.

Over recent years, economists have made a great effort to empirically analyze the possible effects of democracy on economic factors. It has been shown that economic growth is supported by well-developed property rights. If economic freedom is considered more generally, the link to economic growth depends on the measure used. Many researchers hypothesize that democracy positively affects economic growth. However, there is no clear evidence that the extent of democracy fosters economic development. Some studies find that countries that democratize grow faster, while those that become less democratic grow more slowly than comparable countries. There is also evidence that a severe lack of democracy indirectly reduces growth via lower investments. More important for growth is how the democratic rules are implemented. Thus, government instability, political violence and unrest, and policy volatility indeed tend to hamper growth. (For cross-country growth analysis, see, e.g., Barro 1997, Dasgupta 1993, de Haan and Sturm 2000, Minier 1998, or Siermann 1998.) Political and civil liberties are also evaluated with regard to the distribution of income. It has, for example, been shown that democracies pay higher wages. In a combined cross-section time series analysis, the level of manufacturing wages has been shown to be robustly higher in countries with extensive democracy. Average wages in Mexico would increase by 10 to 40 percent if that country had a level of democracy comparable to that in the United States (Rodrik 1999).

Researchers on happiness have taken a further step and have looked at the interaction of democracy with happiness. The extent to which a constitution is democratic and allows its citizens to make decisions according to their own preferences can be captured by various indices of freedom. Figure 8.1 presents a graphical representation of a comprehensive measure of freedom, combined with a four-item measure of happiness, in 38 nations (mainly developed ones) at the beginning of the 1990s (Veenhoven 2000a). A visual test reveals that freedom (horizontal axis) and happiness (vertical axis) are positively related.

The comprehensive index of the constitutional setup used in this figure has been captured in three areas:

(a) *Political freedom* measures the possibility of citizens to engage in the democratic process or, conversely, the restrictions on political

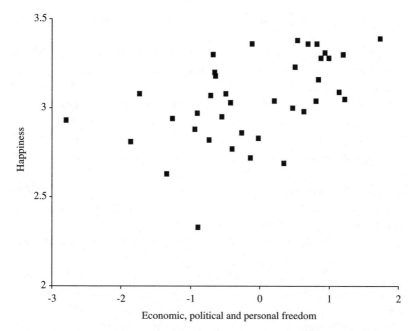

Figure 8.1. Freedom and happiness across nations. Veenhoven (2000a), Appendix 1.

participation. It is composed of two subindices, the first relating to civil rights, such as freedom of speech (with 11 items), and the second to political rights (9 items).

(b) *Economic freedom* measures the opportunity of individuals to engage in the free exchange of goods, services, and labor. It is based on subindices (each in turn composed of a number of items), referring to the security of money, free enterprise, freedom from excessive taxation, and the possibility of undertaking monetary transfers.

(c) *Personal freedom* measures how free one is in one's private life—for example, to practice one's religion, to travel, or to get married.

To combine the subindices, average z-scores are calculated. All three—political, economic, and private freedoms—are strongly correlated in a statistically significant way with happiness in a sample of 46 countries (mainly developed ones) in the early 1990s (Veenhoven 2000a). Controlling for differences in per capita income, the correlation with economic freedom but not political and personal freedoms remains statistically significant. In contrast, no correlation could be found between freedom and happiness in developing countries (Lane 2000, pp. 265–66).

Such studies are certainly illuminating, but they can only inform us in a limited way about the influence of various constitutional conditions on subjective well-being. One reason is that not too much faith should be put in the comparability of happiness measures across nations. Countries differ from each other in many dimensions, and it is not sufficient just to control for unequal per capita incomes to capture the influence of democracy. Moreover, the meaning of happiness may significantly differ between countries, so that it is questionable whether large-scale international comparisons of happiness should be undertaken at all. Finally, the cross-section studies only report correlations and do not deal with causation. Even if we ignore the other problems, it remains open whether democracy fosters happiness, or whether happiness is a precondition for democracy. It has been argued, for instance, that high satisfaction with life in a population increases the legitimacy of the political regime installed and it may thus foster democracy (Inglehart 1990,1999).

In the following, we therefore concentrate on specific institutions of democracy in one particular country.

8.3   How Direct Democracy and Federalism Affect Happiness

8.3.1   Referenda

The possibility of citizens directly participating in politics is an important feature of democracy. The constitutions of many countries allow popular referenda, but they are sometimes only used as a device to inform the government when it no longer knows what to do. Often it is used for the opposite purpose—namely, as a plebiscite in which the voters are asked to support the government's policy. In many cases, it is restricted to local and sometimes trivial issues, while the decisions on important issues are reserved for the professional political actors in parliament and government. However, most members of the European Union (with the exception of Germany) have held referenda concerning entry into the union and its extension, such as the Maastricht Treaty or the introduction of a common currency. In the United States, there are many popular referenda on the local level as well as in some states (especially in California), but the constitution does not allow them at a national level. The only country with an extensive set of direct political participation rights at all levels of government, and with respect to all issues, is Switzerland. Of the roughly 500 referenda made in all the countries in the world at the national level between 1793 and 1978, 300 (or 60 percent) were held in Switzerland. The second most intensive use of referenda is in Australia, with just 40 referenda or 8 percent of the total. (See Butler and Ranney 1994.)

A referendum in which all citizens have the possibility of participating meets the crucial requirement that it gives decision power to people outside the group of (professional) politicians. In an *initiative*, the demands are explicitly directed against the political establishment represented in parliament and government. *Optional* and *obligatory* referenda serve more of a controlling function because, if successful, they overrule the decisions made at an executive or legislative level.

Empirical evidence strongly suggests that referenda are indeed able to break the cartel among the politicians by getting through constitutional provisions and laws totally against the interests of the classe politique. The following cases refer to Switzerland, the referenda nation par excellence. The first two cases concern important historical episodes. (See Blankart 1992.)

(a) During the nineteenth century, the house of representatives (*Nationalrat*) was elected according to the majority rule. The largest party greatly benefited therefrom; for seven decades the Radical-Democratic Party secured a majority of the seats. When the idea was raised that the elections should follow proportional representation in order to allow small parties to enter parliament, the then classe politique in the executive and judicial branches strongly rejected this proposal for obvious reasons of self-interest. Nevertheless, in 1918, the corresponding referendum was accepted by a majority of the population and cantons. In the subsequent elections, the Radical-Democratic Party lost no less than 40 percent of its seats.

(b) Up to the Second World War, Urgent Federal Laws (*dringliche Bundesbeschluesse*) were not subject to the (optional) referendum. In order not to have to seek the population's approval, and in order to pursue policies in their own interests, the classe politique in the government and parliament often declared federal laws to be "urgent" even if that was in fact not the case. In 1946, an initiative was started with the objective of preventing this disregard of the interests of the population. Again, the executive and legislative branches urged the voters to reject the initiative, an urging that was clearly an act of self-interest. However, the initiative was accepted by the voters, and the politicians are now forced to take the citizens' interests into account when they decide on federal laws.

Referenda were not only able to break the politicians' cartel in the past. It still happens regularly, as two more recent cases document: The referenda on Switzerland joining the United Nations (1986) and joining the European Economic Space (1992) had strong support by the classe politique, but were nevertheless rejected by the voters.

The constitutional setting determines to a large extent what issues are put on the political agenda, and which are prevented from appearing. In representative democracies, politicians are often very skillful at not letting problems be discussed in the democratically legitimized institutions if it would be to their disadvantage. For example, they usually succeed at not having their privileges (for example, their income and pensions) discussed in open parliamentary sessions. In direct democracies, however, in which the citizens may bring any issue to the ballot, the agenda is much less under the control of the classe politique. Agenda-setting power has a significant effect on vote outcomes.

An important feature of referenda is the *discussion process* stimulated among the population and between politicians and voters (Bohnet and Frey 1994). Prereferendum discussion may be interpreted as an exchange of arguments among equal citizens, taking place under well-defined rules. This institutionalized discussion meets various conditions of the ideal discourse process, as envisaged by Habermas (1983), but it has one crucial advantage: The exchange of arguments does not take the form of an academic seminar without consequence, since at the end the final decision is with the voters. The relevance of the discussion for politics induces citizens to participate, depending on how important the issue in question is considered to be.

The main function of the prereferendum process is certainly to raise the level of information of the participants. Moreover, the exchange of arguments also forms the participants' preferences. (See Frey and Kirchgässner 1993.) What matters, in our context, is that this preference formation—provided it happens at all—can be influenced but cannot be controlled by the classe politique in a constitutional state with freedom of the media and communication.

In a referendum, a political decision is formally made, but this does not necessarily mean that the politicians and the public administration take the appropriate action to implement it. The more legitimate the constitution is taken to be in a political system, the higher are the costs of not following it. The politicians may also be induced to act accordingly by the threat of not being reelected by the voters, but ultimately the extent of implementation depends on how far the constitutional rules are voluntarily obeyed by the people in power.

The effect of direct democracy on various aspects of society has been carefully analyzed in a number of econometric studies for the United States:

- Government expenditure and government revenues are lower in institutions of direct democracy (Matsusaka 1995).
- Per capita dept is substantially lower with a referendum requiring a qualified majority (McEachern 1978).
- Land prices are higher because people find it attractive to live and work in such areas (Santerre 1986).
- Public expenditure on education is higher when a referendum is possible (Santerre 1989,1993).

The following insights have been gained on the basis of econometric studies for Switzerland:

- A comparison of Swiss communes, with different degrees of institutionalized forms of participation in political decisions, reveals that the outcomes correspond more closely to the voters' preferences, the more directly democratic they are (Pommerehne 1990).
- The growth of public expenditure is more strongly determined by demand factors (that is, by the citizens' willingness to pay) than by supply factors (in particular, by the politicians' and bureaucrats' own interests) (Pommerehne and Schneider 1978).
- Public supply is less costly, the more direct the democratic institutions are (Pommerehne 1978).
- Tax morale is better than in representative democracies (Pommerehne and Weck-Hannemann 1996, Frey 1997a).
- Per capita incomes in cantons with more strongly developed direct participation possibilities for citizens are significantly higher than in cantons with less developed forms of direct participation (Feld and Savioz 1997).

All these results control for a great number of variables unrelated to direct democracy. They provide strong evidence that the deviations from the citizens' preferences are indeed significantly lower in a polity with referenda compared to a representative democracy.

8.3.2 Federalism

The institution of citizens directly deciding on an issue, and the decentralization of decision making, are closely connected. On the one hand, federalism is an alternative means for better fulfillment of the voters' preferences: Individuals tend to leave dissatisfying jurisdictions, while they are attracted to those caring for the population's preferences at low cost. The possibility to vote with one's feet (Tiebout 1956; see also Buchanan 1965, Hirschman 1970) tends to undermine politicians' regional cartels, provided, of course, that the people concerned have political rights.

In more important respects, on the other hand, federalism is a prerequisite for effective referenda rather than a substitute. In small communities, much knowledge needed for informed political decision making is impacted in everyday life: As consumers, producers, and people doing the housework, they are well aware of the benefits and costs of particular public programs and, as taxpayers, they immediately have to carry the burden, provided a sufficient amount of fiscal equivalence exists (Olson 1969,1986). Referenda undertaken on communal and regional issues help the citizens to evaluate political questions to be decided at a higher federal level, and make referenda a more effective institution to undermine politicians' cartels against the voters.

8.3.3 Econometric Estimates

The influence of direct democracy and federalism on happiness is analyzed employing the data on reported subjective well-being for Switzerland in 1992–94 previously used in this book.

The major explanatory variable focused on is the institutionalized rights of individual political participation, which vary considerably between the 26 Swiss cantons. Due to the federal structure of Switzerland, major areas of competence are held by the cantons (states). As at a national level, direct democratic instruments exist besides representative democratic parliaments and governments. The most important direct democratic instruments in cantons are the popular initiatives to change the canton's constitution or laws, a compulsory and optional referendum to prevent new laws or the changing of existing laws, and optional financial referenda to prevent new state expenditure. Citizens' access to these instruments differ from canton to canton. Thus, for example, the number of signatures required to launch an initiative or an optional referendum, or the time frame within which the signatures have to be collected, varies. The referendum on public expenditures may be launched at different levels of additional outlays. For the 26 cantons, we constructed an index designed to reflect the extent of direct democratic participation possibilities. (For details of the index construction, see Appendix B.) This index is defined using a six-point scale with 1 indicating the lowest, and 6 the highest degree of participation possibilities for the citizens.

Figure 8.2 provides an overview. It reveals that there are considerable differences between cantons with respect to direct participation possibilities in politics. The weakest direct democratic institutions are found in canton Geneva, the strongest in canton Basel-Landschaft.

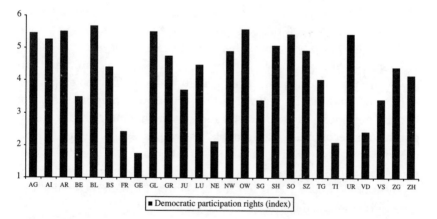

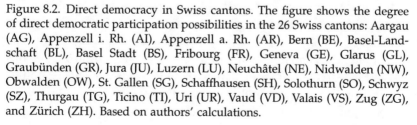

Figure 8.2. Direct democracy in Swiss cantons. The figure shows the degree of direct democratic participation possibilities in the 26 Swiss cantons: Aargau (AG), Appenzell i. Rh. (AI), Appenzell a. Rh. (AR), Bern (BE), Basel-Landschaft (BL), Basel Stadt (BS), Fribourg (FR), Geneva (GE), Glarus (GL), Graubünden (GR), Jura (JU), Luzern (LU), Neuchâtel (NE), Nidwalden (NW), Obwalden (OW), St. Gallen (SG), Schaffhausen (SH), Solothurn (SO), Schwyz (SZ), Thurgau (TG), Ticino (TI), Uri (UR), Vaud (VD), Valais (VS), Zug (ZG), and Zürich (ZH). Based on authors' calculations.

The purpose of our estimate is to show that the extent of direct democratic participation possibilities exerts a statistically significant, robust, and sizable effect on happiness over and above the demographic and economic determinants discussed in the previous chapters.

We also intend to demonstrate that institutional factors in the form of federalism are relevant for happiness. The division of competence between communities and the cantonal government reflects the federal structure of a canton or, from the municipalities' point of view, their autonomy. The extent of local autonomy is measured by an index (due to Ladner 1994). The index over the 26 cantons is based on survey results. Chief local administrators in 1,856 Swiss municipalities were asked to report how they perceived their local autonomy on a 10-point scale, with 1 indicating "no autonomy at all", and 10 "very high" communal autonomy. (The respective numbers are presented in Appendix B.) Again, considerable variation exists across cantons.

The two focal variables included in the estimation models are

• The index for democratic participation rights.
• The index for the extent of local (communal) autonomy.

The two variables refer to the 26 cantons in Switzerland. The structure of Swiss cantons, however, differs not only in respect to direct democracy and federal organization, but also in other respects, such as the degree of urbanization. Therefore, to control for further regional differences, we include five variables for the size of community and seven variables for the type of community in the estimation equations.

Table 8.1 presents the estimated coefficients and marginal effects of two microeconometric happiness functions, taking into account demographic and economic determinants, as well as the institutional variable of direct democratic rights. In the first equation, a weighted least squares model is estimated. In the second one, a weighted ordered probit model is used to exploit the ranking information contained in the originally scaled dependent variable.

The index for democratic participation rights has a highly significant positive effect on happiness. An increase in the index of direct democracy by one point raises average satisfaction by 0.11 units (weighted least squares estimation) and the proportion of persons indicating very high satisfaction with life by 2.8 percentage points. This result is consistent with our hypothesis that the institutions of direct democracy raise reported subjective well-being.

TABLE 8.1
Democratic Participation Rights and Satisfaction with
Life in Switzerland, 1992–94

	Weighted Least Squares	Weighted Ordered Probit	
	Coefficient (t-Value)	Coefficient (t-Value)	Marginal Effect for Score of 10
Democratic participation	0.114	0.081	0.028
rights	(2.82)	(3.01)	
Socio-demographic factors	Included	Included	
Socio-economic factors	Included	Included	
Observations	6,137	6,137	

Source of data: Leu, Burri, and Priester (1997).
Notes: Department variable: level of satisfaction on a 10-point scale. White estimator for variance, t-values are in parentheses. Standard errors are adjusted to clustering in 26 cantons. Additional control variables (not shown) for size of community (five variables) and type of community (one variables).

The effect of democracy on happiness is sizable:

(i) The marginal effect of direct democratic rights on happiness is as large as the effect of living in the second-bottom income category (Sfr. 2,000–3,000) instead of the bottom income category (under Sfr. 2,000).

(ii) The effect is even larger when the full range of the institutional variable is considered—that is, when individuals in canton Basel-Landschaft (with the highest democracy index of 5.69) are compared to citizens in canton Geneva (with the lowest direct participation rights of 1.75). The inhabitants of the former state have an 11–percentage-points higher probability that they are completely satisfied.

(iii) The improvement affects everybody—that is, the institutional factor is important in an aggregate sense. In comparison, getting a job "only" raises the subjective well-being of the unemployed.

Does the causality between direct democracy and subjective well-being work in reverse? Do happy people choose direct democratic institutions? Direct democratic participation possibilities, in the form of referenda and initiatives in Switzerland, started to develop in the middle of the nineteenth century. The adoption of some of the instruments of direct popular participation reflects the spread of

TABLE 8.2
Federalism and Satisfaction with Life in Switzerland, 1992–94

| | Weighted Ordered Probit | | | |
| | (1) | | (2) | |
	Coefficient	t-Value	Coefficient	t-Value
Local autonomy	0.094	2.84	0.032	0.90
Democratic participation rights			0.071	2.29
Socio-demographic factors	Included		Included	
Socio-economic factors	Included		Included	
Observations	6,137		6,137	

Source of data: Ladner (1994) and Leu, Burri, and Prister (1997). Notes: See Table 8.1.

the spirit and ideas behind the American and French revolutions. Equally important were political movements within the citizenry. Citizens fought for direct democratic instruments to gain political power against arbitrary decisions by parliaments and the influence of industrial pressure groups on these authorities in the cantons. (See, e.g., Kölz, 1998.) This historic perspective suggests that the democratic institutions are not simply the result of happy and satisfied citizens. During the past decades, especially, institutional conditions in Swiss cantons have been fairly stable, which suggests that causality runs unambiguously from direct democratic rights to satisfaction with life.

Table 8.2 focuses on federalism in the sense of devolution as a second important political institution hypothesized to raise happiness. Therefore, the variable "local autonomy" is added to the demographic and economic factors in the happiness equation. For simplicity, once again only the coefficients for variables of interest are shown. The coefficients of the variables discussed before remain almost unaltered. The estimate reveals a statistically significant positive effect on subjective well-being. For local autonomy, the proportion of persons indicating being completely satisfied increases by 3.2 percentage points, compared to a situation in which the communes are one index point less autonomous vis-à-vis their canton.

Local autonomy and direct democracy are not independent of each other. On the one hand, direct democracy fosters federal structures at the national and state levels because citizens—in contrast to politicians—are most interested in strong federalism (Blankart 2000). On the other hand, the people bearing the costs and benefits of government action are better identifiable in a decentralized system. Direct legislation, therefore, leads to better political decisions, and federalism thus preserves direct democracy. As a result, the indices for direct democratic rights and local autonomy are correlated ($r = 0.605$). This makes it impossible to clearly separate the effects of the two variables in one model. The second equation in Table 8.2 jointly includes the two constitutional factors: local autonomy and direct democratic rights. The coefficient for the variable measuring federalism is roughly one-third as large as when it is taken alone and it loses its statistical significance. The index for direct democracy has only a slightly smaller marginal effect on life satisfaction than estimated in Table 8.1—namely, 0.024 instead of 0.028. In an adjusted Wald test, the two institutional factors together are significant at the 5 percent level (Prob > F = 0.014). Direct democracy and federalism in Switzerland thus seem to be complements rather than economic substitutes. Local autonomy is one of several "transmission mechanisms" of direct democracy's beneficial effects. Therefore, in the following paragraphs, we focus on direct democracy.

To check the reliability of the results gained so far, several tests for robustness are performed: (i) the influence of outliers is analyzed with a DFBETA-test; (ii) an ordinal measure instead of a cardinal one is applied for the extent of direct democratic rights; (iii) the effect of the four subindices on happiness is tested; and, finally, (iv) four different aggregate control variables are used.

To investigate whether the positive correlation between direct democracy and happiness is largely driven by a single canton, a DFBETA-test is performed. A two-step approach is chosen. In the first step, a further weighted ordered probit model, with a dummy variable for each canton, is estimated. In preparation for the second step, the estimated coefficients are correlated with the index for direct democratic rights. Due to the problem of heteroskedasticity, a weighted least square regression is estimated. Heteroskedasticity arises because the coefficients for the canton's dummy variables are based on samples with largely differing size. Therefore, the weighting variable contains the number of observations per canton. The result is as follows (with t-values in parentheses):

Fixed effects for cantons $= -0.268 + 0.078 \times$ index for democratic
$$(-2.12) \quad (2.65)$$
participation rights, number of observations = 26 and $R^2 = 0.274$.

The results for ordinary least squares are as follows: fixed effects for cantons $= -0.384(-2.20) + 0.120(3.02) \times$ index for democratic participation rights, with adjusted $R^2 = 0.246$.

Using the same estimation model, 26 equations are estimated, with a different canton omitted each time. For each equation, the estimated coefficient for the institutional variable is subtracted from the coefficient in the base equation (0.078) and divided by the estimated standard error. The resulting value is called DFBETA. If it is greater than 1.96 in absolute value, the omitted canton has a significant influence on the coefficient of the institutional variable. Table A.2 in Appendix A shows that not one observation from a single canton has a significant influence. The maximum value of the DFBETA statistic is –0.893 for canton Ticino. If the fixed effect of this canton is omitted, the coefficient for direct democratic rights increases to 0.099. This shows that the positive effect of direct democracy on happiness is not the result of an influential outlier.

The measure applied for the extent of direct democratic participation possibilities is constructed as a cardinal index. However, the same results should be obtained if ordinal dummy variables for democratic participation rights are constructed. To test this claim, cantons were classified into three groups: cantons with an index score lower than four have low direct democratic rights, cantons with an index between four and five have medium direct democratic rights, and cantons with an index score above five are ranked highly with respect to direct democratic rights. The two dummy variables for cantons with a medium or high ranking are included in the estimation equation presented in Table 8.3. As can be seen, satisfaction with life is higher for people living in cantons with medium or high direct democratic rights. The significant coefficient for the top category is 0.178. (The reference group includes people who live in cantons with low direct democratic rights.)

The variable for direct democratic participation possibilities is a nonweighted composite index. (See table B.1 in Appendix B). This aggregation disregards various substitutive and complementary relationships between the single components of the index. Nevertheless, the components can be evaluated by themselves. However, the analysis faces the problem of multicorrelation. The correlation between the four subindices is shown in Table B.2 in Appendix B. The influence of each component is evaluated separately. (See Table 8.3.)

TABLE 8.3
Sensitivity Analysis: Ordinal Variable and Subindices
for Democratic Participation Rights

Variable	Weighted Ordered Probit				
	(1)	(2)	(3)	(4)	(5)
Democratic participation	0.113				
rights, index 4–5	(1.66)				
Democratic participation	0.178				
rights, index above 5	(2.31)				
Index for constitutional		0.060			
initiative		(2.32)			
Index for legislative			0.070		
initiative			(2.85)		
Index for legislative				0.039	
referendum				(1.78)	
Index for financial					0.061
referendum					(3.38)
Socio-democractic factors	———————— Included ————————				
Socio-economic factors	———————— Included ————————				
Observations	6,137	6,137	6,137	6,137	6,137

Source of data: Leu, Burri, and Priester (1997).

Notes: See Table 8.1; t-values in parentheses. In the reference group in equation (1) are cantons with democratic participation rights lower than 4.

All four subindices of direct democratic rights have a positive effect on reported subjective well-being. The coefficient for the subindex for the right to change the canton's law with a legislative popular initiative is the largest. Thus, the possibility of putting new questions on the political agenda seems of special importance for the beneficial effects of direct democracy on citizens' individual well-being.

In order to test for alternative explanations of the cross-regional differences in happiness, the effect of some aggregate control variables is estimated on its own, as well as jointly with the institutional variable. Table 8.4 exhibits the results for the two macroeconomic variables "national income per capita" and "total tax burden" as well as for the two language variables "French-speaking canton" and "Italian-speaking canton." Equation (1) and equation (2) indicate that national income per capita does not influence happiness significantly, whether it is controlled for institutional differences or not. The same holds for the variable total tax burden in equations (3) and (4). As can be seen, the introduction of these two macroeconomic variables does not

TABLE 8.4
Sensitivity Analysis: Aggregate Control Variables

	Weighted Ordered Probit					
Variable	*(1)*	*(2)*	*(3)*	*(4)*	*(5)*	*(6)*
Democratic participation rights		0.086 (3.20)		0.082 (2.60)		0.076 (2.67)
Macroeconomic factors						
National income per capita in canton (in SFr. 1,000) in 1992	−3.1e-4 (−0.09)	−0.004 (−1.28)				
Total tax burden (index) in canton in 1992			−0.002 (−1.43)	1.5e-4 (0.09)		
Majority language						
French-speaking canton					−0.217 (−3.78)	−0.087 (−1.32)
Italian-speaking canton					0.071 (1.95)	0.241 (3.17)
Socio-demographic factors			——— Included ———			
Socio-economic variables			——— Included ———			
Observations	6,137	6,137	6,137	6,137	6,137	6,137

Source of data: Leu, Burri, and Priester (1997) and Swiss Federal Statistical Office (1997).

Notes: See Table 8.1; t-values in parentheses.

greatly affect the size and significance of the direct democracy variable. In contrast, the variables for the language the majority speak are significantly correlated with reported satisfaction with life—that is, living in a French-speaking canton means significantly lower happiness, whereas living in the Italian-speaking canton Ticino means significantly higher reported subjective well-being (equation (5)) than living in a German-speaking canton. However, the lower well-being in the French-speaking cantons can, to a large extent, be explained by weaker direct democratic rights (equation (6)). In equation (6) the coefficient of the institutional variable is almost unchanged and yet still statistically significant ($p < 0.05$). It can be concluded that the extent of direct democracy has a robust influence on happiness.

Are the beneficial effects of direct democracy restricted to some privileged groups? To investigate this important question of equality, we analyze the influence of direct democracy on groups of people sharing common characteristics with regard to sex, education, employment status, and income. Technically, interaction variables are included in the estimation equation, in addition to the demographic and economic variables. The interaction variables are the product of dummy variables for the personal characteristics and the index for direct democratic rights.

The benefits of direct democracy are smaller for women than for men. However, the difference is not statistically significant. There is also no significant difference between the three levels of education and the seven categories of employment status distinguished; that is, the positive effect of direct democracy does not arise with a higher education class and is not bound to a certain employment status. We have also analyzed whether direct democracy raises the happiness of high-income recipients while not doing so for low-income recipients. However, the interaction variables do not show any statistically significant differences. The positive effect of direct democracy on happiness applies to all income classes, and is not restricted to a particular one.

Overall, our analysis indicates that direct democracy is not used to discriminate against certain groups within society. The benefits are distributed rather evenly among social classes. However, as in other countries, a large proportion of residents—namely, foreigners—is formally excluded from participation in the direct democratic process. In the next chapter, it is argued that they can reap only part of the utility derived from direct democracy.

8.4 CONCLUSIONS

Research has revealed that political, economic, and personal freedom are positively related to happiness in developed countries. No such correlation can be detected for developing countries. However, the analysis of this relationship is wrought with difficulties. It is questionable whether happiness data can be compared effectively in cross-country analysis. But more importantly, causality may run in the reverse direction: It may well be that happy citizens are politically more active and therefore achieve more freedom.

Because of the problems connected with cross-country comparisons, we concentrate here on analyzing the effects of different democratic institutions in one country on happiness. Switzerland allows such analyses, because its 26 cantons exhibit considerable differences with respect to the direct participation possibilities of the citizens and the extent of political decentralization. More extensive political participation rights, as well as more autonomous communes, increase people's subjective well-being over and above the demographic and economic factors considered in earlier chapters.

Institutions matter. This holds not only with respect to the effects of institutions on economic activity, as normally analyzed in economics. We are moreover able to show, for the first time, that good political institutions do indeed raise happiness.

HINTS ON THE LITERATURE

International cross-section analyses of the relationship between democratic institutions and happiness are contained in

Diener, Ed, Marissa Diener, and Carol Diener (1995). Factors Predicting the Subjective Well-Being of Nations. *Journal of Personality and Social Psychology* 69(5): 851–64.

Veenhoven, Ruut (2000). Freedom and Happiness: A Comparative Study in Forty-Four Nations in the Early 1990s. In Ed Diener and Eunkook M. Suh (eds.), *Culture and Subjective Well-Being.* Cambridge, Mass.: MIT Press; 257–88.

A survey of the effects of various democratic features on economic growth is given in

Siermann, Clemens L. J. (1998). *Politics, Institutions and the Economic Performance of Nations.* Cheltenham, U.K., and Northampton, Mass: Edward Elgar.

Direct democracy is the subject of

Bowler, Shaun, Todd Donovan, and Caroline J. Tolbert (1998). *Citizens as Legislators: Direct Democracy in the United States.* Columbus: Ohio State University Press.

Butler, David, and Austin Ranney (eds.) (1994). *Referendums around the World: The Growing Use of Direct Democracy.* Washington, D.C.: AEI Press.

Cronin, Thomas E. (1989). *Direct Democracy: The Politics of Initiative, Referendum and Recall.* Cambridge, Mass. Harvard University Press.

Swiss direct democracy is discussed from the economic point of view in

Frey, Bruno S. (1994). Direct Democracy: Politico-Economic Lessons from Swiss Experience. *American Economic Review* 84(2): 338–48.

A survey of the empirical work on direct democracy is presented in

Kirchgässner, Gebhard, Lars Feld, and Marcel R. Savioz (1999). *Die direkte Demokratie: Modern, erfolgreich, entwicklungs- und exportfähig.* Basel et al.: Helbing and Lichtenhahn.

A survey of the traditional economic analysis of federal decentralization is presented by

Oates, Wallace E. (1999). An Essay on Fiscal Federalism. *Journal of Economic Literature* 37(3): 1120–49.

More unorthodox ideas on decentralization are developed in

Frey, Bruno S., and Reiner Eichenberger (1999). *The New Democratic Federalism for Europe: Functional, Overlapping and Competing Jurisdictions.* Cheltenham, U.K.: Edward Elgar.

Chapter 9

OUTCOME AND PROCESS

9.1 Introduction

PEOPLE ARE LIKELY to experience happiness not only from the actual outcomes but also from the process itself: They experience *procedural utility*. Individuals may, for instance, experience a higher subjective well-being when they are treated in a way they consider to be just and fair, or in the absence of favoritism when it comes to being hired or promoted. Another important case in which procedural utility is obviously important has to do with the labor market. As Scitovsky (1976) argued in his *Joyless Economy*, intrinsic work enjoyment is a major source of well-being. (See also Lane 2000, p. 170.) Scitovsky even proposed that "[T]he difference between liking and disliking one's work may well be more important than the differences in economic satisfaction that the disparities in our income lead to" (p. 103). People may also be more satisfied by acting fairly or by being honest, quite independent of the outcome. (See, e.g., Rabin 1993, Tooby and Cosmides 1994.) Thus, utility is reaped from the decision-making process itself over and above the outcome generated. In this chapter, we focus on these *procedural* components of happiness. This expands the analysis of happiness in the previous chapters, where mainly economic and political *outcomes* were considered important for subjective well-being.

In economics, procedural utility has been particularly useful to model the payoffs from gambling. (See Le Menestrel 2001.) Scholars such as Pascal (1670), Marschak (1950), and von Neumann and Morgenstern (1947) were well aware that people derive utility from the mere act of engaging in that activity. Simon (1976,1978) and Sen (1995,1997) argue more generally that economic choice models should combine preferences for outcomes as well as for processes. But such amalgamation is not easy to undertake. Harsanyi (1993, p. 314) states that procedural utility is incompatible with expected utility theory and Rabin (1993, p. 1285), in game theory, believes that procedural utility certainly cannot be analyzed by appropriately transforming the payoffs of a conventional game. Other scholars—in particular, Hammond (1988,1996)—simply deny the existence of process utility beyond expected utility.

Psychologists have done extensive research on "procedural fairness" (in particular, Lind and Tyler 1988, Tyler 1990, Tyler and Blader 2000). They are able to show that people are at least as concerned with procedural justice as with the outcomes of those procedures. They evaluate procedures not only by the results they yield, but by the relational information that they convey. These evaluations may consist of assessments of impartiality, trustworthiness of superiors and authorities, and the extent to which individuals feel they are treated with dignity. (See also the empirical research reported in Shafir and Tversky 1992, Gärling, Axhausen, and Brydsten 1996, Donaldson and Shackley 1997.) Many intrinsic pleasures of a procedure have been identified, among them the utility gained by facing and meeting challenges, by expressing oneself, by showing one's talents, and by reporting one's experiences over and above the instrumental value they may have. But procedures may also lower utility—for instance, by being cognitively taxing or by forcing one into making a decision. Thus, many people prefer not to have to decide between two newly available alternatives (for example, new job offers), even if both of them are superior to the status quo.

This chapter shows that the two types of utility can be measured and isolated. As in chapter 8, the effect on happiness of institutions in the form of participation in democratic decision making is at the center of analysis. In order to distinguish between the two types of utility and measure their sizes, we take the fact that national citizens are allowed to participate politically (and therefore may enjoy satisfaction from both outcome and process), while foreigners have no political participation rights (and therefore only enjoy outcome utility).

Section 9.2 discusses the outcome and process utility of actual *participation* in democratic decision making. Section 9.3 considers the relationship between utility and political participation *rights*. The testable hypotheses are advanced, and the empirical estimation is undertaken in section 9.4. The last section, 9.5, offers conclusions.

9.2 THE UTILITY OF ACTUAL PARTICIPATION

A large literature in the social sciences, especially in psychology, political science, and sociology, attributes a positive value to participation, as it enhances individuals' perceptions of self-determination. (For an extensive survey, see Lane 2000, ch. 13.) It is important to distinguish actual participation from the right to participate. The former refers to the decision of individuals as to whether they choose to engage themselves. The traditional calculus of voting based on expected utility maximization solely considers outcome utility. (See Mueller 1989, Aldrich 1997.) It suggests that rational voters never participate in political decisions, because the probability of affecting the outcome is close to zero with most sizes of electorates, while there are participation costs. However, this prediction is at odds with the empirical observations that citizens do indeed cast their votes, even if their expected influence is virtually nil. This casts doubt on the rational choice approach as traditionally formulated. Some authors therefore have identified the various procedural utilities that voters may derive from political participation—for instance, a sense of civic duty or the value of expressing an ideological view (Hardin 1982, Brennan and Buchanan 1985, Schuessler 2000).

9.3 THE UTILITY OF PARTICIPATION RIGHTS

The *right* to participate in political decisions accords the citizens more encompassing self-determination, because the decision of whether to participate or not is left up to the individual. People may value the right to participate even if they seldom, if ever, actually exercise it. What matters is that they can participate if they find it appropriate. It may therefore be hypothesized that participation rights reflect procedural utility more strongly than actual participation does.

In most countries, the status of a national differs fundamentally from that of foreigners because nationals have the right to vote. In many other ways, the principle of the rule of law demands that the two groups be treated equally. Thus, for example, they have the same human rights and, once admitted into the country, foreigners have (with few exceptions) the same rights as nationals to participate in economic affairs. It cannot, of course, be denied that national legislation and political decisions tend to be rigged in favor of nationals. But what matters for the approach used here is that the *outcome* of the democratic political process is much more equally distributed between nationals and foreigners than are the formal *participation rights*. It follows that, on average, the nationals derive more utility from political participation rights than do foreigners, provided that nationals enjoy both outcome and process utilities, while the foreigners only enjoy outcome utility.

The distinction between nationals and foreigners is largely exogenous. Whether a person may become a citizen of the country or not is determined by law—in particular, the need to have stayed in the host country for a sufficient number of years and to have sufficient knowledge of the local language and the content of the constitution. Only after these very strict requirements have been met does an individual have the choice of becoming a nationalized citizen. Of course, whether people eligible for citizenship indeed accept it also depends inter alia on their expected procedural utility—that is, their wish to become a community member with full participation rights. Thus, some will decide not to change their citizenship. Becoming a naturalized citizen is more or less automatic for young people and spouses once the head of the family has decided to do so. Resident citizens have no possibility of choosing their status of citizenship. They cannot give up their current citizenship without relocation. The distribution of residents in a country between the two categories (foreigners and nationals) thus strongly reflects formal exogenous criteria for citizenship and not revealed preferences for procedural goods. As a result of these considerations, one may assume that the distinction between nationals and foreigners influences the extent to which one benefits from outcome and process utility, while the reverse causation can safely be neglected.

9.4 Empirical Analysis

9.4.1 *Testable Hypotheses*

On the basis of our discussion, two empirically testable hypotheses can be formulated:

(1) The utility derived from the *rights* to participate in the political process (measured by the extent of direct democratic rights across

regions) supports the subjective well-being of the citizens. The foreigners living in the same region, who are excluded from this process, experience lower happiness compared to the citizens.

(2) *Actual* political participation (measured by the differential participation rates between regions in national ballots) is less connected with procedural utility than is the *right* to political participation.

In both hypotheses, the strategy to identify procedural utility is based on the formal distinction between citizens and foreigners. The corresponding statistical approach is in analogy to the differences-in-differences estimator for time series. In a crude formulation then, procedural utility is the additional positive effect of more extended participation *rights* for citizens' compared to that for foreigners' well-being (first hypothesis). With *actual* participation, procedural utility is the difference between the increase in reported subjective well-being of citizens and noncitizens due to citizens' higher participation rates (second hypothesis).

9.4.2   Descriptive Analysis

PARTICIPATION RIGHTS

The individual rights of political participation are the first source of procedural utility proposed. As described in section 8.3.3 of chapter 8, there are several possibilities of directly engaging in three state levels in the political process, in addition to elections, in Switzerland. The most important are the direct democratic instruments. They exist at the national level as well as at the level of the 26 cantons (states). Here again, the cantonal level is taken into consideration (because the participation rights on the national level apply equally across the country) and the same indicator (see Appendix B) for the extent of direct democratic participation rights in the 26 cantons is used as in the empirical analysis in chapter 8. According to the first hypothesis, more extended democratic participation rights are expected to increase reported satisfaction with life, due to a larger gain in procedural utility. In Table 9.1, the difference in life satisfaction between residents living in cantons with weak participation rights (cantons where the index of participation rights is lower than 4) and cantons with strong participation rights is expressed. A cutoff point of 4 is selected in order to split the sample into two subsamples, with an approximately equal number of

TABLE 9.1
Satisfaction with Life and Participation Rights in Switzerland,
Descriptive Statistics, 1992–94

| | Participation Rights | | |
	Weak	Strong	Difference
Whole sample	8.099	8.318	0.218
	(0.033)	(0.029)	(0.044)
Foreigners	7.625	7.602	−0.023
	(0.090)	(0.104)	(0.136)
Swiss citizens	8.176	8.402	0.226
	(0.036)	(0.029)	(0.046)
Difference	0.551	0.800	0.249
(Swiss citizens − foreigners)	(0.096)	(0.092)	(0.133)

Source of data: Leu, Burri, and Priester (1997).
Note: Standard errors in parentheses.

individual observations. On average, residents with strong participation rights report a 0.22-point–higher level of well-being. However, this difference may also be due to a favorable outcome of the political process. As has been demonstrated in the previous chapter, the outcome of the political process is closer to the wishes of the residents in more direct democratic jurisdictions. To differentiate between outcome and procedural utility, the proposed identification criteria (namely, people's nationality) is taken into consideration. As foreigners are excluded from political participation rights but not from the outcome of the political process, differences in levels of satisfaction between citizens and foreigners in cantons with weak and with strong democratic participation rights have to be compared. Where participation rights are weak, a difference in well-being between Swiss citizens and foreigners of 0.55 points is measured. The respective difference in cantons with extended direct democratic rights is 0.80 points. Both gaps in subjective well-being are due to differences in individual characteristics, incomplete assimilation, and, above all, citizens' opportunity to reap procedural utility. The difference in differences between cantons with weak and strong participation rights then reflects the gain in procedural utility of citizens due to more extended participation rights. The raw data show that the effect of procedural utility is large in terms of reported satisfaction with life—namely, 0.25 points. A multiple regression analysis has to test whether this result still holds if individual characteristics are controlled for. An ordered probit estimation and extended discussion of the result are provided in subsection 9.4.3.

ACTUAL PARTICIPATION

Actual participation is hypothesized to contribute to people's feeling of self-determination and thus their experienced procedural utility. Here, participation in national ballots is taken into consideration, in order to keep the content of the ballots equal for all voters. This does not mean that the expected outcome utility of the voting decision is equally distributed across jurisdictions. Consequently, we again use a differences-in-differences approach to conduct a descriptive analysis of the second proposed hypothesis.

The participation rate is measured at the cantonal level. Average actual participation is calculated from 45 national ballots on referenda and initiatives. These ballots were held between February 19, 1992, and December 4, 1994—that is, during the same years that the personal interviews were conducted. An overview of the variation in actual participation rates across cantons is presented in Appendix B. For the analysis in Table 9.2, the data set is divided into two subsamples. In the left-hand column, the subsample consists of people living in cantons with an average participation rate below 49.1 percent; in the right-hand column are those in cantons with an average participation

TABLE 9.2

Satisfaction with Life and Rate of Active Participation in Switzerland, Descriptive Statistics, 1992–94

| | Rate of Active Participation | | |
	Low	High	Difference
Whole sample	8.143	8.287	0.143
	(0.032)	(0.030)	(0.044)
Foreigners	7.556	7.688	0.132
	(0.092)	(0.101)	(0.137)
Swiss citizens	8.235	8.360	0.125
	(0.033)	(0.031)	(0.046)
Difference	0.679	0.672	−0.007
(Swiss citizens − foreigners)	(0.092)	(0.097)	(0.134)

Source of data: Leu, Burri, and Priester (1997) and Swiss Federal Statistical Office (various years).

Note: Standard errors in parentheses.

rate above 49.1 percent. A cutoff point of 49.1 is chosen in order to split the sample into two subsamples with an approximately equal number of individual observations. For the entire sample, a higher reported well-being of 0.14 points is measured in jurisdictions with more active voters. This positive relationship between actual participation and life satisfaction can either be due to spatially different material consequences of the legislative proposals that stimulated participation, or be due to procedural utility. If the difference in well-being is calculated separately for foreigners and citizens, the effects of outcome and procedural utility can be distinguished. As foreigners have no direct democratic participation rights, their procedural utility is expected to be close to nil. Therefore, foreigners' higher life satisfaction of 0.13 points in cantons with high participation rates, in comparison to those living in cantons with low participation rates, is attributed to outcome utility. For citizens, a similar positive difference of 0.13 is computed. A first empirical test thus gives no evidence for procedural utility through more active political participation. The difference in differences is −0.01 points and thus close to zero. In the next section, a detailed analysis of the relationship between participation rates and subjective well-being is presented. A multiple ordered probit regression then allows for the control of correlated effects.

9.4.3 Econometric Analysis

The descriptive analysis just presented offers preliminary evidence of positive procedural utility caused by stronger participation rights, but no evidence of process utility due to higher actual participation. A multiple regression analysis is needed in order to show whether these results are robust. Once more a differences-in-differences estimation strategy is applied to identify procedural utility. Technically, an interaction term is included in the estimation equation, combining the variable that captures the proposed source of procedural utility with the identifying criteria. Here, the identifying characteristic is being a foreigner.

PARTICIPATION RIGHTS

The first hypothesis is tested by estimating a microeconometric happiness function, using a weighted ordered probit model. It takes democratic participation rights into account, in addition to the large set of control variables already considered in the previous chapters.

TABLE 9.3
Procedural Utility and Participation Rights in Switzerland, 1992–94

| | Weighted Ordered Probit | | |
	Coefficient	t-Value	Marginal Effect for Score of 10
Democratic participation rights	0.096	3.25	0.033
Democratic participation rights × foreigner	−0.071	−1.71	−0.024
Foreigner	−0.055	−0.34	−0.019
Socio-demographic factors	Included		
Socio-economic factors	Included		
Observations	6,137		

Source of data: Leu, Burri, and Priester (1997).

Notes: Dependent variable: level of satisfaction on a 10-point scale. White estimator for variance. Standard errors are adjusted to clustering in 26 cantons.

Table 9.3 solely presents the coefficients and marginal effects for the variable we focus on here, participation rights. The coefficients of the control variables are very similar to the ones presented in the basic equation presented in Appendix A.

The estimation results show sizable effects for both variables considered in the first hypothesis. The overall effect of participation rights on reported satisfaction with life is positive. In the ordered probit estimation, a positive coefficient indicates the probability of stating that well-being is greater than, or equal to, any given level of increases. The positive effect can be attributed to a gain in outcome or procedural utility in cantons with more extended participation rights. The interaction term in the second row reveals the difference in the positive effects for Swiss citizens and foreigners. The negative coefficient indicates that foreigners gain less from stronger participation rights than the people in the reference group (the citizens). This result is consistent with the first hypothesis that foreigners reap less procedural utility from direct democratic participation rights than Swiss nationals. If it is further assumed that foreigners do not reap any procedural utility at all but cannot be excluded from the outcome of the political process, the relative size of procedural utility can be assessed. Comparing the negative coefficient of the interaction variable, which under these assumptions captures procedural utility, with the coefficient for the variable participation rights, two-thirds of the positive effect of more extended direct democratic participation rights is due to procedural utility and one-third stems from outcome utility.

An absolute interpretation of the size of the effects is provided by the marginal effects. As was already indicated in earlier chapters, the marginal effect indicates the change in the proportion of people belonging to a stated satisfaction level when the independent variable increases by one unit. In the case of a dummy variable, such as being or not being a foreigner, the marginal effect is evaluated with regard to the reference group. For simplicity, only the marginal effects for the top group expressing complete satisfaction with life (score of 10) are shown in Table 9.3. An increase in the index of participation rights by one point raises the proportion of people indicating very high satisfaction with life by 3.3 percentage points. For foreigners, however, this effect is smaller, as the interaction term has to be considered; 2.4 percentage points of the increased probability to report maximum subjective well-being cannot be reaped by the foreigners. In our interpretation, this is because they are excluded from the political process and thus from procedural utility.

The effect of procedural utility as reflected in reported life satisfaction itself is sizable. This can be seen when compared to the marginal effects of control variables. For instance, the marginal effect capturing procedural utility is almost as large as the effect of living in the second-lowest income category (Sfr. 2,000–3,000) instead of the lowest income category (under Sfr. 2,000). If the total variation in participation rights is considered—that is, when citizens in canton Basel-Landschaft (with the highest democracy index of 5.69) are compared to citizens in canton Geneva (with the lowest direct participation rights of 1.75)—the effect is even larger. The former enjoy procedural utility that increases their probability to be completely satisfied by approximately 12.3 percentage points. In the next section, this procedural effect of participation rights on subjective well-being comes face to face with the effect of actual participation on satisfaction with life.

ACTUAL PARTICIPATION

Participation in political decision making is often explained by the procedural utility gained (e.g., Riker and Ordeshook 1973). The second hypothesis, as outlined in Section 9.4.1, argues, however, that citizens value the right to participate even more. Here, as a first step, the effect on subjective well-being of average actual participation across cantons is evaluated. In the test performed, ballots at the national level are considered in order to guarantee that participation rights are equal to all citizens. If evidence for procedural utility is found, an estimation including participation rights, as well as actual participation rates, will be conducted to assess the relative importance of the two measures.

Table 9.4 shows the results for an ordered probit model. The first variable tests for a partial correlation between average participation rate and reported satisfaction with life. According to the very small and statistically insignificant coefficient, there is no such relationship in the data set at hand. Whether this negligible correlation is due to a net effect that equalizes a positive effect due to procedural utility, and a negative effect caused by low outcome utility in cantons with high participation rates, is tested with the interaction variable. The interaction term between participation rate and being a foreigner identifies the contribution of active participation to subjective well-being that is independent of any outcome considerations. However, the coefficient of the interaction term is quantitatively unimportant and gives no evidence for any procedural utility reaped from actual participation. It is, therefore, superfluous to combine the two measures of political participation to test the second hypothesis. There is clear evidence consistent with the sizable procedural utility reaped from the possibility of participating in the directly democratic political process.

TABLE 9.4
Procedural Utility and Actual Participation in Switzerland, 1992–94

	Weighted Ordered Probit		
	Coefficient	t-Value	Marginal Effect for Score of 10
Actual participation rate/10	0.119	1.28	0.041
Actual participation rate/ 10 × foreigner	−0.012	−0.13	−0.004
Foreigner	−0.266	−0.62	−0.085
Socio-demographic factors	Included		
Socio-economic factors	Included		
Observations	6,137		

Source of data: Leu, Burri, and Priester (1997) and Swiss Federal Statistical Office (various years).
Note: See Table 9.3.

However, no statistical evidence is found for procedural utility from actual participation.

9.4.4 Sensitivity Analysis

To check the sensitivity of the results, two tests for robustness are performed. First, the characteristics known about each individual are taken into consideration in order to control for correlated and contextual effects. Second, aggregate variables are included in the estimation equation to test two alternative hypotheses. As there is no evidence of procedural utility in actual participation, we do not perform any robustness tests based on that result. In order to test for correlated or contextual effects, four variables are included that control for three potential alternative explanations. First, a dummy variable for people's participation in sports or music clubs or neighborhood associations is used to test whether citizens may have accumulated more Putnam (1995) style social capital in cantons with stronger participation rights, and thus enjoy higher subjective well-being than citizens in cantons with less extended democratic rights. Second, a variable for residence in an urban area is included, in order to investigate the argument that direct democratic rights could be weaker in urban areas where most of the foreigners live, and thus the raw effect may reflect urbanization. Third, dummies for the language that is spoken in the canton are included in order to test whether the patterns in the descriptive statistics may capture cultural differences within Switzerland instead of institutional variation. Table 9.5 shows the results of an extended estimation equation.

A comparison of the results in Tables 9.3 and 9.5 reveals that the procedural utility reaped from democratic participation rights remains similar in magnitude if four additional control variables are included. The control factors themselves have a positive effect on reported satisfaction with life in the case of being a member of associations and living in the Italian-speaking canton Ticino. There is no sizable effect of urbanization or of living in a French-speaking canton.

For the aggregate control variables, the first alternative hypothesis refers to the distribution of foreigners across cantons: Foreigners report lower life satisfaction than citizens in cantons with stronger participation rights, because the foreigners are a small minority in these cantons. In order to test this hypothesis, two variables are

TABLE 9.5
Sensitivity Analysis: Correlated and Contextual Effects

| | Weighted Ordered Probit | | |
	Coefficient	t-Value	Marginal Effect for Score of 10
Democratic participation rights	0.087	2.86	0.030
Democratic participation rights × foreigner	−0.071	−1.74	−0.024
Foreigner	−0.015	−0.10	−0.005
Membership in associations	0.159	6.41	0.054
Urbanization	−0.051	−0.51	−0.017
French-speaking canton	−0.094	−1.60	−0.032
Italian-speaking canton	0.249	3.70	0.089
Socio-demographic factors	Included		
Socio-economic factors	Included		
Observations	6,124		

Source of data: Leu, Burri, and Priester (1997).
Note: See Table 9.3.

additionally included in the regression model: the average percentage of foreigners in a canton and an interaction term between the percentage of foreigners and being a foreigner. The overall proportion of foreigners in the total population in Switzerland was 18.5 percent between 1992 and 1994. It varied considerably between cantons, the highest percentage being in canton Geneva with 37.5 percent and the lowest in canton Nidwalden with 7.9 percent. The estimation results in column 1 in Table 9.6 show that the coefficient that identifies procedural utility hardly changes (from −0.071 in Table 9.3 to −0.076). Thus, the distribution of foreigners across cantons cannot explain the different effects of participation rights on subjective well-being for citizens and foreigners. A second alternative hypothesis waters down the assumption that foreigners cannot be discriminated against by the outcome of the political process: Cantons with higher income per capita provide public services that serve the citizens' preferences to a larger extent. In order to test this alternative explanation, estimation 2 in Table 9.6 includes a variable for national income per capita for each individual canton, as well as an interaction variable combining income per capita and being a foreigner. The estimation results reveal that the institutional influence on subjective well-being is not affected.

TABLE 9.6
Sensitivity Analysis: Aggregate Control Variables

	Weighted Ordered Probit			
	(1)		(2)	
	Coefficient	t-Value	Coefficient	t-Value
Democratic participation rights	0.092	3.18	0.101	3.42
Democratic participation rights × foreigner	−0.076	−1.12	−0.071	−1.72
Foreigner	−0.024	−0.05	−0.041	−0.12
Share of foreigners	−0.002	−0.39		
Share of foreigners × foreigner	−0.001	−0.05		
National income per capita/1000			−0.004	−1.29
National income per capita/1000 × foreigner			−0.3e−3	−0.04
Socio-demographic factors	Included		Included	
Socio-economic factors	Included		Included	
Observations	6,137		6,137	

Source of data: Leu, Burri, and Priester (1997) and Swiss Federal Statistical Office (1995; 2000 personal correspondence).
Note: See Table 9.3.

The gain in life satisfaction restricted to citizens due to more extended participation rights is thus a fairly robust result.

9.5 CONCLUSIONS

The concept of procedural utility represents a completely different approach to human well-being than the standard outcome-oriented approaches in social science research. The latter approaches use Bentham's concept of "experienced utility" or, in modern economics, employ "decision utility," which is inferred from observed choices (Kahneman, Wakker, and Sarin 1997, p. 375). In contrast, procedural utility looks at the subjective well-being that people gain from the decision-making process itself, irrespective of the outcome.

In this chapter, participatory decision making in politics is considered a possible source of procedural utility. Rights to directly participate in the democratic process give citizens the feeling and the cognitive understanding that their preferences are seriously taken into account in a fair political process. Foreigners, who are excluded from political decision making, cannot reap such procedural utility. The results of our empirical analysis are consistent with this notion of procedural utility. Citizens, as well as foreigners, who live in jurisdictions with more extended political participation rights, enjoy higher levels of subjective well-being (as is discussed at length in chapter 8). The positive effect on reported satisfaction with life is, however, smaller for foreigners, reflecting their exclusion from procedural utility. It is thus empirically feasible to distinguish between outcome and process utility. Moreover, it is possible to get a notion of the relative sizes of outcome and process utility. The positive effect of participation rights is three times larger for the citizens than it is for the foreigners—that is, a major part of the welfare gain from the favorable political process is due to procedural utility. Actual political participation is often rationalized by individuals' experience of procedural utility. Here it is argued that participation *rights* are more important in terms of a feeling of control, self-determination, or influence in the political sphere than *actual* participation. We indeed find neither statistically significant nor sizable positive effects on individual well-being of high participation rates.

Overall, the evidence suggests that individuals value both outcomes and procedures and, in particular, that they derive substantial utility from political participation rights.

Hints on the Literature

The concept of procedural utility is extensively discussed, and further references are provided, in

Lane, Robert E. (2000). *The Loss of Happiness in Market Economies*. New Haven and London: Yale University Press.

Procedural fairness is analyzed from the psychological perspective, for example, in

Tyler, Tom R., and Steven L. Blader (2000). *Cooperation in Groups: Procedural Justice, Social Identity, and Behavioral Engagement*. Philadelphia: Psychology Press.

PART IV

Conclusions

Chapter 10

HAPPINESS INSPIRES ECONOMICS

10.1 INTRODUCTION

THE RESEARCH on happiness presented in this book inspires economics in several ways:

- The extent to which people are happy or unhappy is an essential quality of the economy and society. The state of the economy strongly affects people's happiness. But even more important, in the long run, is whether the constitution favors or hinders the pursuit of happiness (section 10.2).
- The results of happiness research tell economic policymakers which factors tend to raise or diminish people's well-being. The temptation to maximize the happiness functions econometrically identified is, however, mistaken. Rather, institutional (or constitutional) rules promising higher happiness are to be recommended (section 10.3).
- Happiness research inspires economic research by extending the realm of measurement in an important way and by providing new answers to burning questions concerning the welfare effects of income, unemployment, and inflation (section 10.4).
- The systematic study of happiness by economists is only in its initial stages. Many important issues are unresolved and may serve to inspire future economic research (section 10.5).

10.2 HAPPINESS IN THE ECONOMY AND SOCIETY

10.2.1 Happiness as a Final Goal

"For most people, happiness is the main, if not the only, ultimate objective of life" (Ng 1996, p. 1). Happiness, or subjective well-being, is measured by representative surveys. Nevertheless, standard economic theory clings to an "objectivist" position based on observable choices made by individuals. Individual utility depends only on tangible factors (goods and services), is inferred from revealed behavior (or preferences), and is in turn used to explain the choices made. This seemingly modern view is influenced by the positivist movement. It rejects subjectivist experience (for example, as captured in surveys) as being unscientific because it is not objectively observable. It is assumed that the choices made provide *all* the information required to infer the utility of outcomes. Moreover, the axiomatic revealed preference approach is applied not only to derive individual utility, but also to measure social welfare. To do so, social welfare comparison is based on the consumption behavior of households.

This positivist view is still dominant in economics. Sen (1986, p. 18) observes that "The popularity of this view in economics may be due to a mixture of an obsessive concern with observability and a peculiar belief that choice ... is the only human aspect that can be observed." Its dominance is also reflected in the contents of microeconomic textbooks. However, not all contemporary economists subscribe to this view. Numerous scholars have challenged standard economic theory from different angles.

(a) There are numerous examples of nonobjectivist theoretical analyses in economics. They incorporate emotions (e.g., Elster 1998), such as regret (e.g., Bell 1982), self-signaling (self-esteem), goal completion, mastery, and meaning (Loewenstein 1999), and status (e.g., Frank 1985a,b), as well as even broader considerations beyond the normal use of utility (e.g., Sen's 1982 "entitlements").

(b) Standard theory assumes independent utilities, although interdependent utilities fit particular observed behavior much better (e.g., Clark and Oswald 1998). More importantly, interdependent utilities question traditional welfare propositions (e.g., Boskin and Sheshinski 1978, Holländer 2001).

(c) By focusing on the value of outcomes rather than on observed decisions, various types of utility can usefully be distinguished (Kahneman, Wakker, and Sarin 1997). Predicted utility "refers to beliefs about the experienced utility of outcomes," remembered utility "is inferred from a subject's retrospective reports of the total pleasure or displeasure associated with past outcomes," and instant utility measures "hedonic and affective experience, which can be derived from immediate reports of current subjective experience or from physiological indices" (pp. 376f). The differences between these evoke a number of positive questions that have not yet been answered in a satisfactory way—for example, "How is the remembered utility of extended outcomes determined?" (p. 378). These hedonistic concepts are based on an old tradition. The initiators of the modern analysis of decision making (Bernoulli and Bentham) understood utility as satisfaction, referring to the hedonic quality in terms of pleasure and pain.

(d) The previous remarks reveal that the position of psychologists has differed markedly from the economic position. Psychologists value subjective experience as an important source of information about individual utility. They are less convinced that choices are always rational (see the vast literature on anomalies in decision making—for example, Thaler 1992), and therefore doubt that utility can meaningfully be derived from observed choices. Moreover, they go beyond the tangible carriers of utility and emphasize the importance of emotions, such as fear, hope, disappointment, guilt, and pride.

(e) Psychologists have also transcended consequentialism (of which utilitarianism is a special case) and have considered procedural utility.

The exclusive reliance on an objectivist approach by standard economic theory is thus open to doubt, both theoretically and empirically, and strongly restricts the possibility of understanding and influencing reality. The subjectivist approach to happiness opens a fruitful new way of studying the world in which we live.

Directly measurable subjective happiness and derived "objective" decision utility (as commonly used in economics) enter economic research from different sides. Their mutual aim is to investigate individual and social welfare. However, happiness is a much broader concept than decision utility; it includes experience as well as procedural utility. It may be argued that happiness is a fundamental goal of people: To be happy is a goal in itself. That is not the case for other things we may want, such as job security, status, power, and especially money (income). We do not want them for themselves, but rather to give us the possibility of making ourselves happier.

10.2.2 *Economic Influences on Happiness*

A large part of this book was devoted to showing empirically that the state of the economy has a strong impact on people's subjective well-being. In particular, unemployed persons are much less happy than those with a job—and this is not solely due to loss of income (as many economists are quick to point out). To a large extent, it is due to the psychic stress involved, such as losing one's self-esteem, as well as being cast out of established social relationships. But unemployment also lowers the happiness of people in employment. It is taken as a signal that they could also be affected in the future and, more generally, that social conditions are unfortunate, possibly provoking political trouble in the future.

Research has also shown that inflation is experienced as having a substantial depressing effect on happiness. It not only raises the transaction costs of everyday life, but also introduces uncertainty about the future course of the economy, which people experience as a threat to their well-being.

Income also has a significant effect on happiness. People living in poor countries without any doubt become happier with increasing per capita income. But above the threshold of around U.S. $10,000, a higher average income no longer contributes much to subjective well-being, the most important reason being that people adjust their expectations to the rise in income. The finding that economic conditions systematically and strongly influence happiness stands in stark contrast to the view that happiness is a purely personal issue or depends solely on personality factors. A good state of the economy is indeed crucial for the well-being of individuals and society as a whole.

10.2.3 *Institutional Influences on Happiness*

This book presents an insight that has so far been disregarded when considering the determinants of individual well-being: Happiness is crucially dependent on how the economy and society are organized. The more individuals' preferences are taken into account by the political process, the happier they are. Therefore, increased possibilities of directly participating in public decision making via popular referenda and a decentralized state significantly contribute to happiness. This effect is not only due to public policies more closely linked to what the citizens desire but also to the right to participate as such—that is, to the utility gained by the possibility of taking an active role in the political process. These findings again deviate greatly from a view of happiness as solely depending on intrinsic personal characteristics. Happiness does not only lie within the realm of the individual person. Rather, the fundamental constitutional arrangements, as well as specific institutions, crucially affect how happy people are.

10.2.4 Economic Influences on Personal Characteristics

Part of a person's happiness depends on individual and social characteristics, such as one's genetic endowment (e.g., the tendency to feel depressed) and one's childhood experiences. But these factors are not totally independent of external influences, such as the state of the economy. Indeed, the intrinsic and extrinsic components of happiness interact with each other. Thus, tendencies toward depression may be augmented by being unemployed, but under different circumstances they may become subdued by the need to cope with joblessness. How economic conditions influence happiness via the characteristics of a person is difficult to discern because it depends on a large number of conditioning factors. Thus, for example, it has been shown that people with strong materialistic values reap less happiness from higher income (Kasser 2000).

10.3 Consequences for Economic Policy

10.3.1 Economic Policy Advice

The insights gained about happiness are in many respects useful for economic policy undertaken by governments. Some examples suffice to illustrate the point:

- An important part of *antipoverty policy* deals with the question of what "poverty" is. Traditionally, the definition relies on disposable income. Happiness research allows the problem to be approached more fundamentally by considering reported satisfaction levels. Such complementary measurement also allows equivalence scales to be established. They indicate the increase in income necessary to compensate for a larger family, while maintaining the subjective well-being of the family.

- *Welfare policy* is faced with the question of how much economic destitution is responsible for people feeling unhappy. To what extent can people with low income be helped by financial support? If low income is due to unemployment, the research results suggest that not much is achieved by providing the person with a higher income. Rather, the policy should be directed toward providing the person with appropriate employment.
- The use of measures of happiness allows for a new way of evaluating the *effects of government expenditure*. All too often, the effect is measured by the cost incurred by the state: The more spent, the better. This is obviously not always the case, and in some instances lower expenditure would be better. The problem has been approached scientifically by using cost-benefit analysis. The benefits are the recipients' marginal willingness to pay, which is best measured by a contingent valuation analysis. (See Carson et al. 1994, who list almost 1,700 studies in over 40 countries.) This method relies on carefully designed surveys in which the persons are put into a quasi-experimental situation (Arrow et al. 1993). This method is best suited to relatively small and isolated public projects, but it breaks down when it comes to more extensive expenditure policies. Simulations using microeconometric happiness functions with a large number of determinants may be better able to evaluate the widespread effects of such policies.
- *Tax policy* must consider to what extent various income groups are affected. Is it possible to achieve social goals by redistributing income, or are the negative effects on subjective well-being prohibitive? Recently, it has been argued that the fight for *relative* positions is socially wasteful, and that the high-income recipients, as winners of these status races, should be more heavily taxed (Frank 1999, more generally Layard 1980). This proposal has been influenced by the findings of happiness research, which suggest that people derive more satisfaction from their position in comparison to other income recipients than from the income level as such. If the redistributive tax policy is able to maintain income rankings but reduces the absolute differences between income recipients, subjective well-being is little affected, and presumably work incentives are not reduced. But for an overall evaluation,

this proposal must consider many additional aspects—in particular, what possibilities the high-income recipients have to avoid increased taxes.

10.3.2 Advice for the Constitutional Level

A widespread temptation is to consider happiness functions as the best existing approximation of a *social welfare function* and to maximize them. The optimal values of the determinants thus derived are—according to this view—the goals that economic policy should achieve. It seems that, at long last, the so far empirically empty social welfare maximization of the quantitative theory of economic policy (Tinbergen 1956, Theil 1964) is given a new lease on life.

This is exactly how the influential paper by Di Tella, MacCulloch, and Oswald (2001) proceeds. They open their paper with the following statement: "Modern macroeconomics textbooks rest upon the assumption of a social welfare function defined in terms of inflation, π, and unemployment, U. However, no formal evidence for the existence of such a function has ever been presented in literature. Although an optimal policy rule cannot be chosen unless the parameters of the presumed $W(\pi, U)$ function are known, that has not prevented its use in a large theoretical literature in macroeconomics" (p. 1; without footnotes).

Such an endeavor overlooks some fundamental problems in the social welfare maximization approach (Frey 1983, pp. 182–94). Only one shortcoming, empirical emptiness, has been overcome (provided one is prepared to accept happiness functions as a reasonable approximation of a social welfare function). Two other basic shortcomings remain— namely, the problems of preference aggregation and missing incentives:

- *Preference aggregation.* Since Arrow (1951), it has been known that, under a number of "reasonable" conditions, no social welfare function exists that generally ranks outcomes consistently, except a dictatorship. This impossibility result spawned a huge amount of literature (called social choice), analyzing its robustness to modifications of the assumptions. Theorem after theorem demonstrated that almost all changes in the axiomatic structure left the dictatorial result unchanged. (See, e.g., Sen 1995, Slesnick 1998.) It must be concluded that "There is no way we can use empirical observations on their own to produce an ethically satisfactory cardinalization, let alone an ethically satisfactory social welfare ordering" (Hammond 1991, pp. 220–21). This verdict applies to happiness functions if they are used as quasi social welfare functions.

- *Missing incentives.* Deriving optimal policies by maximizing a social welfare function only makes sense if the government has an incentive to apply the optimal policies in reality. This is only the case if a "benevolent dictator" government is assumed (Brennan and Buchanan 1985). From introspection as well as from empirical analyses in political economy (see, e.g., the collection of papers on political business cycles in Frey 1997c), we know that governments are not benevolent and do not follow the wishes of the population, even in well-functioning democracies, not to mention authoritarian and dictatorial governments. Hence, to maximize social welfare corresponds to a "technocratic-elitist" procedure, neglecting the crucial incentive aspect.

This criticism applies particularly when one tries to derive optimal policies by maximizing happiness.

There is a solution on hand that overcomes the problems posed by the impossibility theorem and by the government's missing incentives. *Constitutional political economy* (e.g., Buchanan 1991, Frey 1983, Mueller 1996, Cooter 2000) redirects attention to the level of the social consensus where, behind the veil of ignorance, the basic rules governing a society—the fundamental institutions—are chosen or emerge. At the same time, the approach shifts from a (vain) effort to directly determine social outcomes to shaping the politico-economic process by setting the institutions.

This book may be seen as an empirical demonstration that the fundamental social institutions do indeed systematically influence happiness. The fundamental social institutions shape the incentives of the policymakers. Once these basic institutions are in place and the incentives are set, little can be done to influence the current politico-economic process. Economic policy therefore must help to establish those fundamental institutions, which lead to the best possible fulfilment of individual preferences. Research in positive constitutional economics helps to identify which institutions serve this goal, and whether they do in fact systematically affect happiness.

Our analysis has identified two basic institutions having an important effect on happiness: direct democracy and federalism.

10.4 EXISTING ECONOMIC THEORY

The insights gained from the research on happiness throw new light on important issues analyzed in economics. Most importantly, it enlarges the scope of empirical measurement and provides new tests for theories.

10.4.1 Extending Measurement

Happiness is not identical to utility, but it does capture people's satisfaction with life. For many purposes, it can be considered a useful approximation to utility, which economists have avoided measuring (except in cost-benefit analysis). This enables us to empirically study problems that so far could only be analyzed on an abstract theoretical level. This extension represents a considerable step toward a social science able to provide useful insights. It again suffices to give two examples for such a useful extension into so far uncharted empirical territory:

- Economics is an outcome-oriented discipline. While it has been noted that people may also derive utility from the process itself, this aspect has been treated relatively lightly, mainly because it was impossible to empirically distinguish the two types of utility in a convincing way. As we have demonstrated, happiness data allow us to measure the size of outcome and process utility in the case of political participation possibilities.
- Institutional analysis has been hampered by the difficulty in assessing the impact of specific institutions on people's utility. Happiness data allow us to identify how much individuals value particular extents of democracy and federalism.

10.4.2 New Tests of Theories

Happiness research adds a considerable number of new insights into well-known theoretical propositions. This can best be shown with the example of how economic theory has tended to deal with unemployment, inflation, and income growth.

- One of the most prominent economic theories looks at unemployment as a voluntary decision. Workers do not lose their jobs, but rather choose to be unemployed. They compare the benefits (income) and costs (work effort) of working with the benefits (unemployment compensation and leisure time) and costs (none) of being out of work. Those who choose to remain in work thereby indicate that their net benefit from doing so is higher than if they were unemployed. Conversely, unemployed persons reveal that they have a higher net benefit in this state than if they seek employment. This view was most useful in explaining the behavioral responses, especially to changes in unemployment benefits. But it tended to play down the cost of being unemployed. The idea was that (subsistence) unemployment compensation would induce people to work. Happiness research suggests that much more is involved. Being out of work produces high psychic costs and sets psychological processes in motion, which may impose additional costs on returning to being employed.
- Most economic theories assume that predictable inflation entails no (or only very minor) cost because people are able to adjust to rising prices. This holds in particular in the long run when institutional rigidities (for example, work contracts) have been overcome. Costs are seen to arise mainly when inflation is unpredicted, so that people are caught by surprise by the actual price changes and some of them therefore suffer unavoidable losses. Happiness research suggests, in contrast, that people are unhappy about inflation, irrespective of whether it is predicted or not.
- Many economic theories, especially those concerned with economic growth, take it for granted that utility is a function of the level of income or consumption. The process identified in the context of happiness research suggests, in contrast, that processes of adjustment and comparison are of great importance.

These examples show that the research on happiness is able to contribute successfully to existing economic theory.

10.5 OPEN QUESTIONS

The study of happiness is only just beginning in economics. It's not surprising, therefore, that the research undertaken, and reported in this book, leaves many questions open. At the same time, it opens up challenging new areas. Further progress is especially needed in these four areas: the effects of happiness on behavior (subsection 10.5.1); consideration of a broader set of institutions on happiness (subsection 10.5.2); application of more advanced estimation approaches in cross-national research (subsection 10.5.3); and improved measurements on happiness (subsection 10.5.4).

10.5.1   The Effects of Happiness on Behavior

Economists have mainly studied the effects of behavior on subjective well-being, as represented by variables such as unemployment, inflation, and income. The reverse effect has so far received scant attention. In the following, we present some ideas for future research that are particularly relevant from the economic point of view.

Psychologists have identified some effects of happy persons on behavior. Happy people, for instance, are more often smiling during social interactions (Fernández-Dols and Ruiz-Belda, 1995); are more prepared to initiate social contacts with friends; are more inclined to respond to requests for help; are less often absent from work; and are less likely to get involved in work disputes (Frank 1997, p. 1833).

There can be little doubt that the affective and cognitive aspects of happiness systematically influence people's motivation and goals and, thus, behavior. On the one hand, the cognitive aspects of subjective well-being can influence behavior, as they activate relevant motives and goals. On the other hand, happiness from positive affects signals, to some extent, one's progress toward goals and the satisfaction of innate needs. Affect can thus support learning and the buildup of intrinsic motivation. *Intrinsic motivation* is the standard term used in the psychological literature for the inner force that drives people toward undertaking an activity for its own sake or because of an internalized norm (Deci 1975, Csikszentmihalyi 1990). The self-perpetuating relation between positive affects and intrinsic motivation and its consequences on behavior shall be described here via the example of the working sphere. A working environment that provides employees with the possibility of utilizing their skills, with supportive supervision and opportunities for personal contacts (that is, intrinsic job features), enables employees to fulfill self-set goals and to satisfy certain needs, such as self-determination. Thus the environment offers optimal preconditions for the experience of positive affect. Moreover, the positive affects from perceived control and self-determination build up or strengthen intrinsic work motivation. As a result, employees can be expected to be more engaged in their work tasks. The crucial condition for this positive causal effect of happiness on productivity lies in the work features that allow the satisfaction of innate needs.

Higher productivity is in itself a positive feedback, causing positive affects. The circular and self-perpetuating process thus includes affect, intrinsic motivation, and behavior. The outcome of this process does not have to be perceived as "good," however, as it can start with negative affect and intrinsic motivation that is directed toward destructive actions. Moreover, in the workplace, more satisfied employees need not necessarily be more productive. Some happy workers may simply spend too much time in unproductive activities, such as chatting with their workmates, instead of contributing to their organization's goal.

A causal inner relation between happiness and behavior, like the one described, is not restricted to the workplace, but can be studied within the family, social clubs, and even the polity.

What matters from the point of view of economic advice is that intrinsic happiness and motivation are systematically related to extrinsic motivation—that is, to motivation activated from outside, in particular by monetary compensation. The direction of the effect of external motivation on internal motivation depends on the perception of the people involved. If an outside intervention is perceived to be controlling by the addressee, intrinsic motivation tends to be crowded out; if it is perceived to be supporting, the intrinsic motivation tends to be reinforced (crowded in). This relationship is based on psychological findings known as "hidden costs of reward" (Lepper and Greene 1978) or cognitive evaluation theory (Deci and Ryan 1985, Deci with Flaste 1995), and has been introduced into economics as "crowding theory" (Frey 1997b). The existence of crowding-out and crowding-in effects has been supported by a great number of laboratory experiments (Deci, Koestner, and Ryan 1999), as well as by real life observations (Gneezy and Rustichini 2000, Frey and Oberholzer-Gee 1997; for a survey, see Frey and Jegen 2001). As a consequence, if intrinsic happiness and motivation are expected (or even desired) to have an effect on behavior, external intervention, for example, in the form of performance pay may have counterproductive effects.

The extent of happiness may also influence many other important decisions. Examples are

- *Consumption activities.* Happy people are most likely to save and spend different proportions of their income, to distribute them differently over time, and to acquire different combinations of particular goods and services than do less happy persons.
- *Investment behavior.* It can be hypothesized that happier people have a different attitude to taking risks than less happy people. They may also prefer different markets and types of financial investments.
- *Environmental behavior.* Happier people may well be more prepared to exhibit an environmental morale.
- *Political behavior.* Happy people are likely to vote for different politicians and parties, and for different alternatives in referenda, than unhappy people. It has, for instance, been found that such a difference exists where attitudes toward the European Union are concerned (Castles 1998).

10.5.2   A Broader Set of Institutions

A novel contribution of this book is to study the impact of institutions on happiness. The analysis has been confined to two elements: direct democracy and federalism. They certainly count among the most important basic aspects of a constitution, but there are many other institutions whose impact on subjective well-being is worth studying. Examples are the institutions of monetary policy, such as the extent of independence of the central bank (see, e.g., Eijffinger 1997), the importance of corporatism in policy making (see, e.g., Schneider and Wagner 2000), and the prevalence of centralized or firm-level wage bargaining between trade unions and employer associations (see, e.g., Iversen, Pontusson, and Soskice 2000).

10.5.3   Application of More Advanced Methods

Most comparative studies of happiness between countries employ multiple cross-section regressions. This has been a very useful starting point, but the next important step is to use panel data—that is, combined cross-section time series analyses. The use of this technique for happiness research is only just beginning (in particular, in the work by Di Tella, MacCulloch, and Oswald 2001); it would be desirable to reach a similar level of econometric sophistication as has been achieved by the empirical comparative growth studies (championed by Barro 1997, 2000). This research is quite closely related to the international happiness literature, as it analyzes the effect both of current economic and political events (such as strikes, demonstrations, and coups d'état) and of institutions (such as the extent of democracy) on economic growth.

10.5.4   Improved Happiness Measurements

Much of the research on happiness has been restricted by the paucity of data. For example, the data set used for Switzerland in this book is rather large (about 6,000 observations), but it is confined to one particular time period. To be able to undertake more refined studies—in particular, using panel data—requires a more extensive data set covering many years. There is also room for methodological concerns and the quality of the happiness data (e.g., Diener et al. 1999, pp. 277–78). Economists should, however, not be too critical, in view of the deficiencies of what they measure and use as a matter of course. National income is a case in point. Its shortcomings are obvious and need not be discussed here. But the same applies to more innocuous concepts, such as real income (for example, Kapteyn 1994). As we have argued repeatedly, the main use of happiness measures is, however, not to compare levels of subjective well-being, but rather to seek to identify the *determinants* of happiness. Moreover, the compilation of data on happiness should not become an exercise in itself. What matters is finding out what type of happiness data is appropriate for answering which questions and issues.

The discussion shows that happiness research is able to provide relevant new insights, and can serve as an inspiration for future research in economics as well as for the other social sciences.

Appendix A

THIS APPENDIX presents in Table A.1 the full microeconometric happiness function for Switzerland, as discussed in this book. Table A.2 shows the results of the DFBETA robustness analysis discussed in chapter 8, section 8.3.3.

The empirical analysis in Table A.1 is based on a survey of more than 6,000 residents of Switzerland by Leu, Burri, and Priester (1997). The survey data were collected between 1992 and 1994. The information contained in the data set is based on personal interviews and tax statistics. The single-item measure for people's subjective well-being is based on answers on a 10-point scale to the following question: "How satisfied are you with your life as a whole these days?" Further information on the data is given in chapter 3, section 3.4.1.

ECONOMETRIC ESTIMATION METHOD

Two statistical approaches are applied to study the correlation between socio-demographic, socio-economic, and institutional factors and people's reported satisfaction with life. The results for both approaches are presented in Table A.1.

First, average satisfaction scores for each differentiated demographic category are calculated. They allow for the assessment of the total effect of a certain demographic characteristic and, compared with means for other categories of the same demographic dimension (e.g., age categories), they offer rough information about simple correlations.

Second, partial correlations are presented. They indicate the effect of a certain demographic characteristic independent of other socio-demographic and socio-economic characteristics and independent of the institutional environment. The latter approach uses multiple regression analysis, which is normally applied to estimate microeconometric happiness functions. In the first such equation, a weighted least squares model is estimated. In the second one, a weighted ordered probit model is used in order to exploit the ranking information contained in the originally scaled dependent variable. The weighting variable that is applied allows representative results on the subject level for Switzerland. Throughout the book, we use a robust estimator of variance, because random disturbances are potentially correlated within groups or clusters. Here, dependence refers to residents of the same canton. Ignoring the clustering in the estimation model is likely to produce downward-biased standard errors, due to the effects of aggregate variables on individual data (Moulton 1990). To get unbiased standard errors for the aggregate variable "democratic participation rights" (see chapter 8), the 26 cantons are used as sampling units. The least squares estimation treats happiness as a cardinal variable. This basic estimation technique is applied to facilitate the interpretation of the results. The coefficients are to be read as follows: People belonging to a certain category on average report happiness scores deviating from that of the reference group on the scale of the coefficient. For a continuous variable (such as the measure for democratic participation rights), the coefficient indicates the increase in happiness scores when the independent variable increases by one unit. In the ordered probit estimation, a positive coefficient indicates that the probability of stating happiness greater than or equal to any given level increases. There is no direct quantitative interpretation of the size of the coefficient. Therefore, marginal effects are calculated. The marginal effect indicates the change in the share of persons belonging to a happiness level of 10 when the independent variable increases by one unit. Alternatively, the marginal effect indicates the change in the probability belonging to a happiness level of 10 when the independent variable increases by one unit. In the case of dummy variables, the marginal effect is evaluated in regard to the reference group.

TABLE A.1 (Part 1)
Satisfaction with Life in Switzerland, 1992–94

	Descriptive Statistics	Weighted Least Squares	Weighted Ordered Probit	
	Mean	Coefficient (t-Value)	Coefficient (t-Value)	Marginal Effect for Score of 10
Socio-demographic factors				
Age 20–29	8.19		Reference group	
Age 30–39	8.03	−0.142 (−1.06)	−0.084 (−0.96)	−0.028
Age 40–49	8.22	−0.001 (−0.01)	0.001 (0.01)	−0.3-e3
Age 50–59	7.97	−0.053 (−0.61)	−0.012 (0.20)	−0.004
Age 60–69	8.45	0.449 (4.53)	−0.313 (4.60)	0.112
Age 70–79	8.41	0.557 (4.48)	0.387 (4.66)	0.141
Age 80 and older	8.22	0.435 (2.73)	0.332 (3.01)	0.121
Male	8.22		Reference group	
Female	8.22	−0.011 (−0.25)	0.006 (0.19)	0.002
Swiss	8.30		Reference group	
Foreigner	7.62	−0.489 (−5.10)	−0.31 (−5.14)	−0.098
Good health	8.31		Reference group	
Bad health	7.48	−0.74 (−8.18)	−0.438 (−7.71)	−0.133
Low education	7.97		Reference group	
Middle education	8.31	0.219 (4.18)	0.091 (2.50)	0.031
High education	8.41	0.209 (2.85)	0.069 (1.58)	0.024
Married	8.36		Reference group	
Separated, no partner	6.62	−0.948 (−1.92)	−0.570 (−2.32)	−0.159
Separated, with partner	6.33	−1.32 (−1.78)	−0.762 (−2.14)	−0.195

TABLE A.1 (Part 2)
Satisfaction with Life in Switzerland, 1992–94

	Descriptive Statistics	Weighted Least Squares	Weighted Ordered Probit	
	Mean	Coefficient (t-Value)	Coefficient (t-Value)	Marginal Effect for Score of 10
Widowed, no partner	8.16	−0.264 (−3.35)	−0.201 (−3.98)	−0.065
Widowed, with partner	8.35	0.104 (0.58)	0.047 (0.32)	−0.016
Divorced, no partner	7.43	−0.633 (−4.66)	−0.354 (−4.11)	−0.109
Divorced, with partner	7.90	−0.179 (−0.91)	−0.083 (−0.66)	−0.028
Single, no partner	8.01	−0.262 (−2.91)	−0.171 (−2.63)	−0.056
Single, with partner	8.17	−0.097 (−1.11)	−0.080 (−1.29)	−0.027
Socio-economic factors				
Employed	8.21	Reference group		
Self-employed	8.31	0.013 (0.18)	0.051 (0.94)	0.018
Unemployed	6.56	−1.615 (−4.84)	−0.815 (−4.93)	−0.206
Student	8.16	0.031 (0.22)	−0.001 (−0.01)	−0.001
Housewife	8.38	0.158 (1.87)	0.130 (2.30)	0.045
Retired	8.23	−0.294 (−2.84)	−0.164 (−2.65)	−0.055
Other employment status	8.37	0.127 (0.65)	0.119 (0.89)	0.042
Equiv. income less than SFr. 2,000	7.98	Reference group		
Equiv. income SFr. 2,000–3,000	8.17	0.155 (2.49)	0.079 (2.05)	0.027
Equiv. income SFr. 3,000–4,000	8.24	0.259 (3.51)	0.149 (3.15)	0.052
Equiv. income SFr. 4,000–5,000	8.49	0.423 (4.91)	0.273 (4.87)	0.098
Equiv. income SFr. 5,000 and more	8.45	0.332 (4.80)	0.208 (4.07)	0.074

TABLE A.1 (Part 3)
Satisfaction with Life in Switzerland, 1992–94

	Descriptive Statistics	Weighted Least Squares	Weighted Ordered Probit	
	Mean	Coefficient (t-Value)	Coefficient (t-Value)	Marginal Effect for Score of 10
Institutional factor				
Democratic		0.114	0.081	0.028
participation rights		(2.82)	(3.01)	
Observations		6,137	6,137	

Source of data: Leu, Burri, and Priester (1997).
Notes: Dependent variable: level of satisfaction on a 10-point scale. White estimator for variance; t-values are in parentheses. Standard errors are adjusted to clustering in 26 cantons. Additional control variables (not shown) for size of community (five variables) and type of community (seven variables).

TABLE A.2
Sensitivity Analysis: DFBETA-Test for 26 Swiss Cantons (Independent Variable: Democratic Participation Rights)

Omitted Observation	β_0	DFBETA	Omitted Observation	β_0	DFBETA
Aargau	0.076	0.060	Nidwalden	0.078	−0.001
Appenzell i. Rh.	0.078	−0.006	Obwalden	0.072	0.215
Appenzell a. Rh.	0.072	0.203	Sankt Gallen	0.081	−0.099
Bern	0.080	−0.069	Schaffhausen	0.082	−0.132
Basel-Landschaft	0.086	−0.274	Solothurn	0.080	−0.059
Basel Stadt	0.076	0.060	Schwyz	0.076	0.060
Fribourg	0.072	0.187	Thurgau	0.077	0.026
Geneva	0.078	0.002	Ticino	0.099	−0.893
Glarus	0.079	−0.037	Uri	0.076	0.061
Graubünden	0.079	−0.034	Vaud	0.057	0.788
Jura	0.078	0.002	Valais	0.078	−0.007
Luzern	0.083	−0.163	Zug	0.077	0.039
Neuchâtel	0.076	0.063	Zürich	0.081	−0.108

Source of data: Leu, Burri, and Priester (1997).
Notes: A value of DFBETA greater than 1.96 in absolute value shows an influential observation.
Weight: inverse of the number of observations per canton.

Appendix B

INDEX FOR DEMOCRATIC PARTICIPATION RIGHTS IN SWISS CANTONS

DEMOCRATIC RIGHTS ARE DEFINED here in terms of individual political participation possibilities. In Switzerland, institutions for the direct political participation of citizens exist on the federal level as well as on the level of cantons. However, the democratic participation rights on the cantonal level are very heterogeneous. Therefore, an index is constructed to measure the different barriers preventing citizens from entering the political process, apart from elections, in the year 1992. The index is based mainly on data collected in Trechsel and Serdült (1999). (For details, see Stutzer, 1999.)

The four main legal instruments directly influencing the political process in Swiss cantons are

(a) The popular initiative to change the canton's constitution.
(b) The popular initiative to change the canton's law.
(c) The compulsory and optional referendum to prevent new law or changing law.
(d) The compulsory and optional referendum to prevent new state expenditure.

Barriers are in terms of

(a) The necessary signatures to launch an instrument (absolute and relative to the number of citizens with the right to vote).
(b) The amount of time legally allowed for collecting signatures.
(c) The level of new expenditure per head allowing a financial referendum.

(Compulsory referenda are treated like referenda, with the lowest possible barrier.)

Each of these restrictions is evaluated on a six-point scale: 1 indicates a high barrier, 6 a low barrier. From the resulting ratings, a nonweighted average is calculated for each instrument (that is, four subindices) and for the composite index, which represents the measure of direct democratic rights in Swiss cantons. The results are presented in Table B.1. The cross-correlations for the four subindices, the composite index, and the measure for local autonomy discussed shortly are shown in Table B.2.

INDEX FOR LOCAL AUTONOMY IN SWISS CANTONS

The index for local autonomy is based on survey results by Ladner (1994). Chief local administrators in 1,856 Swiss municipalities reported how they perceive their local autonomy on a 10-point scale, with 1 indicating "no autonomy at all" and 10 "very high" communal autonomy. Average scores for each canton are also shown in Table B.1.

TABLE B.1

Index for Democratic Participation Rights and
Local Autonomy in Swiss Cantons

	Direct Democracy					
Canton	Index for Constitutional Initiative	Index for Legislative Initiative	Index for Legislative Referendum	Index for Financial Referendum	Composite Index for Democratic Participation Rights	Local Autonomy
Aargau	5.67	5.67	6.00	4.50	5.46	4.9
Appenzell i. Rh.	6.00	6.00	6.00	3.00	5.25	5.0
Appenzell a. Rh.	6.00	6.00	6.00	4.00	5.50	5.8
Bern	2.67	2.67	3.67	5.00	3.50	4.6
Basel-Landschaft	6.00	6.00	6.00	4.75	5.69	4.3
Basel Stadt	4.67	4.67	4.00	4.25	4.40	5.5
Fribourg	2.67	2.67	2.33	2.00	2.42	4.2
Geneva	2.00	2.00	2.00	1.00	1.75	3.2
Glarus	6.00	6.00	6.00	4.00	5.50	5.6
Graubünden	4.00	5.00	6.00	4.00	4.75	5.8
Jura	4.67	4.67	3.00	2.50	3.71	4.0
Luzern	4.67	5.33	3.67	4.25	4.48	4.1
Neuchâtel	2.67	2.67	1.67	1.50	2.13	3.7
Nidwalden	2.67	6.00	6.00	5.00	4.92	5.5
Obwalden	5.33	6.00	6.00	5.00	5.58	6.0
Sankt Gallen	3.33	4.00	3.00	3.25	3.40	4.9
Schaffhausen	5.33	5.33	5.17	4.50	5.08	6.1
Solothurn	5.33	5.33	6.00	5.00	5.42	4.9
Schwyz	5.33	5.33	4.67	4.38	4.93	4.6
Thurgau	3.67	3.67	4.33	4.50	4.04	5.9
Ticino	1.33	2.67	1.67	2.75	2.10	4.3
Uri	5.67	5.67	5.33	5.00	5.42	5.4
Vaud	2.33	2.33	2.00	3.00	2.42	4.7
Valais	3.00	3.67	6.00	1.00	3.42	5.5
Zug	5.00	5.00	3.67	4.00	4.42	6.0
Zürich	3.33	3.33	6.00	4.00	4.17	5.4

Source: Ladner (1994) and own calculations based on Trechsel and Serdült (1999).

TABLE B.2

Correlation of Subindices and Composite Index for Democratic Participation
Rights and Local Autonomy in Swiss Cantons

	CI	LI	LR	FR	DPR	LA
Index for constitutional initiative (CI)	1.000					
Index for legislative initiative (LI)	0.871	1.000				
Index for legislative referendum (LR)	0.669	0.772	1.000			
Index for financial referendum (FR)	0.539	0.632	0.562	1.000		
Composite index for democratic participation rights (DPR)	0.888	0.943	0.877	0.767	1.000	
Local autonomy (LA)	0.410	0.506	0.646	0.531	0.605	1.000

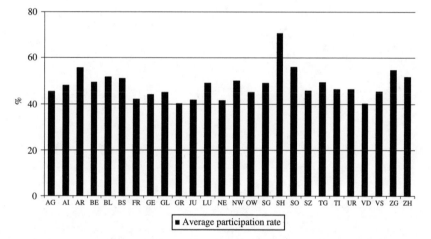

Figure B.1. Actual participation rates in Swiss cantons. The figure shows the average actual participation rate between 1992 and 1994 in the 26 Swiss cantons: Aargau (AG), Appenzell i. Rh. (AI), Appenzell a. Rh. (AR), Bern (BE), Basel-Landschaff (BL), Basel Stadt (BS), Fribourg (FR), Geneva (GE), Glarus (GL), Graubünden (GR), Jura (JU), Luzern (LU), Neuchâtel (NE), Nidwalden (NW), Obwalden (OW), St. Gallen (SG), Schaffhausen (SH), Solothurn (SO), Schwyz (SZ), Thurgau (TG), Ticino (TI), Uri (UR), Vaud (VD), Valais (VS), Zug (ZG), and Zürich (ZH). The high participation rate in canton Schaffhausen is due to compulsory voting. Data from own calculations.

REFERENCES

Ahuvia, Aaron C., and Douglas C. Friedman (1998). Income, Consumption, and Subjective Well-Being: Towards a Composite Macromarketing Model. *Journal of Macromarketing* 18(2): 153–68.

Aldrich, John H. (1997). When Is It Rational to Vote? In Dennis C. Mueller (ed.), *Perspectives on Public Choice: A Handbook*. Cambridge, U.K.: Cambridge University Press, 373–90.

Alesina, Alberto (1987). Macroeconomic Policy in a Two-Party System as a Repeated Game. *Quarterly Journal of Economics* 102(3): 651–78.

Alesina, Alberto (1988). Macroeconomics and Politics. In Stanley Fischer (ed.), *NBER Macroeconomic Annual*, Vol. 3. Cambridge, Mass.: MIT Press, 13–52.

Allen, Roy G. D. (1934). A Reconsideration of the Theory of Value, II. *Economica* 1: 196–219.

Amabile, Teresa M. (1996). *Creativity in Context: Update to the Social Psychology of Creativity*. Boulder, Colo.: Westview Press.

Amabile, Teresa M. (1998). How to Kill Creativity. *Harvard Business Review* 96(5): 77–87.

Andrews, Frank M., and John P. Robinson (1991). Measures of Subjective Well-Being. In John P. Robinson, Phillip R. Shaver, and Lawrence S. Wrightsman (eds.), *Measures of Personality and Social Psychological Attitudes*. San Diego, Calif.: Academic Press, 61–114.

Antonides, Gerrit, and Fred W. Van Raaij (1998). *Consumer Behaviour: A European Perspective*. West Sussex, U.K.: John Wiley & Sons.

Argyle, Michael (1987). *The Psychology of Happiness*. London: Methuen.

Argyle, Michael (1989). *The Social Psychology of Work*, 2nd ed., London: Penguin.

Argyle, Michael (1996). *The Social Psychology of Leisure*. London: Penguin.

Argyle, Michael (1999). Causes and Correlates of Happiness. In Daniel Kahneman, Ed Diener, and Norbert Schwarz (eds.), *Well-Being: The Foundations of Hedonic Psychology*. New York: Russell Sage Foundation: 353–73.

Arrow, Kenneth J. (1951). *Social Choice and Individual Values*. New York: John Wiley & Sons.

Arrow, Kenneth J., Robert S. Solow, Edward Leamer, Paul Portney, Roy Radner, and Howard Schuman (1993). Report of the NOAA Panel on Contingent Valuation. *Federal Register* 58(10): 4601–14.

Barro, Robert J. (1997). *Determinants of Economic Growth. A Cross-Country Empirical Study*. Cambridge, Mass.: and London: MIT Press.

Barro, Robert J. (2000). Inequality and Growth in a Panel of Countries. *Journal of Economic Growth* 5(1): 5–32.

Becker, Gary S. (1962). Irrational Behavior and Economic Theory. *Journal of Political Economy* 70(1): 1–13.

Becker, Gary S. (1974). A Theory of Social Interactions. *Journal of Political Economy* 82(6): 1063–93.

Bell, David E. (1982). Regret in Decision Making under Uncertainty. *Operations Research* 30(5): 961–81.

Bentham, Jeremy (1789). *An Introduction to the Principles of Morals and Legislation*. Reprinted 1948. Oxford: Blackwell.

Biswas-Diener, Robert, and Ed Diener (2000). Making the Best of a Bad Situation: Life in the Slums of Calcutta. Mimeo. Urbana Champaign: University of Illinois.

Blanchflower, David G., and Andrew J. Oswald (1999). Well-Being, Insecurity and the Decline of American Job Satisfaction. Mimeo. Warwick, U.K.: University of Warwick.

Blanchflower, David G., and Andrew J. Oswald (2000a). The Rising Well-Being of the Young. In David G. Blanchflower and Richard B. Freeman (eds.), *Youth Employment and Joblessness in Advanced Countries*. Chicago: National Bureau of Economic Research and University of Chicago Press.

Blanchflower, David G., and Andrew J. Oswald (2000b). Well-Being over Time in Britain and the USA. NBER Working Paper no. 7487. Cambridge, Mass.: National Bureau of Economic Research.

Blankart, Charles B. (1992). Bewirken Referenden und Volksinitiativen einen Unterschied in der Politik? *Staatswissenschaften und Staatspraxis* 3(4): 509–24.

Blankart, Charles B. (2000). The Process of Government Centralization: A Constitutional View. *Constitutional Political Economy* 11(1): 27–39.

Bohnet, Iris, and Bruno S. Frey (1994). Direct-Democratic Rules: The Role of Discussion. *Kyklos* 47(3): 341–54.

Boskin, Michael, and Evtan Sheshinski (1978). Optimal Redistributive Taxation when Individual Welfare Depends on Relative Income. *Quarterly Journal of Economics* 92(4): 589–601.

Bowler, Shaun, Todd Donovan, and Caroline J. Tolbert (1998). *Citizens as Legislators: Direct Democracy in the United States*. Columbus: Ohio State University Press.

Brennan, Geoffrey, and James M. Buchanan (1985). *The Reason of Rules: Constitutional Political Economy*. Cambridge, U.K.: Cambridge University Press.

Brickman, Philip, and Donald T. Campbell (1971). Hedonic Relativism and Planning the Good Society. In Mortimer H. Appley (ed.), *Adaptation Level Theory: A Symposium*. New York: Academic Press.

Brickman, Philip, Dan Coates, and Ronnie Janoff-Bulman (1978). Lottery Winners and Accident Victims: Is Happiness Relative? *Journal of Personality and Social Psychology* 36(8): 917–27.

Brim, Orville G., and Featherman David L. (1998). Surveying Midlife Development in the United States. Mimeo. Ann Arbor: University of Michigan.

Buchanan, James M. (1965). An Economic Theory of Clubs. *Economica* 32(1): 1–14.

Buchanan, James M. (1991). *Constitutional Economics*. Oxford: Basil Blackwell.

Butler, David, and Austin Ranney (eds.) (1994). *Referendums around the World: The Growing Use of Direct Democracy*. Washington, D.C.: AEI Press.

Campell, Angus, Philip E. Converse, and Willard L. Rodgers (1976). *The Quality of American Life: Perceptions, Evaluations, and Satisfactions*. New York: Russell Sage Foundation.

Cantril, Hadley (1976). *The Pattern of Human Concerns.* New Brunswick, N.J.: Rutgers University Press.

Carroll, Christopher D., and David N. Weil (1994). Saving and Growth: A Reinterpretation. *Carnegie–Rochester Conference Series on Public Policy* 40(0): 133–92.

Carson, Richard, et al. (1994). *A Bibliography of Contingent Valuation Studies and Papers.* La Jolla, Calif.: Natural Resources Damage Assessment, Inc.

Carstensen, Laura L. (1995). Evidence for a Life-Span Theory of Socioemotional Selectivity. *Current Directions in Psychological Science* 4(5): 151–55.

Castles, Francis G. (1998). Die Bedeutung der Oekonomie für die politische Unterstützung der Europäischen Union. In Thomas König, Elmar Rieger, and Hermann Schmitt (eds.), *Europa der Bürger? Voraussetzungen, Alternativen, Konsequenzen.* Frankfurt: Campus Verlag, 159–76.

Clark, Andrew E. (1997). Job Satisfaction and Gender: Why Are Women So Happy at Work? *Labour Economics* 4(4): 341–72.

Clark, Andrew E. (2000). Unemployment as a Social Norm: Psychological Evidence from Panel Data. Mimeo. University of Orléans, France.

Clark, Andrew E., Yannis Georgellis, and Peter Sanfey (1999). Scarring: The Psychological Impact of Past Unemployment. Mimeo. University of Orléans, France.

Clark, Andrew E., and Andrew J. Oswald (1994). Unhappiness and Unemployment. *Economic Journal* 104(424): 648–59.

Clark, Andrew E., and Andrew J. Oswald (1996). Satisfaction and Comparison Income. *Journal of Public Economics* 61(3): 359–81.

Clark, Andrew E., and Andrew J. Oswald (1998). Comparison-Concave Utility and Following Behaviour in Social and Economic Settings. *Journal of Public Economics* 70(1): 133–55.

Cohen, Sheldon, Gary W. Evans, David S. Krantz, Daniel Stokols, and S. Kelly (1981). Aircraft Noise and Children: Longitudinal and Cross-Sectional Evidence on Adaptation to Noise and the Effectiveness of Noise Abatement. *Journal of Personality and Social Psychology* 40(2): 331–45.

Cooter, Robert D. (2000). *The Strategic Constitution.* Princeton, N.J.: Princeton University Press.

Cronin, Thomas E. (1989). *Direct Democracy. The Politics of Initiative, Referendum and Recall.* Cambridge, Mass.: Harvard University Press.

Crowne, Douglas P., and David A. Marlowe (1964). *The Approval Motive: Studies in Evaluative Dependence.* New York: Wiley.

Csikszentmihalyi, Mihaly (1990). *Flow: The Psychology of Optimal Experience.* New York: Harper Perennial.

Daly, Herman E., and John B. Cobb (1989). *For the Common Good: Redirecting the Economy towards Community, the Environment, and a Sustainable Future.* London: Green Print.

Darity, William, and Arthur H. Goldsmith (1996). Social Psychology, Unemployment and Macroeconomics. *Journal of Economic Perspectives* 10(1): 121–40.

Dasgupta, Partha (1993). *An Inquiry into Well-Being and Destitution.* Oxford, U.K.: Oxford University Press.

De Haan, Jakob, and Jan Egbert Sturm (2000). On the Relationship between Economic Freedom and Economic Growth. *European Journal of Political Economy* 16(2): 215–41.

Deci, Edward L. (1975). *Intrinsic Motivation*. New York: Plenum Press.

Deci, Edward L., with Richard Flaste (1995). *Why We Do What We Do: The Dynamics of Personal Autonomy*. New York: Putnam.

Deci, Edward L., Richard Koestner, and Richard M. Ryan (1999). A Meta-Analytic Review of Experiments Examining the Effects of Extrinsic Rewards on Intrinsic Motivation. *Psychological Bulletin* 125(6): 627–68.

Deci, Edward L., and Richard M. Ryan (1985). *Intrinsic Motivation and Self-Determination in Human Behavior*. New York: Plenum Press.

DeNeve, Kristina M., and Harris Cooper (1998). The Happy Personality: A Meta-Analysis of 137 Personality Traits and Subjective Well-Being. *Psychological Bulletin* 124(2): 197–229.

Di Tella, Rafael, and Robert MacCulloch (1999). Partisan Social Happiness. Mimeo. Boston: Harvard Business School.

Di Tella, Rafael, Robert J. MacCulloch, and Andrew J. Oswald (1999). How Do Macroeconomic Fluctuations Affect Happiness? Mimeo. Boston: Harvard Business School.

Di Tella, Rafael, Robert J. MacCulloch, and Andrew J. Oswald (2001). Preferences over Inflation and Unemployment: Evidence from Surveys of Happiness. *American Economic Review* 91(1): 335–41.

Diener, Ed, and Robert Biswas-Diener (2000). Will Money Increase Subjective Well-Being? A Literature Review and Guide to Needed Research. Mimeo. University of Illinois Urbana-Champaign.

Diener, Ed, Marissa Diener, and Carol Diener (1995). Factors Predicting the Subjective Well-Being of Nations. *Journal of Personality and Social Psychology* 69(5): 851–64.

Diener, Ed, Carol L. Gohm, Eunkook M. Suh, and Shigehiro Oishi (2000). Similarity of the Relations between Marital Status and Subjective Well-Being across Cultures. *Journal of Cross Cultural Psychology* 31(4): 419–36.

Diener, Ed, Jeff Horwitz, and Robert A. Emmons (1985). Happiness of the Very Wealthy. *Social Indicators Research* 16: 263–74.

Diener, Ed, and Richard E. Lucas (1999). Personality and Subjective Well-Being. In Daniel Kahneman, Ed Diener, and Norbert Schwarz (eds.), *Well-Being: The Foundations of Hedonic Psychology*. New York: Russell Sage Foundation, 213–29.

Diener, Ed, and Shigehiro Oishi (2000). Money and Happiness: Income and Subjective Well-Being across Nations. In Ed Diener and Eunkook M. Suh (eds.), *Culture and Subjective Well-Being*. Cambridge, Mass.: MIT Press, 185–218.

Diener, Ed, Ed Sandvik, William Pavot, and Frank Fujita (1992). Extraversion and Subjective Well-Being in a U.S. National Probability Sample. *Journal of Research in Personality* 26(3): 205–15.

Diener, Ed, Ed Sandvik, Larry Seidlitz, and Marissa Diener (1993). The Relationship between Income and Subjective Well-Being: Relative or Absolute? *Social Indicators Research* 28(3): 195–223.

Diener, Ed, and Eunkook M. Suh (1997). Subjective Well-Being and Age: An International Analysis. *Annual Review of Gerontology and Geriatrics* 17: 304–24.

Diener, Ed, and Eunkook M. Suh (1999). National Differences in Subjective Well-Being. In Daniel Kahneman, Ed Diener, and Norbert Schwarz (eds.), *Well-Being: The Foundations of Hedonic Psychology.* New York: Russell Sage Foundation, 434–50.

Diener, Ed, and Eunkook M. Suh (eds.) (2000). *Culture and Subjective Well-Being.* Cambridge, Mass.: MIT Press.

Diener, Ed, Eunkook M. Suh, Richard E. Lucas, and Heidi L. Smith (1999). Subjective Well-Being: Three Decades of Progress. *Psychological Bulletin* 125(2): 276–303.

Diener, Ed, Eunkook M. Suh, Heidi Smith, and Liang Shao (1995). National Differences in Reported Subjective Well-Being: Why Do They Occur? *Social Indicators Research* 34(1): 7–32.

Dittmar, H. (1992). *The Social Psychology of Material Possessions.* Hemel Hempstead: Harvester Wheatsheaf.

Donaldson, Cam, and Phil Shackley (1997). Does "Process Utility" Exist? A Case Study of Willingness to Pay for Laparoscopic Cholecystectomy. *Social Science Medicine* 44(5): 699–707.

Downs, Anthony (1957). *An Economic Theory of Democracy.* New York: Harper & Row.

Drifill, John, Grayham E. Mizon, and Alistair Ulph (1990). Costs of Inflation. In Benjamin M. Friedman and Frank H. Hahn (eds.), *Handbook of Monetary Economics,* Vol. II. Amsterdam: North-Holland, 1014–66.

Duesenberry, James S. (1949). *Income, Savings and the Theory of Consumer Behavior.* Cambridge, Mass.: Harvard University Press.

Dunning, David, Ann Leuenberger, and David A. Sherman (1995). A New Look at Motivated Inference: Are Self-Serving Theories of Success a Product of Motivational Forces? *Journal of Personality and Social Psychology* 69(1): 58–68.

Easterlin, Richard A. (1974). Does Economic Growth Improve the Human Lot? Some Empirical Evidence. In Paul A. David and Melvin W. Reder (eds.), *Nations and Households in Economic Growth: Essays in Honor of Moses Abramowitz.* New York: Academic Press, 89–125.

Easterlin, Richard A. (1995). Will Raising the Incomes of All Increase the Happiness of All? *Journal of Economic Behaviour and Organization* 27(1): 35–48.

Easterlin, Richard A. (2000a). Income and Happiness: Towards a Unified Theory. Mimeo. Los Angeles: University of Southern California.

Easterlin, Richard A. (2000b). The Worldwide Standard of Living since 1800. *Journal of Economic Perspectives* 14(1): 7–26.

Easterly, William (1999). Life during Growth. *Journal of Economic Growth* 4(3): 239–76.

Edgeworth, Francis Ysidro (1881). *Mathematical Psychics: An Essay on the Application of Mathematics to the Moral Sciences.* London: Kegan Paul.

Ehrhardt, Joop J., Willem E. Saris, and Ruut Veenhoven (2000). Stability of Life-satisfaction over Time. *Journal of Happiness Studies* 1(2): 177–205.

Eijffinger, Sylvester C. W. (ed.) (1997). *Independent Central Banks and Economic Performance*. Cheltenham, U.K.: Edward Elgar.

Ellison, Christopher G. (1991). Religious Involvement and Subjective Well-Being. *Journal of Health and Social Behavior* 32(1): 80–99.

Elster, Jon (1998). Emotions and Economic Theory. *Journal of Economic Literature* 36(1): 47–74.

Estes, Richard (1988). *Trends in World Social Development: The Social Progress of Nations, 1970–1987*. New York: Praeger.

Falk, Armin, and Markus Knell (2000). Choosing the Joneses: On the Endogeneity of Reference Groups. Working Paper no. 59. Institute for Empirical Research in Economics, University of Zurich.

Feather, Norman T. (1990). *The Psychological Impact of Unemployment*. New York: Springer.

Feld, Lars P., and Marcel R. Savioz (1997). Direct Democracy Matters for Economic Performance: An Empirical Investigation. *Kyklos* 50(4): 507–38.

Fernández-Dols, José-Miguel, and María-Angeles Ruiz-Belda (1990). Are Smiles a Sign of Happiness? Gold Medal Winners at the Olympic Games. *Journal of Personality and Social Psychology* 69(6): 1113–19.

Fischer, Stanley (1981). Towards an Understanding of the Costs of Inflation: II. *Carnegie–Rochester Conference Series on Public Policy* 15(0): 5–41.

Fischer, Stanley, and Franco Modigliani (1978). Towards an Understanding of the Real Effects and Costs of Inflation. *Weltwirtschaftliches Archiv* 114(4): 810–33.

Fogel, Robert W. (1993). Economic Growth, Population Theory, and Physiology: The Bearing of Long-Term Processes on the Making of Economic Policy. *American Economic Review* 84(3): 369–95.

Foster, Rick, and Greg Hicks (1999). *How We Choose to Be Happy: The 9 Choices of Extremely Happy People: Their Secrets, Their Stories*. New York: Putnam.

Frank, Robert H. (1985a). *Choosing the Right Pond*. New York: Oxford University Press.

Frank, Robert H. (1985b). The Demand for Unobservable and Other Nonpositional Goods. *American Economic Review* 75(1): 101–16.

Frank, Robert H. (1997). The Frame of Reference as a Public Good. *Economic Journal* 107(445): 1832–47.

Frank, Robert H. (1999). *Luxury Fever: Why Money Fails to Satisfy in an Era of Excess*. New York: Free Press.

Frederick, Shane, and George Loewenstein (1999). Hedonic Adaptation. In Daniel Kahneman, Ed Diener, and Norbert Schwarz (eds.), *Well-Being: The Foundations of Hedonic Psychology*. New York: Russell Sage Foundation, 302–29.

Frey, Bruno S. (1983). *Democratic Economic Policy*. Oxford: Blackwell.

Frey, Bruno S. (1991). Forms of Expressing Economic Discontent. In Helmut Norpoth, Michael S. Lewis-Beck, and Jean-Dominique Lafay (eds.), *Economics and Politics. The Calculus of Support*. Ann Arbor: University of Michigan Press, 267–80.

Frey, Bruno S. (1994). Direct Democracy: Politico-Economic Lessons from Swiss Experience. *American Economic Review* 84(2): 338–48.

Frey, Bruno S. (1997a). A Constitution for Knaves Crowds Out Civic Virtues. *Economic Journal* 107(443): 1043–53.

Frey, Bruno S. (1997b). *Not Just For the Money: An Economic Theory of Personal Motivation*. Cheltenham, U.K., and Brookfield, US: Edward Elgar.

Frey, Bruno S. (ed.) (1997c). *Political Business Cycles*. Cheltenham, U.K.: Edward Elgar.

Frey, Bruno S., and Reiner Eichenberger (1999). *The New Democratic Federalism for Europe: Functional Overlapping and Competing Jurisdictions*. Cheltenham, U.K.: Edward Elgar.

Frey, Bruno S., and Reiner Eichenberger (2001). Marriage Paradoxes. In Bruno S. Frey, *Inspiring Economics: Human Motivation in Political Economy*. Cheltenham, U.K., and Brookfield: Edward Elgar, 37–51.

Frey, Bruno S., and Beat Heggli (1999). An Ipsative Theory of Human Behaviour. In Bruno S. Frey, *Economics as a Science of Human Behaviour*, 2nd ed. Boston: Kluwer Academic Publishers, 195–212.

Frey, Bruno S., and Reto Jegen (2001). Motivation Crowding Theory: A Survey of Empirical Evidence. Forthcoming in *Journal of Economic Surveys*.

Frey, Bruno S., and Gebhard Kirchgässner (1993). Diskursethik, Politische Ökonomie und Volksabstimmungen. *Analyse und Kritik* 15(2): 129–49.

Frey, Bruno S., and Felix Oberholzer-Gee (1997). The Cost of Price Incentives: An Empirical Analysis of Motivation Crowding-Out. *American Economic Review* 87(4): 746–55.

Frey, Bruno S., and Margit Osterloh (2000). Motivation—der zwiespältige Produktionsfaktor. In Bruno S. Frey and Margit Osterloh (eds.), *Managing Motivation: Wie Sie die neue Motivationsforschung für Ihr Unternehmen nutzen können*. Wiesbaden: Gabler, 19–42.

Frey, Bruno S., and Friedrich Schneider (1978a). An Empirical Study of Politico-Economic Interaction in the United States. *Review of Economics and Statistics* 60(2): 174–83.

Frey, Bruno S., and Friedrich Schneider (1978b). A Political-Economic Model of the United Kingdom. *Economic Journal* 88(350): 243–53.

Frey, Bruno S., and Friedrich Schneider (1979). An Economic Model with an Endogenous Government Sector. *Public Choice* 34(1): 29–43.

Frey, Bruno S., and Alois Stutzer (1999). Measuring Preferences by Subjective Well-Being. *Journal of Institutional and Theoretical Economics* 155(4): 755–88.

Frey, Bruno S., and Alois Stutzer (2000). Happiness, Economy and Institutions. *Economic Journal* 110(446): 918–38.

Friedlaender, Ann F. (1973). Macro-Policy Goals in the Postwar Period: A Study in Revealed Preference. *Quarterly Journal of Economics* 87(1): 25–43.

Froyen, Richard T. (1974). A Test of the Endogeneity of Monetary Policy. *Journal of Econometrics* 2(2): 175–88.

Fukuyama, Francis (1995). *Trust: The Social Virtues and the Creation of Property*. New York: Free Press.

Furnham, Adrian, and Michael Argyle (1998). *The Psychology of Money*. London and New York: Routledge.

Galbraith, John Kenneth (1958). *The Affluent Society*. Harmondsworth: Penguin Books.

Galetovic, Alexander, and Ricardo Sanhueza (2000). Citizens, Autocrats, and Plotters: A Model and New Evidence on Coups D'Etat. *Economics & Politics* 12(2): 183–204.

Gallup, George H. (1976). Human Needs and Satisfactions: A Global Survey. *The Public Opinion Quarterly* 41: 459–67.

Gardner, Jonathan, and Andrew J. Oswald (2001). Does Money Buy Happiness? A Longitudinal Study Using Data on Windfalls. Mimeo. Warwick, U.K.: Warwick University.

Gärling, Tommy, Kay Axhausen, and Monika Brydsten (1996). Travel Choice and the Goal/Process Utility Distinction. *Applied Cognitive Psychology* 10(1): 65–74.

Gerlach, Knut, and Gesine Stephan (1996). A Paper on Unhappiness and Unemployment in Germany. *Economics Letters* 52(3): 325–30.

Glatzer, Wolfgang (1992). Lebensqualität und subjektives Wohlbefinden: Ergebnisse sozialwissenschaftlicher Untersuchungen. In Alfred Bellebaum (ed.), *Glück und Zufriedenheit*. Opladen, Germany: Westdeutscher Verlag, 49–85.

Gneezy, Uri, and Aldo Rustichini (2000). A Fine Is a Price. *Journal of Legal Studies* 29(1): 1–18.

Graham, Carol, and Stefano Pettinato (2000). Happiness, Markets, and Democracy: Latin America in Comparative Perspective. Working Paper no. 13. Washington D.C.: Center on Social and Economic Dynamics, Brookings Institution.

Greene, William H. (1997). *Econometric Analysis*, 3rd ed. Upper Saddle River, N.J.: Prentice Hall.

Habermas, Jürgen (1983). Diskursethik—Notizen zu einem Begründungsprozess. In Jürgen Habermas (ed.), *Moralbewusstsein und kommunikatives Handeln*. Frankfurt: Suhrkamp, 53–125.

Hamermesh, Daniel S. (1999). The Changing Distribution of Job Satisfaction. NBER Working Paper no. 7332. Cambridge, Mass.: National Bureau of Economic Research.

Hammond, Peter J. (1988). Consequentialist Foundation of Expected Utility. *Theory and Decision* 25(1): 25–78.

Hammond, Peter J. (1991). Interpersonal Comparisons of Utility: Why and How They Are and Should Be Made. In Jon Elster and John E. Roemer (eds.), *Interpersonal Comparisons of Well-Being*. Cambridge, U.K.: Cambridge University Press, 200–54.

Hammond, Peter J. (1996). Consequentialism, Rationality and Game Theory. In Kenneth J. Arrow, E. Colombatto, M. Perlman, and Christian Schmidt (eds.), *The Rational Foundations of Economic Behaviour*. IEA Conference Vol. 114. New York: St. Martin's Press; London: Macmillan Press, 25–42.

Hardin, Russell (1982). *Collective Action*. Baltimore: Johns Hopkins University Press.

Harsanyi, John C. (1993). Normative Validity and Meaning of von Neumann-Morgenstern Utilities. In Ken Binmore, Alan Kirman, and Piero Tani (eds.), *Frontiers of Game Theory*. Cambridge, Mass., and London: MIT Press, 307–20.

Headey, Bruce, and Alexander Wearing (1989). Personality, Life Events, and Subjective Well-Being: Toward a Dynamic Equilibrium Model. *Journal of Personality and Social Psychology* 57(4): 731–39.

Headey, Bruce, and Alexander Wearing (1991). Subjective Well-Being: A Stocks and Flows Framework. In Fritz Strack, Michael Argyle and Norbert Schwarz (eds.), *Subjective Well-Being: An Interdisciplinary Perspective.* Oxford: Pergamon Press, 7–26.

Headey, Bruce, and Alexander Wearing (1992). *Understanding Happiness.* Melbourne, Australia: Longman Cheshire.

Helson, Harry (1964). *Adaptation-Level Theory: An Experimental and Systematic Approach to Behavior.* New York: Harper & Row.

Hibbs, Douglas A. (1977). Political Parties and Macroeconomic Policy. *American Political Science Review* 71(4): 1467–87.

Hibbs, Douglas A. (1981). Economics and Politics in France: Economic Performance and Mass Political Support for President Pompidou and Giscard D'Estaing. *European Journal of Political Research* 9: 133–45.

Hibbs, Douglas A. (1987). *The American Political Economy: Macroeconomics and Electoral Policy.* Cambridge, Mass.: Harvard University Press.

Hicks, John R. (1934). A Reconsideration of the Theory of Value, I. *Economica* 1: 52–75.

Hirsch, Fred (1976). *The Social Limits to Growth.* Cambridge, Mass.: Harvard University Press.

Hirschman, Albert O. (1970). *Exit, Voice and Loyalty.* Cambridge, Mass.: Harvard University Press.

Hochschild, Arlie Russell (1997). *The Time Bind: When Work Becomes Home and Home Becomes Work.* New York: Metropolitan Books.

Holländer, Heinz (2001). On the Validity of Utility Statements: Standard Theory versus Duesenberry. *Journal of Economic Behavior and Organization* 45(3): 227–49.

Holmström, Bengt, and Paul Milgrom (1991). Multi-Task Principal Agent Analysis: Incentive Contracts, Asset Ownership and Job Design. *Journal of Law, Economics and Organization* 7(0): 24–52.

Horley, James, and John J. Lavery (1995). Subjective Well-Being and Age. *Social Indicator Research* 34(2): 275–82.

Houthakker, Hendrik S. (1950). Revealed Preference and the Utility Function. *Economica* 17: 159–74.

Iaffaldano, Michelle T., and Paul M. Muchinsky (1985). Job Satisfaction and Job Performance: A Meta-Analysis. *Psychological Bulletin* 97(2): 251–73.

Inglehart, Ronald F. (1990). *Culture Shift in Advanced Industrial Society.* Princeton, N.J.: Princeton University Press.

Inglehart, Robert F. (1999). Trust, Well-Being and Democracy. In Mark E. Warren (ed.), *Democracy and Trust.* Cambridge, U.K.: Cambridge University Press, 88–120.

Inglehart, Ronald F., and Hans-Dieter Klingemann (2000). Genes, Culture, Democracy, and Happiness. In Ed Diener and Eunkook M. Suh (eds.), *Culture and Subjective Well-Being.* Cambridge, Mass.: MIT Press, 165–83.

Inkeles, Alex, and Larry Diamond (1986). Personal Development and National Development: A Cross-Cultural Perspective. In Alexander Szalai and Frank M. Andrews (eds.), *The Quality of Life: Comparative Studies*. Ann Arbor: Institute for Social Research, University of Michigan, 73–109.

Irwin, F. W. (1944). The Realism of Expectations. *Psychological Review* 51: 120–26.

Iversen, Torben, Jonas Pontusson, and David Soskice (eds.) (2000). *Unions, Employers, and Central Banks: Macroeconomic Coordination and Institutional Change in Social Market Economies*. Cambridge, U.K.: Cambridge University Press.

James, William (1902). *Varieties of Religious Experience*. New York: Mentor.

Jarvis, George K., and Herbert C. Northcott (1987). Religion and Differences in Morbidity and Mortality. *Social Science and Medicine* 25(7): 813–24.

Judge, Timothy A., and Edwin A. Locke (1993). Effect of Dysfunctional Thought Processes on Subjective Well-Being and Job Satisfaction. *Journal of Applied Psychology* 78(3): 475–90.

Judge, Timothy A., and Shinichiro Watanabe (1993). Another Look at the Job Satisfaction–Life Satisfaction Relationship. *Journal of Applied Psychology* 78(6): 939–48.

Kahneman, Daniel (1999). Objective Happiness. In Daniel Kahneman, Ed Diener, and Norbert Schwarz (eds.), *Well-Being: The Foundations of Hedonic Psychology*. New York: Russell Sage Foundation, 3–25.

Kahneman, Daniel (2000). Experienced Utility and Objective Happiness: A Moment-Based Approach. In Daniel Kahneman and Amos Tversky (eds.), *Choices, Values, and Frames*. New York: Cambridge University Press and Russell Sage Foundation.

Kahneman, Daniel, Ed Diener, and Norbert Schwarz (eds.), (1999). *Well-Being: The Foundations of Hedonic Psychology*. New York: Russell Sage Foundation.

Kahneman, Daniel, and Amos Tversky (1979). Prospect Theory: An Analysis of Decision under Risk. *Econometrica* 47(2): 263–91.

Kahneman, Daniel, and Carol Varey (1991). Notes on the Psychology of Utility. In Jon Elster and John E. Roemer (eds.), *Interpersonal Comparisons of Well-Being: Studies in Rationality and Social Change*. Cambridge, U.K.: Cambridge University Press, 127–63.

Kahneman, Daniel, Peter P. Wakker, and Rakesh Sarin (1997). Back to Bentham? Explorations of Experienced Utility. *Quarterly Journal of Economics* 112(2): 375–405.

Kapteyn, Arie (1994). The Measurement of Household Cost Functions: Revealed Preference versus Subjective Measures. *Journal of Population Economics* 7(4): 333–50.

Kapteyn, Arie (2000). Saving and Reference Groups. Mimeo. Tilburg University, Netherlands.

Kapteyn, Arie, and Tom Wansbeek (1982). Empirical Evidence on Preference Formation. *Journal of Economic Psychology* 2(2): 137–54.

Kapteyn, Arie, and Tom Wansbeek (1985). The Individual Welfare Function: A Review. *Journal of Economic Psychology* 6(4): 333–63.

Kasser, Timothy J. (2000). Two Versions of the American Dream: Which Goals and Values Make for a High Quality of Life? In Ed Diener and Don R. Rahtz (eds.), *Advances in Quality of Life Theory and Research*. Dordrecht: Kluwer Academic Publishers, 3–12.

Kelvin, P., and J. Jarrett (1985). *The Social Psychological Effects of Unemployment*. Cambridge, U.K.: Cambridge University Press.

Kenny, Charles (1999). Does Growth Cause Happiness, or Does Happiness Cause Growth? *Kyklos* 52(1): 3–26.

Kessler, Ronald C., Katherine A. McGonagle, Christopher B. Nelson, and Michael Hughes (1994). Sex and Depression in the National Comorbidity Survey: II. Cohort Effects. *Journal of Affective Disorders* 30(1): 15–26.

Kirchgässner, Gebhard (1985). Rationality, Causality, and the Relation between Economic Conditions and the Popularity of Parties: An Empirical Investigation for the Federal Republic of Germany, 1971–1982. *European Economic Review* 28(1–2): 243–68.

Kirchgässner, Gebhard, Lars Feld, and Marcel R. Savioz (1999). *Die direkte Demokratie: Modern, erfolgreich, entwicklungs—und exportfähig*. Basel et al.: Helbing and Lichtenhahn/Vahlen/Beck.

Kölz, A. (1998). *Der Weg der Schweiz zum modernen Bundesstaat: Historische Abhandlungen*. Chur and Zürich, Switzerland: Rüegger.

Komlos, John (ed.) (1994). *Stature, Living Standards, and Economic Development: Essays in Anthropometric History*. Chicago and London: University of Chicago Press.

Konow, James, and Joseph Earley (1999). The Hedonistic Paradox: Is Homo Economicus Happier? Mimeo. Los Angeles: Loyola Marymount University.

Korpi, Tomas (1997). Is Well-Being Related to Employment Status? Unemployment, Labor Market Policies and Subjective Well-Being among Swedish Youth. *Labour Economics* 4(2): 125–47.

Kosicki, George (1987). A Test of the Relative Income Hypothesis. *Southern Economic Journal* 54(2): 422–34.

Kwan, Virginia S. Y., Michael H. Bond, and Theodore M. Singelis (1997). Pan-cultural Explanations for Life Satisfaction: Adding Relationship Harmony to Self-Esteem. *Journal of Personality and Social Psychology* 73(5): 1038–51.

Lachman, Margie E., and Suzanne L. Weaver (1998). The Sense of Control as a Moderator of Social Class Differences in Health and Well-Being. *Journal of Personality and Social Psychology* 74(3): 763–73.

Ladner, Andreas (1994). Finanzkompetenzen der Gemeinden—ein Ueberblick über die Praxis. In Franz Eng, Alexander Glatthard, and Beat H. Koenig (eds.), *Finanzföderalismus*. Bern: Emissionszentrale der Schweizer Gemeinden, 64–85.

Landau, Simha F., Benjamin Beit-Hallahmi, and Shilomit Levy (1998). The Personal and the Political: Israelis' Perception of Well-Being in Times of War and Peace. *Social Indicators Research* 44(3): 329–65.

Lane, Robert E. (1991). *The Market Experience*. Cambridge, U.K.: Cambridge University Press.

Lane, Robert E. (1998). The Joyless Market Economy. In Avner Ben-Ner and Louis Putterman (eds.), *Economics, Values, and Organization*. Cambridge, U.K.: Cambridge University Press, 461–88.

Lane, Robert E. (2000). *The Loss of Happiness in Market Economies*. New Haven and London: Yale University Press.

Larsen, Randy J. (1992). Neuroticism and Selective Encoding and Recall of Symptoms: Evidence from a Combined Concurrent–Retrospective Study. *Journal of Personality and Social Psychology* 62: 480–88.

Lawton, Mortimer P. (1996). Quality of Life and Affect in Later Life. In Carol Magai and Susan H. McFadden (eds.), *Handbook of Emotions, Adult Development and Aging*. San Diego, Calif.: Academic Press, 327–48.

Layard, Richard (1980). Human Satisfactions and Public Policy. *The Economic Journal* 90(363): 737–50.

Le Menestrel, Marc (2001). A Process Approach to the Utility for Gambling. *Theory and Decision* 50(3): 249–62.

Lebergott, Stanley (1993). *Pursuing Happiness: American Consumers in the Twentieth Century*. Princeton, N.J.: Princeton University Press.

Lee, Gary R., Karen Seccombe, and Constance L. Shehan (1991). Marital Status and Personal Happiness: An Analysis of Trend Data. *Journal of Marriage and the Family* 53 (November): 839–44.

Lepper, Mark R., and David Greene (eds.) (1978). *The Hidden Costs of Reward: New Perspectives on Psychology of Human Motivation*. Hillsdale, N.Y.: Erlbaum.

Leu, Robert E., Stefan Burri, and Tom Priester (1997). *Lebensqualität und Armut in der Schweiz*. Bern: Haupt.

Lind, Allan E., and Tom R. Tyler (1988). *The Social Psychology of Procedural Justice*. New York: Plenum Press.

Lindenberg, Siegwart, and Bruno S. Frey (1993). Alternatives, Frames, and Relative Prices: A Broader View of Rational Choice Theory. *Acta Sociologica* 36: 191–205.

Loewenstein, George (1999). Because It Is There: The Challenge of Mountaineering . . . for Utility Theory. *Kyklos* 52(3): 315–43.

Loewenstein, George, and David Schkade (1999). Wouldn't It Be Nice? Predicting Future Feelings. In Daniel Kahneman, Ed Diener, and Norbert Schwarz (eds.), *Well-Being: The Foundation of Hedonic Psychology*. New York: Russell Sage Foundation, 85–105.

Lucas, Richard E., Ed Diener, Alexander Grob, Eunkook M. Suh, and Liang Shao (2000). Cross-Cultural Evidence for the Fundamental Features of Extraversion. *Journal of Personality and Social Psychology*. 79(3): 452–68.

Lucas, Richard E., Ed Diener, and Eunkook M. Suh (1996). Discriminant Validity of Well-Being Measures. *Journal of Personality and Social Psychology* 71(3): 616–28.

Lucas, Robert E. Jr. (1981). Discussion of: Stanley Fischer, "Towards an Understanding of the Costs of Inflation: II." *Carnegie–Rochester Conference Series on Public Choice* 15(0): 43–52.

Lynn, Peter, and Justin Davis Smith (1991). *The 1991 National Survey of Voluntary Activity in the UK*. Berkhamstead, U.K.: The Volunteer Centre.

Makin, John H. (1976). Constraints on Formulation of Models for Measuring Revealed Preferences of Policy Makers. *Kyklos* 29(4): 709–32.

Marks, Gary N., and Nicole Fleming (1999). Influences and Consequences of Well-Being among Australian Young People: 1980–1995. *Social Indicators Research* 46(3): 301–23.

Marschak, Jacob (1950). Uncertain Prospects, and Measurable Utility. *Econometrica* 18: 111–41.

Marshall, Alfred (1890). *The Principles of Economics*, 8th ed. (1920). London: Macmillan.

Mastekaasa, Arne (1995). Age Variations in the Suicide Rates and Self-Reported Subjective Well-Being of Married and Never Married Persons. *Journal of Community and Applied Social Psychology* 5(1): 21–39.

Matsusaka, John G. (1995). Fiscal Effects of the Voter Initiative: Evidence from the Last 30 Years. *Journal of Political Economy* 103(2): 587–623.

McEachern, William A. (1978). Collective Decision Rules and Local Debt Choice: A Test of the Median Voter Hypothesis. *National Tax Journal* 31(2): 129–36.

Meyer, Herbert M. (1975). The Pay-for-Performance Dilemma. *Organizational Dynamics* 3(3): 39–50.

Michalos, Alex C. (1991). *Global Report on Student Well-Being. Volume 1: Life Satisfaction and Happiness*. New York: Springer.

Mill, John Stuart (1863). Utilitarianism. In Roger Crisp (ed.), *Utilitarianism: John Stuart Mill* (1998 Reprint). Oxford: Oxford University Press.

Minier, Jenny A. (1998). Democracy and Growth: Alternative Approaches. *Journal of Economic Growth* 3(3): 241–61.

Modigliani, Franco (1949). *Fluctuations in the Saving-Income Ratio: A Problem in Economic Forecasting*. Conference on Research in Income and Wealth. New York.

Moller, Valerie (1989). Cant't Get No Satisfaction. *Indicator South Africa* 7: 43–46.

Moulton, Brent R. (1990). An Illustration of a Pitfall in Estimating the Effects of Aggregate Variables on Micro Units. *Review of Economics and Statistics* 72(2): 334–38.

Mroczek, Daniel K., and Christian M. Kolarz (1998). The Effect of Age on Positive and Negative Affect: A Developmental Perspective on Happiness. *Journal of Personality and Social Psychology* 75(5): 1333–49.

Mueller, Dennis C. (1989). *Public Choice II*, 2nd ed. Cambridge, U.K.: Cambridge University Press.

Mueller, Dennis C. (1996). *Constitutional Democracy*. New York: Oxford University Press.

Murphy, Gregory C., and James A. Athanasou (1999). The Effect of Unemployment on Mental Health. *Journal of Occupational and Organizational Psychology* 72(1): 83–99.

Myers, David G. (1993a). *The Pursuit of Happiness: Discovering the Pathway to Fulfillment, Well-Being, and Enduring Personal Joy*. New York: Avon.

Myers, David G. (1993b). *The Pursuit of Happiness: Who Is Happy and Why?* New York: Avon.

Myers, David G. (1999). Close Relationship and Quality of Life. In Daniel Kahneman, Ed Diener, and Norbert Schwarz (eds.), *Well-Being: The Foundations of Hedonic Psychology*. New York: Russell Sage Foundation, 374–91.

Myers, David G. (2000). The Funds, Friends, and Faith of Happy People. *American Psychologist* 55(1): 56–67.

Nannestad, Peter, and Martin Paldam (1994). The VP-Function: A Survey of the Literature on Vote and Popularity Functions after 25 Years. *Public Choice* 79(3–4): 213–45.

Neumark, David, and Andrew Postlewaite (1998). Relative Income Concerns and the Rise in Married Women's Employment. *Journal of Public Economics* 70(1): 157–83.

Ng, Yew-Kwang (1996). Happiness Surveys: Some Comparability Issues and an Exploratory Survey Based on Just Perceivable Increments. *Social Indicators Research* 38(1): 1–27.

Ng, Yew-Kwang (1997). A Case for Happiness, Cardinalism, and Interpersonal Comparability. *Economic Journal* 107(445): 1848–58.

Nisbett, Richard, and Lee Ross (1980). *Human Inference: Strategies and Shortcomings of Social Judgement.* Englewood Cliffs, N.J.: Prentice Hall.

Niven, David (2000). *The 100 Simple Secrets of Happy People: What Scientists Have Learned and How You Can Use It.* San Francisco: Harper.

Nolen-Hoeksema, Susan, and Cheryl L. Rusting (1999). Gender Differences in Well-Being. In Daniel Kahneman, Ed Diener, and Norbert Schwarz (eds.), *Well-Being: The Foundations of Hedonic Psychology.* New York: Russell Sage Foundation, 330–50.

Nordhaus, William (1975). The Political Business Cycle. *Review of Economic Studies* 42(2): 169–90.

Nordhaus, William, and James Tobin (1972). *Is Growth Obsolete?* NBER General Series no. 96. New York: Columbia University Press.

Nye, Joseph S., Philip D. Zelikow and David C. King (eds.) (1997). *Why People Don't Trust Government.* Cambridge, Mass.: Harvard University Press.

Oates, Wallace E. (1999). An Essay on Fiscal Federalism. *Journal of Economic Literature* 37(3): 1120–49.

Offer, Avner (2001). On Economic Welfare Measurement and Human Well-Being over the Long Run. In Paul A. David, Peter Solar, and Mark Thomas (eds.), *The Economic Future in Historical Perspective.* London: British Academy.

Olson, Mancur (1969). The Principle of "Fiscal Equivalence": The Division of Responsibilities among Different Levels of Government. *American Economic Review* 59(2): 479–87.

Olson, Mancur (1986). Towards a More General Theory of Governmental Structure. *American Economic Review* 76(2): 120–25.

Opp, Karl-Dieter, Peter Voss, and Christiane Gern (1995). *The Origins of a Spontaneous Revolution: East Germany 1989.* Ann Arbor: University of Michigan Press.

Ormel, Johan, Siegwart Lindenberg, Nardi Steverink, and Lois M. Verbrugge (1999). Subjective Well-Being and Social Production Functions. *Social Indicators Research* 46(1): 61–90.

Oswald, Andrew J. (1997). Happiness and Economic Performance. *Economic Journal* 107(445): 1815–31.

Paldam, Martin (1981). A Preliminary Survey of the Theories and Findings on Vote and Popularity Functions. *European Journal of Political Research* 9: 181–99.

Parducci, Allen (1995). *Happiness, Pleasure, and Judgment: The Contextual Theory and Its Applications*. Hillsdale, N.J.: Erlbaum.

Pascal, Blaise (1670). *Pensées*. Paris: Port-Royal.

Pavot, William, and Ed Diener (1993). The Affective and Cognitive Context of Self-Reported Measures of Subjective Well-Being. *Social Indicators Research* 28(1): 1–20.

Pissarides, Christopher A. (1972). A Model of British Macroeconomic Policy 1955–1969. *Manchester School of Economic and Social Studies* 40(3): 245–59.

Pollak, Robert A. (1970). Habit Formation and Dynamic Demand Functions. *Journal of Political Economy* 78(4): 745–63.

Pollak, Robert A. (1976). Interdependent Preferences. *American Economic Review* 66(3): 309–20.

Pommerehne, Werner W. (1978). Institutional Approaches to Public Expenditure: Empirical Evidence from Swiss Municipalities. *Journal of Public Economics* 9(2): 225–80.

Pommerehne, Werner W. (1990). The Empirical Relevance of Comparative Institutional Analysis. *European Economic Review* 34(2–3): 458–69.

Pommerehne, Werner W., and Friedrich Schneider (1978). Fiscal Illusion, Political Institutions and Local Public Spending. *Kyklos* 31(3): 381–408.

Pommerehne, Werner W., and Hannelore Weck-Hannemann (1996). Tax Rates, Tax Administration and Income Tax Evasion in Switzerland. *Public Choice* 88(1–2): 161–70.

Prager, Dennis (1998). *Happiness Is a Serious Problem: A Human Nature Repair Manual*. New York: Regan.

Putnam, Robert D., with Robert Leonardi and Raffaella Y. Nanetti (1993). *Making Democracy Work*. Princeton, N.J.: Princeton University Press.

Putnam, Robert D. (1995). Tuning In, Tuning Out: The Strange Disappearance of Social Capital in America. *PS: Political Science and Politics* 28(4): 664–83.

Rabin, Matthew (1993). Incorporating Fairness into Game Theory and Economics. *American Economic Review* 83(5): 1281–302.

Riker, William H., and Peter C. Ordeshook (1973). *An Introduction to Positive Political Theory*. Englewood Cliffs, N.J.: Prentice Hall.

Robbins, Lionel C. (1932). *An Essay on the Nature and Significance of Economic Science*. London: Macmillan. Selections reprinted in Daniel M. Hausman (ed.) (1984), *The Philosophy of Economics: An Anthology* (New York: Cambridge University Press).

Rodrik, Dani (1999). Democracies Pay Higher Wages. *Quarterly Journal of Economics* 114(3): 707–38.

Roy, Kakoli, and Susanne Ziemek (2000). On the Economics of Volunteering. Discussion Papers on Development Policy no. 31. Center for Development Research, University of Bonn, Germany.

Russell, Bertrand (1930). *The Conquest of Happiness*. London: George Allen & Unwin.

Ryan, Richard M., and Edward L. Deci (2000a). Self-Determination Theory and the Facilitation of Intrinsic Motivation, Social Development, and Well-Being. *American Psychologist* 55(1): 68–78.

Ryan, Richard M., and Edward L. Deci (2000b). To Be Happy or to Be Self-Fulfilled: A Review of Research on Hedonic and Eudaimonic Well-Being. Mimeo. Rochester, N.Y.: University of Rochester.

Ryan, Richard M., Kennon M. Sheldon, Tim Kasser, and Edward L. Deci (1996). All Goals Are Not Created Equal: An Organismic Perspective on the Nature of Goals and Their Regulation. In Peter M. Gollwitzer and John A. Bargh (eds.), *The Psychology of Action: Linking Cognition and Motivation to Behavior*. New York and London: The Guilford Press, 7–26.

Salamon, Lester M., and Helmut K. Anheier (1997). *Defining the Nonprofit Sector: A Cross-National Analysis*. Manchester, U.K., and New York: Manchester University Press.

Samuelson, Paul A. (1938). A Note of the Pure Theory of Consumer's Behaviour. *Economica* 5(17): 61–71.

Santerre, Rexford E. (1986). Representative versus Direct Democracy: A Tiebout Test of Relative Performance. *Public Choice* 48(1): 55–63.

Santerre, Rexford E. (1989). Representative versus Direct Democracy: Are There Any Expenditure Differences? *Public Choice* 60(2): 145–54.

Santerre, Rexford E. (1993). Representative versus Direct Democracy: The Role of Public Bureaucrats. *Public Choice* 76(3): 189–98.

Scheier, Michael F., and Charles S. Carver (1985). Optimism, Coping, and Health: Assessment and Implications of Generalized Outcome Expectancies. *Health Psychology* 4(3): 219–47.

Schneider, Friedrich, and Dominik Enste (2000). Increasing Shadow Economy All over the World—Fiction or Reality? *Journal of Economic Literature* 38(1): 77–114.

Schneider, Friedrich, and Bruno S. Frey (1988). Politico-Economic Models of Macroeconomic Policy: A Review of the Empirical Evidence. In Thomas D. Willett (ed.), *The Political Economy of Money, Inflation and Unemployment*. Durham, N.C., and London: Duke University Press, 240–75.

Schneider, Friedrich, and Alexander F. Wagner (2000). Korporatismus im europäischen Vergleich: Förderung makroökonomischer Rahmenbedingungen? Working Paper no. 15. Linz, Austria: University of Linz.

Schor, Juliet B. (1992). *The Overworked American: The Unexpected Decline of Leisure*. New York: Basic Books.

Schuessler, Alexander A. (2000). Expressive Voting. *Rationality and Society* 12(1): 87–119.

Schwarz, Norbert, and Fritz Strack (1999). Reports of Subjective Well-Being: Judgmental Processes and Their Methodological Implications. In Daniel Kahneman, Ed Diener, and Norbert Schwarz (eds.), *Well-Being: The Foundations of Hedonic Psychology*. New York: Russell Sage Foundation, 61–84.

Schyns, Peggy (2000). The Relationship between Income, Changes in Income and Life Satisfaction in West Germany and the Russian Federation: Relative, Absolute, or a Combination of Both? In Ed Diener and D. R. Rahtz (eds.), *Advances in Quality of Life Theory and Research*, Vol. 1. Dordrecht: Kluwer, 83–109.

Scitovsky, Tibor (1976). *The Joyless Economy: An Inquiry into Human Satisfaction and Dissatisfaction*. Oxford: Oxford University Press.

Seidlitz, Larry, and Ed Diener (1993). Memory for Positive versus Negative Events: Theories for the Differences between Happy and Unhappy Persons. *Journal of Personality and Social Psychology* 64(4): 654–64.

Sen, Amartya K. (1979). The Welfare Basis of Real Income Comparisons: A Survey. *Journal of Economic Literature* 17(1): 1–45.

Sen, Amartya K. (1980). Equality of What? In Sterling M. McMurrin (ed.), *The Tanner Lectures on Human Values*, Vol. I. Cambridge, U.K.: Cambridge University Press, 257–80.

Sen, Amartya K. (1982). *Choice, Welfare and Measurement*. Oxford: Basil Blackwell.

Sen, Amartya K. (1986). The Standard of Living. In Sterling McMurrin (ed.), *Tanner Lectures on Human Values*, Vol. VII. Cambridge, U.K.: Cambridge University Press.

Sen, Amartya K. (1993). Capability and Well-Being. In Amartya K. Sen and Martha Nussbaum (eds.), *The Quality of Life*. Oxford et al.: Oxford University Press, 30–53.

Sen, Amartya K. (1995). Rationality and Social Choice. *American Economic Review* 85(1): 1–24.

Sen, Amartya K. (1997). Maximization and the Act of Choice. *Econometrica* 65(4): 745–79.

Shafir, Eldar, Peter Diamond, and Amos Tversky (1997). On Money Illusion. *Quarterly Journal of Economics* 112(2): 341–74.

Shafir, Eldar, and Amos Tversky (1992). Thinking through Uncertainty: Nonconsequential Reasoning and Choice. *Cognitive Psychology* 24: 449–74.

Shiller, Robert J. (1997). Why Do People Dislike Inflation? In Christina D. Romer and David H. Romer (eds.), *Reducing Inflation: Motivation and Strategy*. Chicago and London: University of Chicago Press, 13–65.

Siermann, Clemens L. J. (1998). *Politics, Institutions and the Economic Performance of Nations*. Cheltenham, U.K., and Northampton, Mass.: Edward Elgar.

Simon, Herbert A. (1976). From Substantive to Procedural Rationality. In S. J. Latsis (ed.), *Methods and Appraisal in Economics*. Cambridge, Mass.: Cambridge University Press.

Simon, Herbert A. (1978). Rationality as a Process and Product of Thought. *American Economic Review* 68(2): 1–16.

Slesnick, Daniel T. (1998). Empirical Approaches to the Measurement of Welfare. *Journal of Economic Literature* 36(4): 2108–65.

Smith, Adam (1776). *An Inquiry into the Nature and Causes of the Wealth of Nations*. Reprinted 1980, London: Deut and Sane.

Smith, Stephen, and Peter Razzell (1975). *The Pools Winners*. London: Caliban Books.

Sousa-Poza, Alfonso, and Andrés A. Sousa-Poza (2000). Taking Another Look at the Gender/Job-Satisfaction Paradox. *Kyklos* 53(2): 135–52.

Spector, Paul E. (1997). *Job Satisfaction: Application, Assessment, Causes, and Consequences*. Thousand Oaks, Calif.: Sage.

Strack, Fritz, Michael Argyle, and Norbert Schwarz (eds.) (1991). *Subjective Well-Being: An Interdisciplinary Perspective*. Oxford: Pergamon Press.

Stroebe, Margaret S., Wolfgang Stroebe, and Robert O. Hansson (eds.) (1993). *Handbook of Bereavement: Theory, Research, and Intervention*. Cambridge, U.K.: Cambridge University Press.

Stroebe, Wolfgang, and Margaret S. Stroebe (1987). *Bereavement and Health: The Psychological and Physical Consequences of Partner Loss*. New York: Cambridge University Press.

Stutzer, Alois (1999). Demokratieindizes für die Kantone der Schweiz. Working Paper no. 23, Institute for Empirical Research in Economics, University of Zurich.

Stutzer, Alois, and Rafael Lalive (2000). The Role of Social Work Norms in Job Searching and Subjective Well-Being. Working Paper no. 51, Institute for Empirical Research in Economics, University of Zurich.

Sullivan, Oriel (1996). The Enjoyment of Activities: Do Couples Affect Each Others' Well-Being? *Social Indicators Research* 38(1): 81–102.

Sumner, Leonard W. (1996). *Welfare, Happiness, and Ethics*. Oxford: Oxford University Press.

Swiss Federal Statistical Office (ed.) (various years). Statistisches Jahrbuch der Schweiz. Zurich: Neue Zürcher Zeitung.

Tajfel, Henri (1981). *Human Groups and Social Categories. Studies in Social Psychology*. London: Cambridge University Press.

Taylor, Shelley E., and Jonathon D. Brown (1988). Illusion and Well-Being: A Social-Psychological Perspective on Mental Health. *Psychological Bulletin* 103(2): 193–210.

Thaler, Richard H. (1980). Toward a Positive Theory of Consumer Choice. *Journal of Economic Behavior and Organization* 1 (March): 39–60.

Thaler, Richard H. (1992). *The Winner's Curse: Paradoxes and Anomalies of Economic Life*. New York: Free Press.

Theil, Henry (1964). *Optimal Decision Rules for Government and Industry*. Amsterdam: North Holland.

Tiebout, Charles M. (1956). A Pure Theory of Local Expenditure. *Journal of Political Economy* 64 (October): 416–24.

Tinbergen, Jan (1956). *Economic Policy: Principles and Design*. Amsterdam: North Holland.

Tooby, John, and Leda Cosmides (1994). Better than Rational: Evolutionary Psychology and the Invisible Hand. *The American Economic Review* 84(2): 327–32.

Trechsel, Alexander, and Uwe Serdült (1999). *Kaleidoskop Volksrechte: Die Institutionen der direkten Demokratie in den schweizerischen Kantonen 1970–1996*. Basel: Helbing & Lichtenhahn.

Tullock, Gordon (1987). *Autocracy*. Dordrecht: Kluwer.

Tyler, Tom R. (1990). *Why People Obey the Law*. New Haven: Yale University Press.

Tyler, Tom R., and Steven L. Blader (2000). *Cooperation in Groups: Procedural Justice, Social Identity, and Behavioral Engagement*. Philadelphia: Psychology Press.

Uzawa, Hirofumi (1960). Preference and Rational Choice in the Theory of Consumption. In Kenneth J. Arrow, Simon Karlin, and Peter Suppes (eds.), *Mathematical Methods in the Social Sciences*. Stanford, Calif.: Stanford University Press.

Van Praag, Bernard M. S., and Paul Frijters (1999). The Measurement of Welfare and Well-Being: The Leyden Approach. In Daniel Kahneman, Ed Diener, and Norbert Schwarz (eds.), *Well-Being: The Foundations of Hedonic Psychology*. New York: Russell Sage Foundation, 413–33.

Van Praag, Bernard M. S., Paul Frijters, and Ada Ferrer-i-Carbonell (2000). A Structural Model of Well-Being. Discussion Paper no. 53/3. Amsterdam and Rotterdam: Tinbergen Institute.

Van Praag, Bernard M. S., and Arie Kapteyn (1973). Further Evidence on the Individual Welfare Function of Income: An Empirical Investigation in the Netherlands. *European Economic Review* 4(1): 33–62.

Veblen, Thorstein (1899). *The Theory of Leisure Class*. New York: Modern Library.

Veenhoven, Ruut (1989). Does Happiness Bind? Marriage Changes of the Unhappy. In Ruut Veenhoven (ed.), *How Harmful Is Happiness? Consequences of Enjoying Life or Not*. Rotterdam: University of Rotterdam Press, 44–60.

Veenhoven, Ruut (1991a). Is Happiness Relative? *Social Indicators Research* 24(1): 1–34.

Veenhoven, Ruut (1991b). Questions on Happiness: Classical Topics, Modern Answers, Blind Spots. In Fritz Strack, Michael Argyle, and Norbert Schwarz (eds.), *Subjective Well-Being: An Interdisciplinary Perspective*. Oxford: Pergamon Press, 7–26.

Veenhoven, Ruut (1993). *Happiness in Nations: Subjective Appreciation of Life in 56 Nations 1946–1992*. Rotterdam: Erasmus University Press.

Veenhoven, Ruut (1995). Satisfaction and Social Position: Within Nation Differences, Compared across Nations. In Willem E. Saris, Ruut Veenhoven, Annette C. Scherpenzeel, and Brendan Bunting (eds.), *A Comparative Study of Satisfaction with Life in Europe*. Budapest: Eotvos University Press, 254–62.

Veenhoven, Ruut (1997). Progres dans la comprehension du bonheur. *Revue Quebecoise de Psychologie* 18: 29–74.

Veenhoven, Ruut (2000a). Freedom and Happiness: A Comparative Study in Forty-Four Nations in the Early 1990s. In Ed Diener and Eunkook M. Suh (eds.), *Culture and Subjective Well-Being*. Cambridge, Mass.: MIT Press, 257–88.

Veenhoven, Ruut (2000b). Well-Being in the Welfare State: Level Not Higher, Distribution Not More Equitable. *Journal of Comparative Policy Analysis* 2: 91–125.

Von Neumann, John, and Oskar Morgenstern (1947). *Theory of Games and Economic Behavior*. 2nd ed. Princeton, N.J.: Princeton University Press.

Warr, Peter (1999). Well-Being and the Workplace. In Daniel Kahneman, Ed Diener, and Norbert Schwarz (eds.), *Well-Being: The Foundations of Hedonic Psychology*. New York: Russell Sage Foundation, 392–412.

Waterman, Alan S. (1993). Two Conceptions of Happiness: Contrasts of Personal Expressiveness (Eudaimonia) and Hedonic Enjoyment. *Journal of Personality and Social Psychology* 64(4): 678–91.

Weede, Erich, and Edward N. Muller (1998). Rebellion, Violence and Revolution: A Rational Choice Perspective. *Journal of Peace Research* 35(1): 43–59.

Weinstein, Neil D. (1981). Unrealistic Optimism about Future Life Events. *Journal of Personality and Social Psychology* 39(5): 806–20.

Weinstein, Neil D. (1982). Community Noise Problems: Evidence against Adaptation. *Journal of Environmental Psychology* 2(2): 87–97.

Weitzman, Martin (1976). On the Welfare Significance of National Product in a Dynamic Economy. *Quarterly Journal of Economics* 90(1): 156–62.

White, James M. (1992). Marital Status and Well-Being in Canada. *Journal of Family Issues* 13: 390–409.

Wilson, William Julius (1996). *When Work Disappears*. New York: Knopf.

Winkelmann, Liliana, and Rainer Winkelmann (1998). Why Are the Unemployed So Unhappy? Evidence from Panel Data. *Economica* 65(257): 1–15.

Wintrobe, Ronald (1998). *The Political Economy of Dictatorship*. Cambridge, U.K.: Cambridge University Press.

Wood, John H. (1967). A Model of Federal Reserve Behavior. In G. Horwich (ed.), *Monetary Process and Policy*. Homewood, Irwin, Ill.: 135–66.

Wood, Wendy, Nancy Rhodes, and Melanie Whelan (1989). Sex Differences in Positive Well-Being: A Consideration of Emotional Style and Martial Status. *Psychological Bulletin* 106(2): 249–64.

Zeckhauser, Richard J., and Donald S. Shepard (1976). Where Now for Saving Lives? *Law and Contemporary Problems* 40(4): 5–45.

Zolatas, Xenophon (1981). *Economic Growth and Declining Social Welfare*. Athens: Bank of Greece.

DATA SOURCES

American National Election Studies
  http://www.umich.edu/~nes/
Bureau of Economic Analysis of the U.S. Department of Commerce
  http://www.bea.doc.gov/
  http://www.bea.doc.gov/bea/dn1.htm
General Social Survey
  National Opinion Research Center (1985). *General Social Survey [United States] and German Social Survey [Allbus] Combined Files*, 1982 (computer file). Chicago Ill.: National Opinion Research Center (producer), 1985. Ann Arbor, Mich.: Inter-university Consortium for Political and Social Research (distributor).
  http://www.icpsr.umich.edu/GSS99/
International Social Survey Program
  International Social Survey Program (ISSP) (2000). *International Social Survey Program: Work Orientations II*, 1997 (computer file). ICPSR version. Koeln, Germany: Zentralarchiv für Empirische Sozialforschung (producer), 1999. Koeln, Germany: Zentralarchiv für Empirische Sozialforschung / Ann Arbor, Mich.: Inter-university Consortium for Political and Social Research (distributors.)
  http://www.issp.org/
Penn World Tables
  Summers, Robert, and Alan Heston (1991). The Penn World Table (Mark 5): An Expanded Set of International Comparisons, 1950–1988. *Quarterly Journal of Economics* 106(2): 327–68.
  http://pwt.econ.upenn.edu/
U.S. Bureau of the Census, U.S. Department of Commerce
  U.S. Bureau of the Census (2000). *Historical National Population Estimates.* Population Estimates Program, Population Division.
  http://www.census.gov/population/www/estimates/popest.html
World Database of Happiness
  Veenhoven, Ruut (2001). World Database of Happiness: Catalog of Happiness in Nations.
  www.eur.nl/fsw/research/happiness
World Development Indicators
  World Bank (various years). *World Development Report.* New York et al.: Oxford University Press.
  http://www.worldbank.org/data/wdi/home.html
World Value Survey
  Inglehart, Ronald, et al. (2000). *World Values Surveys and European Values Surveys*, 1981–1984, 1990–1993, and 1995–1997 (computer file). ICPSR version. Ann Arbor, Mich.: Institute for Social Research (producer), 1999. Ann Arbor, Mich.: Inter-university Consortium for Political and Social Research (distributor).
  http://wvs.isr.umich.edu/

INDEX